Cambridge Studies in Ethnomusicology

General Editor: John Blacking

Cantonese Opera

Cantonese opera is one of the grandest of the traditional musical theaters in China. This book investigates the creative process involved in the performance of these operas, in which as many as fifty or sixty singers/actors/dancers and a dozen or more instrumentalists take part.

With the guidance of only a written script and an extensive repertory of preexistent tunes, operas are staged as a rule without rehearsal or reference to any musical notation. The few lead singers often sing as many as six or seven different operas in as many consecutive days, each one lasting about four hours.

Based on fieldwork conducted in Hong Kong and upon transcription and analysis of the music from live performances, this book investigates this extraordinary performance, focusing on the social function, the script, the language, and the individual singer's creative input. Bell Yung suggests a model of creative process that involves a set of rules according to which singers operate, improvise, and interact. He also considers other theoretical issues, most importantly the relationship between text and music and the question of the variance or invariance of melodies.

A cassette illustrating the music discussed in the book is also available.

Cambridge Studies in Ethnomusicology

General Editor: John Blacking

Ethnomusicological research has shown that there are many different ingredients in musical systems. The core of this series will therefore be studies of the logics of different musics, analyzed in the contexts of the societies in which they were composed and performed. The books will address specific problems related to potential musical ability and practice, such as how music is integrated with dance, theater and the visual arts, how children develop musical perception and skills in different cultures and how musical activities affect the acquisition of other skills. Musical transcriptions will be included, sometimes introducing indigenous systems of notation. Cassettes will accompany most books.

Already published:
Bonnie C. Wade, *Khyāl: creativity within North India's classical music tradition*
Regula Burckhardt Qureshi, *Sufi Music of India and Pakistan: sound, context and meaning in Qawwali*
Peter Cooke, *The Fiddle Tradition of the Shetland Isles*
Anthony Seeger, *Why Suyá Sing: a musical anthropology of an Amazonian people*
James Kippen, *The Tabla of Lucknow: a cultural analysis of a musical tradition*
John Baily, *Music of Afghanistan: professional musicians in the city of Herat*

Cantonese Opera

Performance as creative process

Bell Yung
Associate Professor of Music
University of Pittsburgh

Cambridge University Press
Cambridge
New York   New Rochelle
Melbourne   Sydney

Published by the Press Syndicate of the University of Cambridge
The Pitt Building, Trumpington Street, Cambridge CB2 1RP
32 East 57th Street, New York, NY 10022, USA
10 Stamford Road, Oakleigh, Melbourne 3166, Australia

© Cambridge University Press 1989

First published 1989

Printed in Great Britain at the University Press, Cambridge

British Library cataloguing in publication data
Yung, Bell
Cantonese opera: performance as creative
process. – (Cambridge studies in ethnomusicology).
1. Opera in Cantonese
I. Title
782'.1'09517

Library of Congress cataloguing in publication data
Yung, Bell.
Cantonese opera: performance as creative process / Bell Yung.
  p.   cm. – (Cambridge studies in ethnomusicology)
Bibliography: p.
Includes index.
ISBN 0-521-30506-3
1. Operas, Chinese – History and criticism.   I. Title.
II. Series.
ML1751.C4Y9 1989   88-20209 CIP
782.1'0951'27 – dc 19

ISBN 0 521 30506 3
ISBN 0 521 35632 6 cassette

For my parents Durbin Yung and Greer Chi-cheng Tung

FP

Contents

		page
	List of figures	vi
	Preface	ix
1	Introduction to Chinese Opera	1
2	Essential elements of Cantonese opera as performing art	11
3	Musical instruments	23
4	Social context	32
5	The opera script	42
6	Speech types	57
7	Aria types	67
8	Linguistic tones	82
9	Padding syllables	92
10	*Sin*	106
11	Fixed tunes	128
12	Narrative songs	138
13	Three levels of creative process	145
Appendix 1	Linguistic tones, romanization system, and pronunciation guide	158
Appendix 2	Notes on transcription symbols	161
Appendix 3	Text of musical examples in translation, romanization, and linguistic tones	162
Appendix 4	Text of musical examples in Chinese characters	170
Appendix 5	Sources of musical examples	176
	Items on the cassette	178
	Notes	179
Glossary 1	Names of performers, plays, and opera companies	190
Glossary 2	Other terms	191
	Bibliography	195
	Index	203

Figures

		page
2.1	Categories of oral delivery types	14
2.2	Music scale in Cantonese opera	15
2.3	*Dainty Steps* in *gongche* notation	16
2.4	*Dainty Steps* in staff notation	17
2.5	Cantonese heptatonic scale in three octaves	17
3.1	Large woodblock	23
3.2	Medium woodblock	23
3.3	Placement of woodblocks	24
3.4	*Erhu*	28
3.5	*Sanxian*	28
3.6	*Pipa*	30
3.7	*Yueqin*	30
3.8	*Yangqin*	30
3.9	*Dizi*	30
6.1	*Comic Rhymed Speech*	59
6.2	*Percussion Speech*	59
6.3	Verse structure of *Poetic Speech*	61
6.4	*Poetic Speech*	61
6.5	Verse structure of *Rhymed Speech*	62
6.6	*Rhymed Speech*	63
6.7	Verse structure of *Patter Speech*	64
6.8	*Patter Speech*	65
7.1	Two versions of *Chatjiching*	68
7.2	Nine versions of *Chatjiching*	69
7.3	Verse structure of *Chatjiching*	70
7.4	Syllable placement of *Chatjiching*	70
7.5	Principal pitches of *jingsin*	71
7.6	Role types and voice types	74
7.7	Verse structure of *Faansin Jungbaan*	75
7.8	Syllable placement of *Faansin Jungbaan*	75
7.9	Line-ending pitches for the *bongji* family of tunes	75
7.10	Instrumental prelude of *Faansin Jungbaan*	76
7.11	Three lines of *Faaidim*	76
7.12	Syllable placement of *Faaidim*	76
7.13	Instrumental prelude of *Faaidim*	76
7.14	Four couplets of *Gaamji Fuyung*	77
7.15	Verse structure of *Gaamji Fuyung*	77

List of figures

		page
7.16	Syllable placement of *Gaamji Fuyung*	77
7.17	Syllable placement of *Bongji Maanbaan*	78
7.18	Instrumental prelude of *Bongji Maanbaan*	78
7.19	Three couplets of *Gwanfa*	79
7.20	Instrumental interludes of *Gwanfa* (*bongji, jingsin*)	79
7.21	Instrumental interludes of *Gwanfa* (*bongji, yifaansin*)	79
7.22	Comparison of *Gwanfa* instrumental interludes (in *bongji* and *yiwong*)	80
8.1	Distribution of 136 syllables among 9 tonal categories	83
8.2	Frequency of occurrence for pitches	87
8.3	Table of pitch matching	89
8.4	Table of pitch matching for "big" voice	89
8.5	Table of pitch matching for *Gaamji Fuyung* (last phrase)	89
9.1	Verse structure of *Bongji Maanbaan*	93
9.2	Syllable placement of *Bongji Maanbaan*	93
9.3	An upper line of *Bongji Maanbaan* showing an added phrase	94
9.4	Comparison of (A) syllable placement of an actual performance transcribed in figure 9.3 with (B) prescribed syllable placement, showing an added phrase	95
9.5	A lower line of *Bongji Maanbaan* showing phrase leader syllables	96
9.6	Comparison of (A) syllable placement of an actual performance transcribed in figure 9.5 with (B) prescribed syllable placement, showing phrase leader syllables	96
9.7	Two phrases of *Bongji Maanbaan*	96
9.8a	Transcription of two versions of *Bongji Maanbaan*	97
9.8b	Comparison of the text of the two versions and the script	98
9.9	Comparison of (A) syllable placement of an actual performance transcribed in figure 9.7 with (B) prescribed syllable placement, showing multiplets	99
9.10	Syllable placement of one phrase from *The Royal Beauty*	99
9.11	A possible syllable placement of the same phrase from figure 9.10	99
9.12	One line of *Faansin Yiwong* with instrumental interlude	100
9.13	One line of *Faansin Yiwong* with interlude fillers	101
9.14	Verse structure and syllable placement of *Yiwong*	102
9.15	Verse structure and syllable placement of one line of *Long Yiwong*	102
9.16	One couplet of *Long Yiwong*	103
9.17	One line of *Bongji Maanbaan* showing five kinds of padding syllables	104
10.1	Cantonese heptatonic scale in three octaves	106
10.2	Comparison of the same tune played in (A) *Chewusin* and in (B) *Hochesin*	108
10.3	Intervals for the seven *sins*	109
10.4	Seventeen lines of *Jingsin Jungbaan*	112
10.5	Seventeen lines of *Faansin Jungbaan*	114

viii *List of figures*

		page
10.6	Sixteen lines of *Yifaansin Jungbaan*	116
10.7	Table of matching between linguistic tones and musical pitches	119
10.8	Matrix of eighteen graphs showing result of pitch counting	120
10.9	The aggregate "weight" of pitches for the three *sins*	121
10.10	The principal scales for the three *sins*	122
10.11	Intervals of the principal scales	122
10.12	Intervals of the transposed scales	123
10.13	*Jingsin* tuning of *yangqin*	125
10.14	*Faansin* tuning of *yangqin*	125
10.15	*Yifaansin* tuning of *yangqin*	125
10.16	Predominant and cadential pitches and range for the three *sins*	127
11.1	Four versions of *Autumn Moon on the Calm Lake*	130
11.2	Sections of the tune *Autumn Moon* used in the three performed versions	132
11.3	Version A measure 1	134
11.4	Version B measure 1	134
11.5	Alternate renditions of figure 11.4	135
11.6	Measure 4	135
11.7	Measure 16	136
12.1	Verse structure of main quatrain of *Naamyam*	139
12.2	Verse structure of opening couplet of *Naamyam*	139
12.3	Verse structure of closing quatrain of *Naamyam*	139
12.4	An opening couplet and two quatrains of *Naamyam*	140
12.5	Syllable placement of three variants of *Naamyam*	141
12.6	Line-ending pitches for *Naamyam*	142
12.7	Prelude to *Naamyam* sung to a poem	142
12.8	Three interludes of *Naamyam*	143
12.9	Placement of interludes	143
12.10	Line-ending pitches for *Muk'yu*	143
12.11	Two quatrains of *Muk'yu*	144
13.1	Summary of oral delivery types in act 1 of *The Magic Pearl*	146
13.2	Oral delivery types in a speech–song spectrum	151
13.3	A "slow" version of *Chatjiching*	153
13.4	"Slow" and "fast" versions of *Jingsin Sapji Yiwong Maanbaan*	155
13.5	Rules on melodic expansion by Qiu	156
A1.1	Table of linguistic tonal symbols	158

Preface

What first attracted me to the study of Cantonese opera was one single structural aspect: the close relationship between the linguistic tones of the text and the melody of the singing. A little exploration of recorded samples revealed a musical sound rich in texture and various in its expressive means. The initial investigation was concerned mainly with transcription and analysis and a structural study of the large number of tunes in the opera, most of which are repeatedly sung in the same and different plays. The repetitions always differ from one another to varying degrees. The main question was, what makes one tune different from, or the same as, another? The tunes are not notated but have titles which are clearly labeled in the script; using these titles as a guide, it is possible to see what Cantonese opera performers consider to be the same or different tunes.

During field trips to Hong Kong, I was able to study Cantonese opera in its proper context by observing live performances and interviewing the singers, musicians, audience, and other members of the operatic community. A striking characteristic is what I called "living" – it is a "living" opera in the sense that, despite a long tradition, it is ready to change and adapt itself to the current tastes of the audience. Some performance practices in Cantonese opera reflect what other regional operas have long lost; yet it is in many ways the most progressive of all Chinese operas in view of its development over the last eighty years. It is also "living" because of its intimate relationship with the lives of the Cantonese people: its role as ritual as well as entertainment is still very much evident in the cosmopolitan city of Hong Kong today. Finally and most importantly to this study, it is "living" in its performance practice: a performance on stage can be considered a continual "creative process" rather than a static "display." Without musical notation and with little or no rehearsal, the singers and musicians interact with one another and, in the process, spin out a stream of music.

Such a performance has a "creative" element because a play seldom remains unchanged in different performance situations, and a tune, when repeated, almost never sounds the same. On the other hand, being "creative" is not being "free"; a performer is bound, or led, by a complex set of rules which emanates from a tradition he shares with the community, from his individual habits and preferences, and from the unique performance situation. A performance may perhaps be compared to some forms of game or competitive sport in that the participants interact according to a set of general rules, but the details of the operation of the rules and the outcome of the "game" are left to the players' own skill and ingenuity and the circumstances of the moment. An important difference is that, while "rules" in a game or sport are explicitly stated, those in the performance of Cantonese opera are not even in the conscious mind of most of the performers. This characteristic is, of course, found in many kinds of traditional performing art. What makes Cantonese opera special in this respect is the large number of people involved and the complexity of its musical structure.

The present study focuses on the performance of Cantonese opera as a "creative process," and attempts to isolate and define the "rules" and their operation in a performance situation. It is the premise of this study that the dynamic "creative process" is as essential to the understanding of a musical tradition as its static, structural features. The author recognizes that, in abstracting "rules" of any process, particularly when it is the complex process of making music, there is a danger of oversimplification to the extent that the result obscures the true understanding of the process. The book does not claim to present the complete picture of the creative process in Cantonese opera. By consciously limiting the scope and depth of the questions posed, it hopes to bring us one small step closer to such an understanding, not only of Cantonese opera, but of music in general.

In musical traditions (both East and West) that have received the bulk of interest of scholars, how a performer creates a passage of music depends to a large extent on musical notation and rehearsal. When such means are not employed, the creative process involves complex factors: first, historically determined and socially enforced and shared tradition, second, individualized habit and aesthetic judgement, and third, performance situations unique to a particular event. This study is limited, to a large extent, to the first group of factors. In other words, based upon different performing situations (a varied repertory and physical and social context) and different performers, the study examines the creative process that defines or reflects a tradition (or a style) that is known as "Cantonese opera." The idiosyncracies of individual performers and the effect of specialized performing situations on musical outcome are left for future studies.

The book further limits its investigation of the creative process mainly to that of the singer and the scriptwriter, discussing the role of the instrumental ensemble and other operatic personnel only as a complementary component to that of the singer. Since the study deals more with how musicians perform than with the end-product of their performance, it does not claim to give an exhaustive description of all the musical material of the opera. The emphasis is on isolating the different "processes" involved in the creation of diverse musical passages.

There have been very few scholarly investigations of Cantonese opera. In regard to its history, the first extensive one is an article "Guangdong xiqu shilüe" [A brief history of Cantonese opera] by Mai Xiaoxia, written in 1940, which contains information on the history, the performance practice, and the repertory of Cantonese opera. It remains the most authoritative work on the subject. A later article "Shitan yueju" [A preliminary study of Cantonese opera] by Ouyang Yuqian, written in 1956, complements Mai's by providing many details of performance practice. A short article on the early history of the opera "Qingdai liusheng xiban zai Guangdong" [Opera troupes from six outside provinces in Guangdong during the Qing dynasty] by Xian Yuqing is also significant. The most recent work, written in 1982, is Leung Puikam's historical survey, *Yueju yanjiu tonglun* [Study of Cantonese opera].

The music of the opera is discussed in several publications mainly for pedagogical purposes, including the two-volume *Yuequ xiechang changshi* [Guide to writing and singing Cantonese opera] by Chen Zhuoying, and the committee-authored *Yueju changqiang yinyue gailun* [General discussion of the style of vocal music of Cantonese opera]. Both works are valuable reference sources because they systematically survey the great variety of tunes used in Cantonese opera and give specific examples in cipher notation. The latter work includes a section on the instrumental ensemble and a summary of the opera's development in recent decades. In the English language, aside from the work of the author, the only other studies are Sauyan Chan's doctoral dissertation "Improvisation in Cantonese operatic music," and a Master's thesis by Chewpah Lim, "The two main singing styles in Cantonese opera."

Studies of the social context of Cantonese opera have appeared in recent years, the most important of which is Tanaka Issei's *Chugoku saishi engeki kenkyu* [Ritual theaters in China], which contains an enormous amount of material on the ritual context of several kinds of Chinese regional operas (including Cantonese opera) in Hong Kong and is based upon exhaustive field work conducted during the 1970s. The late anthropologist Barbara Ward, who spent many years studying village life in Hong Kong, published a series of important articles on Cantonese opera (see bibliography).

The main source of information for the present study is contacts and interviews with performers and other personnel in the operatic circle in Hong Kong, including scriptwriters, managers, theater owners, backstage workers and journalists. Another source is published song texts and musical notation. The most important source materials, however, are sound recordings, which include recordings made during live performances and commercially released records of studio performances. The field work was conducted between December 1972 and August 1973, and between September 1974 and August 1975. The commercial recordings used in this study were almost all made in Hong Kong during the late 1960s and early 1970s (one disk was made in Peking, two in San Francisco). Thus the result of this study represents the state of Cantonese opera in Hong Kong during that period. This is an important point for two reasons. First, Cantonese opera continues to change in Hong Kong since the mid-1970s. Second, after 1949, the development of Cantonese opera in Hong Kong began to diverge from that on the Mainland. Minor differences in nomenclature, and to a certain extent in performance practice itself, appeared between the two branches. While most of the observations and theoretical constructs in this study apply to both, some may apply only to the Hong Kong branch.

Another point to note is that Cantonese opera performed on stage can be quite different from that performed in a studio for commercial recording. The chief difference is that, while a stage performance usually lasts between three to four hours, two sides of a record limits the performance duration drastically and rigidly. (Multi-disk recordings of complete operas are rare.) Furthermore, a studio performance dispenses with many of the purely dramatic elements of a play so that, as a consequence, there is usually much less percussion music and dialogue. But in all other respects, including the creative process of individual song passages, the two kinds of performance are quite similar. Since the focus of this study is the creative process of song passages, it is justified to consider both live performances and studio recordings without belaboring their differences.

This book began as a revision of the author's Ph.D. dissertation "The music of Cantonese opera", but the completed work is quite different from the original goal. Chapters 1, 10, 12, and 13 are entirely newly written, chapter 7 contains essentially new material, chapter 2 is greatly revised, and the other chapters have undergone varying degrees of revision. Earlier versions of chapters 8, 9, and 11 were published separately in 1983 as articles in *Ethnomusicology*, and part of chapter 7 appeared in 1981 in the *IMS Congress Report of 1979*. These four articles have been translated and published in journals on Mainland China and Taiwan under the author's Chinese name Rong Hongzeng. Part of chapter 1 has been translated into Japanese and will appear as part of "China: history and structure of music-dramas," in *Music*

Traditions of Japan, Asia and Oceania (Tokyo: Iwanami Shoten Publishers, in preparation).

A note of explanation must be given for the use of the term "opera" in this book. The Chinese terms *xi* and *qu* have been variously translated depending upon the primary scholarly interest of the translator. The musicologist prefers "opera" (Pian, Yung), the literary scholar prefers "drama" (Johnson, Dolby), and the student of theater arts prefers "theater" (Scott). The term "drama" could be misleading since it may be understood to emphasize the non-musical elements of performance, whereas in the traditional Chinese *xi* or *qu*, singing and musical instrumental accompaniment are obligatory. "Theater" probably has the broadest scope since it can imply a great variety of entertainments including drama, singing, ballet, mime, skit, farce, and so forth; for this reason, it is in many ways perhaps the most appropriate term to apply to the Chinese genre. Nevertheless, since this study is essentially musicological, "opera" seems to be a more suitable translation than either "drama" or "theater." The major problem with this term is the social context it implies: "opera" in the West refers specifically to the kind of musical theater created by composers such as Mozart, Verdi, and Wagner, and which today caters to audiences of a particular social class. The Chinese counterpart has a much broader audience base, providing popular entertainment and serving important ritual functions in the society. This difference will be made clear in the course of the book.

The Chinese names and terms are romanized in some chapters according to the Peking dialect, in others to the Cantonese dialect, and in the rest to both. Names and terms in earlier chapters are romanized according to the Peking dialect because they are not specific to Cantonese opera but are known in other regions of China; they often appear in scholarly literature of a more general nature, where they are almost always romanized in the Peking dialect. Cantonese romanization is used in the second half of the book because most of the names and terms are used exclusively in reference to Cantonese opera, including technical terms and song texts. The technical terms are meaningless when pronounced in any other dialect, and the songs are always sung, of course, in the Cantonese dialect. A few terms in the second half of the book are romanized according to the Peking dialect if they have already appeared as such earlier. In a few chapters, both romanizations are given because, while the terms and names are specific to the Canton area, they may be related to some nationally known terms; examples of these are names of musical instruments. In summary, the following is a table of the scheme of romanization (unless otherwise specified in several isolated places):

Chapter 1   Peking
         2   Peking (Cantonese in parenthesis)
         3   Peking (Cantonese in parenthesis)
         4   Peking (Cantonese in parenthesis)
         5   Peking (Cantonese in parenthesis)
      6–13 Cantonese (Peking in parenthesis).

The Peking dialect is romanized according to the *pinyin* system, with which the reader is assumed to be familiar because of its wide usage today. However, certain names such as Peking in "Peking opera" and "Peking dialect" and Canton in "Cantonese opera" and "Cantonese dialect" are allowed to retain their old, well-established spelling. (Their roma-

Preface

nized form according to the *pinyin* system are, respectively, Beijing and Guangzhou.) The Cantonese dialect, romanized according to the so-called Yale system, is discussed in appendix 1, which also includes a guide to its pronunciation and a brief introduction to its linguistic tones. The reader is advised to read it before approaching chapter 6 and beyond.

All musical examples, unless otherwise noted, are transcribed by the author from field recordings of live performances or commercial records, the sources of which are found in appendix 5. With few exceptions, only the vocal line is transcribed. When the instrumental accompaniment is included, only a "composite" line abstracted from the heterophonic texture is given. Unless otherwise noted, the text is represented only by the linguistic tonal symbols of the syllables, in which case the text in romanization and translation, together with linguistic tonal symbols, can be found in appendix 3, and the Chinese characters in appendix 4. A guide to the symbols used in the transcription of music and in the representation of verse structure of song text can be found in appendix 2.

My greatest debt is owed to the large number of musicians and other personnel of Cantonese opera with whom I studied and consulted in the course of my research. Consistently generous in sharing their knowledge, experience, and artistry, many of the singers and instrumentalists graciously allowed me to watch private practice sessions and rehearsals, sometimes held in their homes. I particularly wish to mention the *erhu* players Mai Huiwen and Wang Yuesheng (who posed for the photographs in chapter 3), and the singers Chen Feinong, Mai Bingrong, He Feifan, Guan Dexing, Lin Jiasheng, Li Baoying, Ruan Zhaohui, and Nan Hong. Guo Lun gave me lessons on the *yangqin*, *erhu*, and *sanxian*. I am also grateful to the singers Fenghuang Nü, Guan Haishan, Jiang Yanhong and Liang Hanwei; the instrumentalists Chen Shao, Chen Wenda, Feng Bingheng, Feng Hua, Lü Wencheng, Zhu Yigang, Zhu Qingxiang, and Zhu Zhaoxiang; the scriptwriters Su Weng, Liu Yuefeng, and Pan Yifan; the opera managers Huang Xuan, Huang Yan, and He Shaobao; the theater-owner Yuan Zhanxun; the puppeteers Mai Shaotang and Chen Hongyu; and the amateur musicians He Chuyun, Li Yuezu, and Luo Jiazhi.

Amy Chan introduced me to her father, the theater-owner Yuan Zhanxun, who opened the door for me to the operatic world by introducing me to several major singers mentioned above. I had useful conversations with the writers Chen Tie'er, Huang Zhanhua, Leung Puikam, Lü Dalü, Sun Baoling, and others. My fieldwork benefited from interactions with fellow research workers in Hong Kong at the time: Masato Nishimura, Rulan Chao Pian, Tanaka Issei, and Barbara Ward.

The doctoral dissertation on which this book is based could not have been completed without the guidance of Rulan Chao Pian and John Ward of Harvard University. Since beginning to revise the dissertation in 1984, I have had many stimulating discussions with, and valuable advice from, Professor Pian. I had useful conversations with Huang Jinpei and Li Yan of the Canton Conservatory of Music, and many discussions with Sauyan Chan and with students in a seminar on Chinese opera which I conducted in winter 1986 at the University of Pittsburgh: Xiwei Li, Poonyeh Tsao, Yingfen Wang, and J. Lawrence Witzleben. Others who made helpful comments at various stages of the writing include John Blacking, Pinghui Li, Mae Smethurst, and John Spitzer. Andrew Miller read the entire manuscript and offered numerous valuable suggestions on matters of style.

I am grateful to John Blacking, the editor for the Cambridge Series on Ethnomusicology,

xiv   Cantonese opera

for his encouragement and support, to Penny Souster of the Cambridge University Press for her patience and understanding, and to Susan Whimster for tirelessly working through the details. Ricardo Schulz assisted in making the cassette tape and Tianwei Xie prepared the Chinese characters.

The field trips to Hong Kong in 1972–73 and 1974–75 were supported by a Graduate Prize Fellowship from Harvard University and a Fulbright-Hays Travel Fellowship respectively. The initial stages of the revision of the dissertation in 1984–85 were funded by an ACLS Grant. The final stages in the preparation of the manuscript were supported in part by grants from the Asian Studies Program and the Contemporary China Program of the University of Pittsburgh.

1 Introduction to Chinese opera

Brief history

Operas in China exist in a great variety of forms and styles, and have a long history. While no one knows when opera first appeared, various sources that could have led to its development have been identified and acknowledged. Some theatrical elements, such as formalized role-playing, existed in religious rituals from antiquity: a shaman would assume the role of a deity or a medium to facilitate communication between the gods and men. The element of entertainment was also apparent when a shaman sang and danced during religious rituals for the gods. Court jesters from the Spring and Autumn period (722–481 BC) mimicked individuals or types of individuals and acted out their stories in order to entertain or to subtly criticize their masters. Primitive forms of puppetry are known to have flourished as early as opera with human actors, if not indeed earlier, and could have played a part in shaping the latter. Various kinds of performances involving song, dance, mimicry, and narrative that served as popular entertainment were mentioned in historical documents centuries before the first appearance of opera scripts. There are also speculations on the influence of Sanskrit drama. That the origin of Chinese opera involved many sources of influence is certain. The questions of when and how these different sources shaped the early development of what has become today's opera may never be completely answered due to the lack of written documentation.[1]

By the time of the Northern Song dynasty (960–1127), a form of entertainment called *zaju*, literally "miscellany play" or "variety play," was in existence. It consisted of enactments of stories in the form of skits for the purposes of social satire, moral advice, and entertainment. The performance appears to have embodied some basic features of present-day operas: singing and dancing, musical accompaniment by percussion and melodic instruments, recitation and dialogue, make-up and costume, acrobatics and clowning. Skits with narrative content were often interwoven with segments of dance, acrobatic display, martial arts, slapstick, and other forms of non-narrative entertainment. Dolby compared these performances to the English stage during the Elizabethan period when drama had yet to establish itself as an independent art-form with its own distinctive institutions and traditions.[2] Incidental references to *zaju* in the literature suggest that it was one of the most popular forms of entertainment of the time, that a large repertory existed, and that written scripts were used. None of the scripts, however, have been preserved to our day.

The earliest complete scripts that have survived are from the Southern Song dynasty (1127–1279); they are for the kind of opera known as Wenzhou *zaju* (the *zaju* from the town of Wenzhou, in modern Zhejiang province in southern China by the eastern seaboard). Despite the fact that no musical notation is included, the few surviving scripts and fragments offer a glimpse of the structure of the opera and its various theatrical and musical elements and prove that the Wenzhou *zaju* was a mature form of theater with the essential characteristics of the present-day operas.[3]

Yuan *zaju*

There is general agreement that, by the Yuan dynasty (1271–1368), a sophisticated form of opera, also called *zaju*, had developed in northern China and, significantly, had become a vehicle for creative output by the literati class. The direct involvement of the literati resulted in a large number of opera scripts, among which more than 160 have been preserved in complete form to this day; most of these are attributable to known writers. None of the scripts, however, contain musical notation. Because for centuries these scripts were recognized as great achievements in literature, the Yuan dynasty was traditionally considered as the golden age of Chinese opera. The scripts and other source materials indicate that the Yuan *zaju* is more than literature: it is also a performing art that attained a high degree of sophistication and complexity.[4]

The rigid formal structure of the Yuan *zaju* is apparent from its scripts. With few exceptions, each opera has four acts (*zhe*) plus an optional interlude (*xiezi*). The interlude is a supplement to the regular acts for the purpose of enhancing the clarity and continuity of the dramatic development. It may fall between any of the four acts or, more often than not, before the first act of the opera, in which case it should more appropriately be considered as a prelude.

The nucleus of the act is the suite (*taoshu*), to which may be added a prologue, an interlude, and an epilogue. The suite is a series of single arias (*qu*) unified by the same tonal mode (*diao*) for the tunes, and by a single rhyme which runs through all the verses of the text. The sequence of arias within the suite is determined by traditionally established patterns. The general practice is that all the arias in an opera are assigned to only a single performer, who plays the principal male or female role.

An important feature of the Yuan *zaju*, found also in Cantonese opera and most other regional operas of today, is the concept and use of *jiaose*, or role types. The characters in all the operas are categorized into a limited number of role types, each of which has its own styles of acting, speaking, singing, costume, and make-up. These oral and visual means of expression define the gender, approximate age, social status, profession, and personality of the role type, and thus the identity of the character, in an opera. An actor or an actress is usually trained in a particular role type, and plays the characters from different operas that belong to this role type. In Yuan *zaju*, there were over twenty role types, among which only a few were singing roles.

It is not known whether or not the music of the opera was notated during the Yuan dynasty even though musical notation was certainly in use in theoretical writings on music at that time; if the music was notated, none has been preserved to the present time. The scripts merely give the titles of the tunes to which the text is to be sung. It is possible that some of the music is represented in a mid-eighteenth-century publication called *Jiugong dachengpu*, a collection of about 4,500 arias with both text and music.[5] A great many of these arias have titles that are identical to those in the Yuan operas. To what degree the music corresponds to those performed in the original operas of four centuries ago is not known.

While little is known about the tunes themselves, it is nevertheless clear that as a rule they are not "composed" by individuals, but are preexistent tunes, each of which identified by a literary title. Even though opera scripts do not contain any musical notation in terms of pitches and rhythm, they do indicate tunes by their titles. The vast repertory of tunes used in the Yuan *zaju* came from a variety of sources, including folk tunes and other kinds of vocal and instrumental music. The poet-scriptwriter selected the tunes from this repertory appropriate to the dramatic and structural demands of the scene, wrote texts to them, and arranged them into a suite. A suite usually consists of from ten to fifteen individual tunes, or a smaller number, of which some are repeated one or more times.

Some tunes became extremely popular among poets; a single tune might be chosen to fit a large number of verses in the same opera or in different operas. This was feasible partly because of the flexibility of the tunes, and partly because the poet-scriptwriter chose the words carefully so that the text conformed to a prescribed prosodic structure, one that could be readily fitted into the tune.[6] This basic compositional process of Yuan operas is found in all operas of later ages and styles, including the Cantonese opera, and is, from the musicologist's point of view, one of the most important characteristics of Chinese opera.

Little information on the musical instruments used in the performance is available today. Paintings and occasional documentation suggest that the performance might be accompanied by an instrumental ensemble of a *dizi* [transverse flute], *ban* [wooden clappers], *gu* [drum], and *luo* [gong]. Other instruments such as the *sanxian* [three-string plucked lute] and the *pipa* [four-string plucked lute] might also have been used.[7]

While the *zaju* flourished in northern China, operatic activities continued to develop in the south more or less independently as a result of the north–south political division of the country for a century and a half during the Southern Song dynasty. The southern style (known as *zaju* in the Song dynasty) was called *nanxi* [southern operas] in the Yuan dynasty, apparently as a way of distinguishing it from the more sophisticated and prestigious opera in the north at that time. Sixteen complete scripts of *nanxi* and a large number of fragments have been preserved from the Yuan dynasty. They show that the southern style differs from its northern counterpart in having a more flexible structure. The number of acts is not fixed, often running up to forty or fifty; more than one singer may sing in an act. The pattern for the sequence of arias is also more flexible, and their choice is not restricted to a single tonal mode within an act. The basic musical unit is still the aria, which uses preexistent tunes of southern origin.

As the more prestigious *zaju* spread to the south after the unification of the country during the Yuan dynasty, it exerted strong influence over the *nanxi*. Many northern style tunes were gradually adopted in the southern opera. By the beginning of the Ming dynasty (1368–1644), the *zaju* had suffered a decline in popularity, while the *nanxi*, having been enriched with musical material from *zaju*, rose in prominence. It developed during the Ming dynasty into a kind of opera called *chuanqi* [marvel tales].[8]

The close association of *zaju* and *nanxi* with the literati class resulted in their relatively high social status, the proliferation of opera scripts, and their prominence in historical documents, all of which contribute to their visibility today. There were doubtless more than the two kinds of opera in China due to regional differences in music and dialect. Other kinds of opera flourished in many areas of the vast country, about which little is known due to the lack of written source material. Nevertheless incidental references indicate that as early as the Song dynasty at least one kind of opera, known as Haiyan opera, developed in the town of Haiyan in Zhejiang province.

Kunqu and Wei Liangfu

A word of explanation is needed on the Chinese terms *shengqiang* and *juzhong*. The term *shengqiang*, or *qiang*, is widely used and could mean different things in different contexts. Principally, it refers to systems of tunes; but it could also imply general modal characteristics and vocal ornamentations of the music. Contemporary musicologists have identified a number of major *qiang* by the early Ming dynasty, among which the most important are the Haiyanqiang in Zhejiang and Jiangxi provinces, the Yuyaoqiang in Jiangsu and Anhui provinces, the Kunshanqiang in the Kunshan area of Jiangsu province, and, apparently the most widespread at that time, the Yiyangqiang in many parts of northern and southern China.

Juzhong, or regional opera, refers to kinds of opera which flourish in different regions; they differ from one another mainly in regional dialect, but often share plot-repertory, styles of costume, and styles of acting. A large number of regional operas share the same *qiang*, while some regional operas combine more than one *qiang*. The different local dialects and aesthetic preferences introduce regional flavors to the music and the performance practice so that the same *qiang* might be manifested in different guises.[9] It is not known how many different regional operas existed during the early Ming dynasty. But the large number of local dialects which had developed by that time suggests that the number of regional operas must be quite large.

Among the major *qiang*, the Kunshanqiang, later known as Kunqu [Kun opera], eventually became the most popular during the middle of the Ming dynasty and exerted the greatest influence on other regional operas throughout China from the sixteenth to the nineteenth centuries. The many scripts of *chuanqi* opera from the Ming dynasty and later were sung in this *qiang*.[10]

The Kunshanqiang is known to have first appeared around the end of the Yuan dynasty (mid-fourteenth century), made popular by a versatile and innovative singer, Gu Jian, who lived near the town of Kunshan. But its eventual dominance in popularity over all other *qiang* is largely attributable to one of the greatest performers in Chinese operatic history, Wei Liangfu (active *c*. mid-sixteenth century), who has been credited by many historians with being the creator of the *qiang*. Little is known about him except that he was from the province of Jiangxi, was blind, and at one point worked as a healer. But he was best known as an accomplished performer of the opera, specializing in the singing of the female roles.

He introduced important musical innovations in his performance and published his theory of singing in a monograph called *Qulü* [Rules on singing] which, according to the late Chinese musicologist Yang Yinliu, can be summarized as follows.[11] First, he paid special attention to *budiao* and *shouyin*. *Budiao* means the matching of the tonal movement of the melody with the linguistic tones of the text; *shouyin* is equivalent to the modern term *yaozi* – the accurate enunciation and projection of the text. Second, melodically, he created a particular style called "shuimoqiang" noted for its refinement and delicacy. Third, rhythmically, he created a style called "lengbanqu" in which the tempo was exceptionally slow, creating a distinctive "lengqing" [cool and clear] atmosphere.

Today, Wei Liangfu is often considered a "composer."[12] Yet he never composed a single tune in the sense that Mozart or Schubert did, but sang only preexistent tunes. Nevertheless he created a new and distinctive *qiang* by introducing innovations into the singing of old

Introduction to Chinese opera

tunes. What Wei accomplished can be considered as composition in a sense different from that usually recognized in European Art music. He did not compose individual "pieces" of music with structural elements such as melody, rhythm, harmony, and so forth, unique to each "piece." Rather, he invented a *qiang* which is not specific to a single "piece" of music (a tune), but is applied to an entire category of music (an entire repertory of tunes).[13]

Wei Liangfu did not create the Kunshanqiang from a vacuum; he was the heir of a long line of singers, such as Gu Jian, who had already cultivated this *qiang* at various stages of its development. The difference is that Wei's contribution was probably greater than anyone else's. A cliché-laden statement such as "The opera of our country is the fruit of the communal creativity of the working masses,"[14] which is typical of the writings of many contemporary Chinese music historians, has greater truth than may appear at first glance. Wei and the other singers of Kunshanqiang also illustrate the truism that, in music that is transmitted principally by oral means, most performers are, to a certain degree, unrecognized composers. Only a few performers, due to their greater impact on performance practice, are recognized as such.

The popularity of Kunqu began to decline by the eighteenth century and since the late nineteenth century, public performances have been rare, although a small group of *aficionados* continues to sing it even today. Its decline was partly due to the rising popularity of several rival *qiang* that spread to many parts of China and spawned a large number of regional operas. Among the ones that played important roles in the course of the next two centuries were the Yiyangqiang, the Bangziqiang, and the Pihuangqiang, each of which was adopted, with local variations, by a number of regional operas. Among them, Pihuangqiang was itself an amalgamation of two systems, or families, of tunes called Xipi and Erhuang.[15] Around the end of the eighteenth century, the Pihuangqiang was introduced into Peking, the capital of the country, and soon became the most popular among the various *qiang*; significantly, it won the royal patronage of the Qing dynasty (1644–1911). Known since then as *jingju*, or the Capital opera, it soon extended its popularity to the other parts of the country and replaced Kunqu as the most influential opera. This is the opera that is commonly known today in the West as Peking opera.[16]

Some features of Chinese opera

The history of Chinese opera in the last four centuries was dominated first by Kunqu, then by Peking opera. Despite their dominance, a large number of regional operas developed and flourished. A survey conducted in the 1950s revealed the existence of some 350 different kinds of dramatic stage performance in China.[17] A small number of these, such as ballet and spoken drama, were developed in the twentieth century under strong Western influence. The vast majority, however, are regional operas which can be called "traditional" in so far as they developed during the past several hundred years as an integral part of the Chinese cultural fabric and share many features of content and structure with one another and particularly with Kunqu and Peking opera.

One distinctive feature of Chinese opera is its multifacetedness. A story is told through speech and mime, song and dance, as well as slapstick and acrobatics. Also indispensable is a generous display of visual splendor in terms of make-up, costume, and sometimes backdrop, stage set, and prop. Dramatic coherence often gives way to pure entertainment and spectacle.

An accomplished performer must be simultaneously an actor, a dancer, and a singer; most performers must also have rigorous training in acrobatics.

Music plays a central role in an opera performance. Before the introduction of Western theater, purely spoken drama was not known in China; all stage performances involved some form of singing and instrumental music. Even when performers "speak," the delivery almost always departs from ordinary speech in its stylized tones and rhythmic patterns. Even non-verbal utterances such as laughing and sighing display formalized structures. Consequently the oral utterances are not solely vehicles for the purpose of telling the story, but are also means of artistic expression in their own right. That is, they are "music" as well as speech. Noted dramatist and scholar Qi Rushan correctly observed that in Chinese operas "all utterances are a form of singing."[18]

The movements and gestures of the performers are also highly stylized and symbolic. For example, the trembling of arms denotes fear; the slow and deliberate raising of an outstretched palm in front of the face suggests weeping. Very few movements are directly representative of real-life gestures. As a parallel to the ubiquity of song, Qi Rushan has said that "all movements on stage are dance."[19] His point is that all movements and gestures on stage are formalized and stylized according to theatrical tradition and a sense of beauty and design. Even mundane movements such as sitting or walking, and everyday gestures such as looking or pointing, must be stylized. Consequently these movements and gestures are not solely vehicles for the purpose of telling the story, but are also means of artistic expression in their own right. That is, they are "dance" in the traditional sense of the word.

The aural and visual means of expression may be generalized to a more basic principle of "theatricality" that seems to underline all aspects of performance in traditional operas. In telling the story on stage the performance does not strive to imitate the sights and sounds of real life, even though the characters portrayed and the emotions expressed are verisimilar, but instead seems deliberately to depart from the familiar and the usual in order to remind the audience that they are witnessing something fantastic and out of the ordinary. Through stylization, the performance seems to say: we are play-acting.

The theatricality of Chinese opera is enhanced by the staging, which traditionally involves a bare space with no realistic backdrop or scenery.[20] The stage props are very often limited to a simple table and two chairs, which, in different scenes, may be used to represent anything from a mountain to a bedchamber. The illusions are achieved through the performers' formalized miming, occasionally using props, and through the use of percussion music. The performers don elaborate and colorful costumes and wear equally colorful and exaggerated make-up. Their design and color are seldom intended as a visual representation of objects in real-life.

Occasionally a performer removes himself from the context of the drama by addressing the audience directly, a breach in dramatic illusion. The dramatist Bertolt Brecht has suggested that Chinese opera practices what he calls the "alienation effect," a device by which the attention of the audience is deliberately redirected from the story being enacted to the fact of performance itself in order that the message can be delivered objectively and clearly.[21]

Another characteristic of Chinese operas is the concept and use of the *jiaose*, or role types, which has already been mentioned in connection with the Yuan opera. Each regional opera has its own system of role types; the systems may differ from one another. As an example, Peking opera has four major role types known as *sheng*, *dan*, *jing*, and *chou*, often translated in

Introduction to Chinese opera

English as "male role," "female role," "painted face role," and "comic role" respectively. On a simple level, the system of role types relies on formulaic visual and aural means to project character-stereotypes in the telling of a story. However, the existence of many subcategories and the flexibility in the application of visual and aural formulae allow complex characterizations on stage.

An important feature of the music of Chinese operas to which allusion has already been made is the use of preexistent tunes. Until recent decades, the tunes are seldom notated, but are preserved and transmitted orally, and are known by literary titles. Each regional opera has its own repertory of tunes from which to draw its musical material, although much overlapping exists among the repertories. Some tunes are used in different regional operas under different names, while some otherwise unrelated tunes might share the same name. Due to the migration of tunes and their evolutionary nature, there is yet to be any systematic understanding of the demography of tunes among the different operas.

There are two ways in which preexistent tunes are combined to form larger units or suites in an opera. First, a suite may comprise a number of entirely different tunes. Called the *lianquti*, this kind of suite might appropriately be termed the "medley" form in English because of its obvious similarity to the "medley" of Western music. Second, a suite may consist of a string of variant forms of the same tune. A certain tune, through many generations of transmission and recreation, has developed into a family of a limited number of variants. Although each variant assumed its structural identity and unique dramatic associations, all are accepted by performers and listeners alike as belonging to the same family. Such family relationships are usually reflected in the names by which the tunes are known. In most cases, they share similar tonal and modal features but differ from each other in what is called *ban*. Literally meaning "wooden clappers" in the context of Chinese theater, the term might be equated with tempo because a pair of wooden clappers mark the beats in some operas. But it implies in addition metrical structure and a degree of melismaticness in the text–tune relationship. A suite of this sort is called the *banqiangti*, or tempo-variant form.[22]

The choice of tunes in both forms may depend on dramatic requirements; the tunes or tune variants in general are associated with certain dramatic moods, and are selected accordingly. The choice may also depend on traditionally established structural patterns. For example, in the medley form, only tunes of the same tonal mode may be allowed in the same suite, or certain tunes may follow or precede certain others. In the tempo-variant form, a suite is often limited to variants of the same tune family, and the sequential arrangement of the variants themselves often determined by established patterns.

All Chinese operas organize their tunes according to a combination of the medley form or the tempo-variant form. Most operas, however, utilize one organization more than the other. For example, the Yuan *zaju* and the Kunqu organize the suites to a large extent in the medley form,[23] while Peking opera uses almost exclusively the tempo-variant form.[24] The size of the repertory of prexistent tunes for an opera that uses the medley form is usually quite large and draws on a wide variety of sources. The size of the repertory for an opera that uses the tempo-variant form, on the other hand, is usually small. For example, in Peking opera only two tunes, or tune families, are used in most of its repertory, each family comprising a dozen or so variant forms.

Regional operas

At the peak of their popularity, Kunqu and Peking opera were performed in many parts of the country and enjoyed by people of different social levels. Kunqu was particularly cultivated by the literati class, while Peking opera had the royal patronage of the Qing court. These intimate associations with the privileged classes enabled the two kinds of opera to achieve high levels of refinement and sophistication. Social prestige and financial rewards, unmatched by other operas, attracted performers and scriptwriters of exceptional talent. The operas came to be appreciated as more than entertainment. Aesthetic theories were proposed and established; repertories were stabilized and systematized; scripts and, to a certain extent, musical notation, were published; biographies and histories were written. In short, each of these two operas evolved into a generally recognized "High Art."

In contrast, almost all other regional operas serve as popular entertainment for the masses with little formalized aesthetic value attached to them. They share two other important social functions, however, in addition to their entertainment value. First, operatic performances had always been an integral part of religious ceremonies, calendrical festivities, and rites of passage in Chinese society.[25] And in some parts of China at least, this ritual function remains largely unchanged today despite the drastic political, social, and economic changes since the turn of the century.[26] Secondly, the operas served for centuries as a source of information and an arbiter of moral standards and social behavior for their audiences, the majority of which were illiterate or semi-literate; it was thus an important medium for mass communication and education. In recent decades, the importance of this function has been reduced by the rise in the level of literacy and the flourishing of other mass media such as cinema and television.[27]

There are, of course, differences among the large number of operas, each of which developed and flourished in a particular geographical area and in some instances a particular social stratum with its own regional and sub-cultural flavor. The size of the troupes and the scale of performances can vary greatly, ranging from a handful of performers to as many as fifty or sixty. Although for most of the operas performances are confined to small geographical regions, a few are known and occasionally performed on a national level.

Foremost among the differences is the dialect used in performance, which is usually that spoken in the area in which the opera flourished.[28] The operas are, of course, musically quite different if they belong to different *qiang*; the differences include scale, tonal mode, ornamentation, the repertory of tunes, accompanying instruments, and the manner of accompaniment. In cases where the operas belong to the same *qiang*, they share the same repertory of tunes and other musical matters to a large extent; but the regional aesthetic preferences inevitably result in different treatments of the same tune by the singers. Thus, on a more detailed level, the music of regional operas belonging to the same *qiang* differ from one another: knowledgeable audiences could easily identify the differences.[29] Visually (that is, in terms of costumes, make-up, and movements), the operas differ from one another only to a small degree. They share for the most part a common repertory of stories drawn from legends, myths, and historical and semi-historical narratives that are nationally known.

Among the many regional operas is the Cantonese opera, which has flourished mainly in the Pearl River Delta in the southern province of Guangdong, one of the most densely populated areas in China. Within this region are urban centers such as Canton, Foshan, and Hong Kong. The Chinese call Cantonese opera Yueju or *daxi*; the former term appears generally in writing, while the latter is more commonly used colloquially by Cantonese-speaking people. The word "Yue" refers to the province of Guangdong, sometimes also including the neighboring province of Guangxi to its west. The term Yueju therefore means "opera of Guangdong and Guangxi." *Daxi*, which literally means "grand opera," reflects its physical grandeur on the one hand, and on the other, its leading social status in relation to the six or seven other kinds of smaller-scale opera that flourish in the Guangdong and Guangxi provinces. The English word "Cantonese," however, refers to the city "Canton" and the dialect used in the opera.

Little is known about early theatrical activities in the Canton area. Sources indicate that, not later than the mid-sixteenth century, various *qiang* such as Yiyangqiang, Kunshanqiang, and others from northern provinces were introduced into the region by visiting musicians. Northern influence is further suggested by the deity Master Zhang, whose name plaque can be found backstage in every theater today and to whom all Cantonese opera personnel pay their respects. He is said to be a real person and an accomplished opera performer from Peking who, in the early eighteenth century, settled in Foshan, a large city about ten miles southwest of Canton, and introduced northern operas to the region. When Canton was declared the only port to handle China's trade with foreign countries in 1759, a large number of businessmen from various northern provinces converged on the city, bringing great wealth as well as attracting operatic troupes from their native areas. Some of the troupes stayed on, trained local Cantonese as performers, and slowly adopted local musical elements.

By the mid-nineteenth century, the identification of two different kinds of opera troupes in the Canton area first appeared in the literature: the *waijiangban* [outside troupes] and the *bendiban* [local troupes]. Significantly, around the same period, the Cantonese vernacular began to be spoken on stage and, for the next half century or so, slowly replaced the original stage dialect called *zhongzhou yin* [the central dialect], which is of northern origin. One may assume that some time around or before the mid-nineteenth century, the identity of Cantonese opera emerged.[30]

For the next century, Cantonese opera continued to develop its stamp of identity by adopting local musical elements as well as absorbing and assimilating new influences from other kinds of theater. For example, when Peking opera became popular throughout the country in the late nineteenth and early twentieth centuries, Cantonese opera readily adopted some of its musical instruments and tunes. When Western performing arts from Europe and America exerted strong influences in the early twentieth century, including the spoken play and the cinema, Cantonese opera again embraced much of its musical instruments, tunes, stories, costume, and staging.

During the first half of the twentieth century, Cantonese opera reached its height of popularity. It was performed in large cities as well as rural areas throughout the Pearl River Delta area, and was also occasionally performed in other parts of China. Furthermore, it has probably spread further and struck deeper roots overseas than any other kind of Chinese opera. During the late nineteenth and early twentieth centuries, it was regularly performed in those parts of Southeast Asia where large colonies of Cantonese have settled for many generations, including Indonesia, the Philippines, Vietnam, Thailand, the Malayan Peninsula, and Singapore.[31] In addition, its popularity extended to North American Chinatowns, San Francisco in particular, where, at one time, several resident Cantonese opera troupes performed regularly.[32]

10   Cantonese opera

From the 1940s, due to complex political and social factors, Cantonese opera has suffered a decline in popularity in China as well as abroad. In particular, official policy during the Cultural Revolution and the so-called Gang-of-Four period (1966–76) banished Cantonese opera with traditional content and style from the stage almost completely,[33] with the result that Hong Kong became almost the only place where such operas continued to be performed. Since 1976, however, there has been a revival of the traditional repertory and style of performance on the Mainland.

2 Essential elements of Cantonese opera as performing art

Cantonese opera as performed today is grand spectacle and total theater in the sense that a story is told on stage by a large number of actors, singers, dancers, acrobats, and instrumentalists, against a backdrop of elaborate sets and costumes. A performance by a major troupe generally involves forty or more performers on stage, about sixteen musical instrumentalists, and a small number of backstage workers. In most plays six performers have roles that involve extensive speaking, singing, and acting; a few play minor supporting roles. Other performers serve in non-speaking, walk-on parts such as the court maidens, attendants, soldiers, and servants, who appear regularly in almost all plays. Many of them are specially trained dancers or acrobats who appear on stage exclusively in scenes that call for such displays.

While the number of performers may vary from a dozen to over fifty or sixty, depending upon the size of the troupe and the performing context, the essential visual, aural, and dramatic elements are always present in any performance. This chapter surveys these elements.

Visual elements

One important feature found in all Chinese operas is the element of dance. A performer's movements and gestures are in general highly stylized. In Cantonese opera, despite a continuing trend towards realistic acting since the 1920s and 1930s, this element of dance is still evident today. An individual performer's stage actions involve a mixture of realism and stylization, the degree of mixture depending upon the role type; the movements and gestures of a scholar-official or an aristocratic maiden are likely to be more stylized, while those of a comic role would be more realistic and natural.

Group activities on stage, such as the maneuvering of soldiers on the battlefield or of a bevy of maids in the palace, involve patterns of interlocking movements performed by a large number of actors and actresses who specialize in these so-called "mute" roles. The sometimes complex patterns, or "dances," are generally formulaic, following rules that have been established by tradition for many generations, and are shared by many plays. Only rarely are original patterns created especially for a specific play. Sometimes such a "dance" provides a decorative background for the hero's feature aria, a kind of human prop, not unlike the role often served by the *corps de ballet* in Western ballet. Occasionally specifically choreographed pieces appear as "dances" within the context of the drama.

Related to dance is the display of martial arts and acrobatics. Many plays have plots that involve some form of combat, either between two groups of men or between two individuals. The encounters might involve bare fists or various kinds of weapons such as swords, sabers, knives, sticks, and axes. Each weapon allows the performers to show off a specific dance-like routine in the martial arts. In the course of such combats displays of breathtaking tumbling are frequent. The routines may be performed by a soloist who shows off special individual skills or by two or more actors interacting with one another in carefully choreographed patterns. Occasionally the dramatic momentum seems to stop with the result that the displays take on the appearance of circus acts designed to exhibit strength and dexterity purely for their own sake. These routines take many years of training and form some of the most spectacular moments in the opera.

A major visual attraction is the costumes of the performers, which have always been an essential element of Chinese opera. Traditionally the costumes were made of embroideries and brocades, but in recent decades the subtle beauty of these fabrics has given way to less expensive yet brighter and louder synthetic materials. Some gowns are covered with colored plastic beads. Under strong stage lights their bright colors, rich textures, and shimmering glitter form a tableau of extraordinary splendor. During one performance in the early 1970s the heroine wore a costume draped with battery-powered lightbulbs. Some members of the audience frown on such visual opulence as excessive; for others the colorful, glittering dresses and gowns are among the opera's major attractions.

It is not uncommon to judge the status and popularity of a performer by the number of *yixiang* (*yiseung*) [costume trunks] he or she possesses.[1] Often a significant portion of a performer's earning goes into the acquisition of new costumes. Given the primacy of spectacle, far less thought is given to choosing the costumes appropriate to the historical period in which the story is laid than to satisfying the audience's desire for gorgeous display for its own sake. The same set of gowns might be worn for a play set in the Warring States period of more than two thousand years ago and for a play set in the last days of the Qing dynasty in the twentieth century.

Unlike Peking opera, which has a single fixed backdrop of simple design and a minimum of stage sets and properties, the Cantonese opera indulges in richly painted backdrops that are normally changed from scene to scene as the dramatic context requires. Sometimes three-dimensional, realistic stage sets are employed. Occasionally use is made of sophisticated lighting systems as well as ingenious special effects such as thunder, lightning, mist, and cloud, and slides and movies may be projected as backdrops to enhance the visual effect.

By Western theatrical standards, the use of make-up by many of the performers is heavy, the amount depending on the individual role. The make-up not only highlights the normal features of the face for projection in a large theater but has important dramatic functions. Its color and design, which depend on the role and are determined by tradition, always have symbolic significance, and contribute to the characterization of the roles. For some roles the face is painted a basic white, with strong shades of red around the eyes, which generally signals a character being "normal" in type. In the case of a more unusual character such as a demon, god, super-villain or hero the design is bolder and involves contrasting colors separated by sharp, distinct lines. Besides its symbolic and dramatic significance, the bright make-up complements the colorful costumes and backdrops and helps to form the fantastic visual palette that is one of the distinctive features of Cantonese opera.

Aural elements

Cantonese opera, when compared to other Chinese operas, is characterized by a great variety of tunes, a lyrical style of singing, a large instrumental ensemble, and spirited and clamorous percussion music, characteristics that were firmly established during the period of bold experimentation and reform in the 1920s and 1930s. The music may be divided into vocal with instrumental accompaniment and purely instrumental, the latter to be discussed after the musical instruments are introduced.

As in other kinds of Chinese operas, the vocal music in Cantonese opera, with very few exceptions, is based on preexistent tunes, each of which is identified by a title. Depending upon their historical origin, their musical structure and style, their dramatic function, and above all, their creative process, the tunes can be grouped into three categories known as, first, the *banghuang* (*bongwong*), second, the *xiaoqu* (*siukuk*) and the *paizi* (*paaiji*), and third, the *shuochang* (*syutcheung*). For reasons that will be explained in subsequent chapters, they are translated respectively as "aria types," "fixed tunes," and "narrative songs." Aria types and fixed tunes are the more important, comprising about 90 per cent of the total vocal music. Collectively, all the songs are known as *chang* (*cheung*) [to sing, or sung].

Complementary to the *chang* is the *bai* (*baak*) [to speak, or spoken]. A passage of text can be delivered in speech in a variety of manners (to be called "speech types" in this study), each of which is characterized by specific verse structures, and metrical and rhythmic patterns; some have instrumental accompaniment. Each speech type is also identified by a title.

The distinction between "song" and "speech" appears to be based upon the presence or absence of musical tones, which are defined here as ones with stable pitches and with consistent intervallic relationships among them such that, theoretically, a scale can be abstracted.[2] Although speech types do not involve musical tones, they often exhibit identifiable metrical and rhythmic patterns, and verse structures that involve patterns in phrase lengths, rhymes, and linguistic tones. All such features can be considered as musical elements that make speaking sound like singing.

Two other factors blur the distinction between speech and song. First, in the course of performing certain songs, a singer often slips for brief moments into speech-like tones. Second, the Chinese speech itself is so constituted that the linguistic tones of individual syllables in a passage can easily produce a tonal contour very similar to that of a melody. This kind of song-like melody in speech is especially noticeable at moments of excitement when the contrasts in pitch levels and pitch contours of linguistic tones are exaggerated. Thus, speaking may verge at times on singing and singing may lapse into speech. The overlap between the two modes of oral expression results in an aural palette rich in variety.

Because of the lack of a clear distinction between "speech" and "song," the term "oral delivery" will be used occasionally in this study for convenience to include both of those concepts, and the various tunes in the "song" category and the speech types will be collectively called "oral delivery types," which are summarized in figure 2.1.

The exceptionally large instrumental ensemble, in comparison to other kinds of Chinese operas, produces a musical texture which is full and rich. Its melodic instrumental ensemble in particular has developed into a small orchestra of about twelve musicians (for a full-sized troupe) with a great variety of instruments that few other operas can match (compared to

Cantonese opera

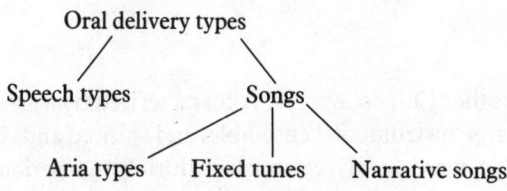

Figure 2.1 Categories of oral delivery types

Peking opera which has a melodic ensemble of two or three instruments). The use of recently developed instruments with low registers has expanded the palette of orchestral color. The number of instruments in a performance varies depending on the size of the troupe as a whole. One musician may handle more than one instrument, switching from one to another in the course of the performance.

The instruments and the instrumentalists are collectively called the *pengmian* (*paangmin*) [face of the shed][3] and are divided into two groups: the *wenchang* (*mancheung*) [civil section], consisting of about twelve instrumentalists who play string and wind instruments, and the *wuchang* (*moucheung*) [military section], consisting of four instrumentalists who play mostly percussion instruments. The percussion ensemble is also among the largest in Chinese operas: it uses two different sets of gongs and cymbals, as well as a wide array of woodblocks and drums.

The two ensembles function as distinct units with distinct functions in the performance. The main functions of the string and wind instruments, herein referred to as the melodic ensemble, are to accompany singing, and, occasionally, to provide background music during non-singing moments. The main functions of the percussion ensemble, although it also accompanies singing to a limited extent, are to underscore the dramatic atmosphere on stage, to accentuate speech, bodily action, and facial expression, to accompany stage movement, dance, and acrobatic display, and to suggest thoughts and moods of a character. Since the percussion ensemble plays a critical role in all aspects of the opera, it is hardly surprising that percussion music should be ubiquitous in performance.

Musical notation and scale

Musical notation generally is not used before or during a performance. The opera script merely specifies the titles of the oral delivery types, based upon which the singer would know the preexistent tunes (or the manner of delivery for speech types). Notation is written into the script on rare occasions when a less-familiar fixed tune is employed or when a new tune is composed. Percussion patterns are never written out beyond their titles. For this reason, notation is not important in the Cantonese operatic tradition.

When notation is necessary in an opera script, a version of the so-called *gongche* (*gungche*) notation is used. Many kinds of opera and other kinds of Chinese vocal and instrumental music use some variant forms of this notation, the origin of which can be traced to at least the Northern Song dynasty. The version used in Cantonese opera comprises two kinds of symbols: tonal and rhythmic. The former consists of a set of names, each of which denotes a particular tone in the total tonal gamut, or scale. Since the names do not imply absolute

Cantonese opera as performing art

pitches, it is more accurate to describe them as names for scale degrees which define a set of tonal intervals.[4]

The music in Cantonese opera uses a heptatonic scale; its seven tones in the octave, or scale degrees, named *ho, si, yi, saang, che, gung,* and *faan* (romanized according to the Cantonese dialect; in Peking dialect, they are *ho, shi, yi, shang, che, gong, fan*), are roughly equivalent to the tones of the Western major diatonic scale. Even though the tones do not imply absolute pitches, the general practice in Cantonese opera today is to equate the seven tones approximately with the following absolute pitches on the piano: G (below middle C), A, B⁻, C, D, E and F+ respectively. B⁻ refers to a pitch halfway between B and B♭, and F+ refers to a pitch halfway between F and F#. The Cantonese scale can therefore be considered as being composed of two intervals: the major second (a whole tone) and the neutral second (a three-quarter tone), arranged in the order shown in figure 2.2.[5] (To accommodate Western

Figure 2.2 Music scale in Cantonese opera

readers, the Western solmization will be used to represent the Cantonese names. Thus: *ho* = Sol, *si* = La, *yi* = Si, *saang* = Do, *che* = Re, *gung* = Mi, *faan* = Fa. It should be understood that the pitch height of Si and Fa here is different from that implied in the usual solmization.)

The Cantonese musicians do not in general use a pitch pipe or tuning fork, but a survey of live performances and commercial recordings shows that the value of *ho* rarely deviates from G for larger than a whole tone. One may describe this practice as one of "flexible absolute pitch," and all transcriptions in this book, which equate *ho* with G for convenience, reflect actual pitch (or octave equivalent) to within a whole tone. It should also be noted that male and female singers sing the same *gongche* notation at an octave apart; in other words, the notational system does not distinguish the octave difference of the two voices. All musical examples in this book follow this practice and do not distinguish between male and female octaves; they are all transcribed in the female octave. Note that the staff notation in figure 2.2 represents the female octave; for the male voice, it should be notated an octave lower if it is to reflect actual pitch. An instrumentalist has the freedom to choose the appropriate octave for his instrument when reading the notation.

There are four rhythmic symbols: "X," "\," "X," and "L." "X" is called *ban (baan)* which refers to "strong beat" in this context; "\" is called *ding (ding)* which refers to "weak beat." Having one of these symbols placed immediately to the side of the name of a tone (or a textual syllable) in the script specifies that the tone (or syllable) is to be sung either on a strong beat or on a weak beat. All Cantonese tunes that have regularly recurring beats have one of the following three metrical patterns: one strong beat followed by (or following) three weak beats (one-*ban*-three-*ding*), strong beats alternating with weak beats (one-*ban*-one-*ding*), and evenly stressed beats (all *ban*). "X" and "L" refer to *ban* and *ding* that are not filled with a tone or a syllable. Tones or syllables that do not have any rhythmic symbol on their sides mean that they occur in between the beats; in other words, the beat is being subdivided. The

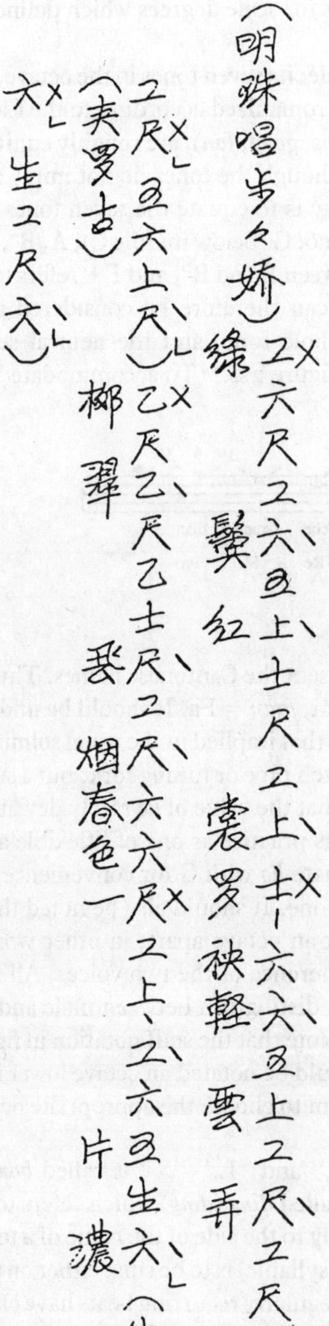

16   Cantonese opera

（明珠唱步々嬌）乙㐅六尺乙㐅六五上士尺乙上士㐅六六五上乙尺乙尺乙（六反
緣　鬢　裊　雲　
（夷罗古）乙尺五六上尺㐅乙尺乙士尺乙尺六六尺乙上乙六五生六㐅（生紀五
榔翠　红　罗　袂輕　弄
六㐅　娑　煙春色一　片濃
生乙尺六㐅

Figure 2.3 *Dainty Steps* in *gongche* notation

Cantonese opera as performing art

subdivision of a beat is never spelled out in the notation, but depends upon the interpretation of the performer. A general rule is that the subdivision is duple.

Figure 2.3 shows an excerpt of the notation for the fixed tune called *Dainty Steps* from the play *Giving the Magic Pearl at Rainbow Bridge* as it appeared in the script. It should be read from right to left and from top to bottom. From right to left, it consists of three columns, the first of which begins, in parenthesis, with the direction to performers: "Lady Pearl sings *Dainty Steps*." The notation proper consists of three subcolumns for each column. From right to left, they are: rhythmic symbols, tonal symbols, and song text. The rhythmic symbols show clearly that *Dainty Steps* has a metrical pattern of one-*ban*-three-*ding*. The tonal symbols in parenthesis in the second subcolumn indicate instrumental interlude. At the top of column 2, the third subcolumn has a short phrase in parenthesis which is not a song text but is a direction for the percussion ensemble: "add percussion music." Figure 2.4 is a transcription of the excerpt in staff notation (stems pointing down indicate voice, stems pointing up indicate instrumental accompaniment).[6]

Figure 2.4 *Dainty Steps* in staff notation

While the singer's vocal range generally does not extend beyond an octave, the complete range of tonal material theoretically comprises three octaves: the core octave given in figure 2.2, one lower octave, and one higher octave. The names of the scale degrees are slightly different for the lower and higher octaves from those of the core octave. Such a three-octave gamut is shown in figure 2.5, with the names of each scale degree given in Chinese characters and romanization.

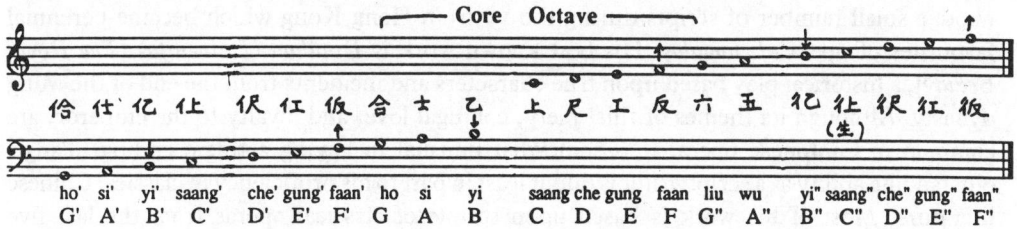

Figure 2.5 Cantonese heptatonic scale in three octaves

Note that the Chinese names for the scale degrees in the lower and the higher octaves are derived from the names of the middle, or core, octave. For example, the scale degree *che* in the core octave is written as 尺; the corresponding scale degree in the lower octave is written as 伬 and the one in the higher octave is written as 仅. It is not difficult to recognize that the lower octave *che* is simply the ideogram for the core *che* with the addition of the partial ideogram 亻 to its left; while the higher octave *che* is simply the core *che* with the addition of a slightly different partial ideogram 纟 . All three ideograms are pronounced identically as *che*. Two exceptions to this simple rule are the octave equivalents of the scale degrees *ho* and *si* in the higher octave; these have entirely different ideograms which are pronounced as *liu* and *wu*. For the scale degree *saang*, the higher octave equivalent has a different character, but is pronounced identically. The reasons for these anomalies in nomenclature are unknown.

In this study, the romanized form of the scale degrees and the letter names representing the pitches from different octaves are distinguished from each other by a method analogous to that used in the Chinese ideograms: a single prime (') is added to the name of the scale degree in the core octave to indicate that it is an octave equivalent in the lower octave; double primes (") are added to the names to indicate those in the higher octave.

Dramatic elements

For all the visual and aural elements, the primary focus of Cantonese opera remains the telling of stories. These are mostly adaptations from China's large body of folk tales, legends, myths, and historical and semi-historical narratives. Most of the stories are widely known throughout China; a small fraction is specific to the Canton region. As in other kinds of Chinese opera, only stories set in the distant past are performed.[7]

Unlike the better-known Peking opera, in which a performance may consist of either a single play or a string of independent acts drawn from different plays, a performance of Cantonese opera always consists of a single play of four to eight acts lasting about four hours.[8] The plot as a whole is often extremely involved and complicated. Largely standardized scenes – weddings, battles, court trials, lovers' farewells and so forth – are shared by many plays. Frequent use is made of such formulaic plot elements as mistaken identities, forced separations, and chance encounters. A hero may have to go through many adventures before he attains his goal, and lovers may have to overcome various obstacles before their final happy union. With few exceptions, stories culminate in a wedding scene in which the protagonists are merrily united. Sometimes even the villains repent and find their appropriate mates.

There are of course exceptions to the above generalization. Tang Disheng (Tong Diksang), one of the most highly respected scriptwriters of Cantonese opera in this century, wrote a small number of scripts during the 1950s in Hong Kong which became perennial favourites of opera *aficionados*. His best known work is *Dinühua (Daineuifa)* [*The Royal Beauty*], a historical play based upon true characters and incidents from the end of the Ming dynasty. Although its themes of filial piety, conjugal love, and loyalty to the emperor, are common in Cantonese opera, it is somewhat unusual in having a tragic ending. Tang's outstanding ability as a scriptwriter is due at least in part to his proficiency in classical Chinese literature. Most of his work is based upon scripts of classical operas from the last five centuries that have long been recognized as literary masterpieces. His scripts are well-structured, dramatically coherent, and elegantly written.

The great majority of Cantonese operas, however, cater to more popular tastes. A typical example is the play *Hongqiao Zengzhu (Hungkiu Jangjyu)* [*Giving the Magic Pearl at Rainbow Bridge*], to be henceforth referred to and abbreviated as *The Magic Pearl*.[9] The story, which is a loose adaptation of a Peking opera of the same title, is also found in other regional operas such as that of Hunan opera.[10] Briefly summarized, the plot is as follows:

Act 1

In Lake Hung Jaak under Rainbow Bridge have lived two female demons, Lady Pearl and her maid Little Bou.[11] After years of self-cultivation, they have acquired the ability to assume the form of two beautiful female human beings. Lady Pearl possesses a magic pearl which has immense power. Golden Scale, the young son of the Dragon King of the nearby Bin River, is attracted to the beautiful Lady Pearl, but she has not returned his love. The activities of the two demons and the visits of Golden Scale to the lake have caused great flooding in the surrounding territory. The magistrate of the lakeshore town of Sei Jau has offered sacrifices to the Goddess of Mercy in heaven and prayed for the return of peace to his land. The Goddess of Mercy sends the God of Law to deal with the demons and to restore peace.

One day, a young scholar named Si Tingfong arrives by the lake. Betrothed by his parents to the magistrate's daughter ten years ago, he has come to claim his bride, whom he has never met. Wanting to cross the lake, he hires a boat. Just then Lady Pearl and Little Bou, strolling by the lake in human form, catch sight of Si and, being immediately attracted to him, ask to share the boat trip with him. The boatman is actually the God of Law in disguise, and recognizes the demons, but because they have the magic pearl, he can do nothing to stop them. While they are all in the boat, Lady Pearl expresses her love for Si and he also falls in love with her. He feels, however, that he must abide by the marriage contract, and hence cannot return her love. Feeling greatly saddened, they part at the other side of the lake.

When the magistrate meets Si, he finds out that Si's family has become poor and that Si has not passed any high level Royal Examination. He wants to break the marriage contract, but Si refuses out of a sense of propriety, and they part acrimoniously.

Act 2

Back by the side of the lake, Si meets Little Bou again, who, learning that he has been rejected by the magistrate, invites him to visit their home underneath the water. Si and Lady Pearl meet once again and declare their love for each other. Si decides to break the marriage contract so that he can stay with Lady Pearl. Suddenly Golden Scale appears and, raging with jealousy, tries to kill Si. Lady Pearl subdues him with her magic pearl and tells him that he can never win her love. Convinced of this, he promises to remain her friend and to help her in her need. Before Si goes back to see the magistrate, Lady Pearl gives him her magic pearl as a token of her love. The pearl also enables him to ascend to land from the depth of the lake.

Act 3

As soon as Si comes up to land, he is seized by the God of law, who has been waiting for him, and the magic pearl is taken away from him. Learning of this, Lady Pearl plans a battle with the God of Law in order to rescue Si; she also solicits the help of Golden Scale. Her plan is to flood the whole land with water from the lake. The God of Law, however, tricks her while disguised as an old woman and averts the flooding. He also obtains help from six other gods, including well-known mythological figures such as the Monkey King, the Green Dragon, the White Tiger, and the Red Bird. After several fierce battles Lady Pearl, Little Bou, and Golden Scale are defeated. Captured by the God of Law, Lady Pearl bids sad farewell to Si before being banished to confinement.

Act 4

A few years have passed. Si has taken the Royal Examination and passed with the highest honors, and has become a high government official. The magistrate now welcomes him and asks him to fulfill the marriage contract with his daughter, he consents reluctantly. The magistrate's daughter, in the meantime, has become gravely ill. The magistrate insists that the wedding ceremony be held because he believes that it would have a curing effect on her illness. On the wedding night, the God of Law arrives with Lady Pearl. He explains to her that the Goddess of Mercy has pardoned her; not only because she has already atoned for her wrongdoings, but because the Goddess is moved by her true and undying love for Si. Since the magistrate's daughter is destined to die that night, Lady Pearl has been allowed to live a proper human life by assuming the physical form of the magistrate's daughter. The opera ends happily with the lovers united in marriage, and with the magistrate possessed of a new daughter in Lady Pearl.

This play, while not necessarily regarded as a masterpiece, can serve to illustrate certain typical plot elements in Cantonese opera. The battle scenes in act 3 offer an excellent excuse for a display of martial arts including acrobatic skills. Comic relief is provided mainly by the God of Law, who disguises himself as a boatman in act 1 and as an old woman in act 3. Long passages of lyrical singing occur between the lovers in act 2 and again in act 4. The scene in the demons' underwater palace allows an opportunity for spectacular stage sets. Although there is no wedding scene *per se*, the wedding chamber in act 4 offers a sufficient excuse for a lavish display of traditional furnishings, costumes and other paraphernalia associated with a wedding, including a pair of red candles, a large piece of red cloth embroidered with the character *xi* (*hei*) [double happiness], and the newlyweds' elaborate wedding gowns. The unexpected plot development in the last act, which crowns a potential tragedy with a happy ending, is a common feature in many plays.

In Chinese folklore demons are not necessarily evil; in this play, Lady Pearl and Little Bou are treated sympathetically. Since they cause flooding and misery to the townspeople of Sei Jau, they must properly atone for their sins. Their defeat by the God of Law and eventual capture and confinement serve as punishment. Lady Pearl's unselfish love (she first gave up her magic pearl to her lover and then risked her life to save him) moves the heavens, and, by taking the place of the magistrate's dead daughter and fulfilling filial duty, she further proves her worth as a human being. She is thus permitted to reunite with her love and find happiness. The young scholar shows respect for his elders by honoring the marriage contract made by his parents, and is rewarded by passing the Royal Examination with the highest honors and by eventually achieving the love-match that he deserves. Didactic messages of this kind are quite common in Cantonese operas.

Role type system

Through its history, Cantonese opera has adopted different sets of role types, the concept and practice of which were as old as Chinese opera itself (see chapter 1). The 1940s and 1950s saw the emergence of a set of six role types which has still prevailed in the 1970s and 1980s. Many of the names of these types are identical to those used in historical times or to those in other kinds of opera; for example, the name *xiaosheng* is also used in Peking opera to refer to young

Cantonese opera as performing art

male roles. In Cantonese opera, however, the classification is less rigid as regards characterizations. The following are the six role types.

1. Wenwusheng. The word "wen" means "literary" or "refined" in this context, while the term "wu" means "military" or "martial." The name *wenwusheng* therefore implies that the role incorporates the two seemingly contrasting characterizations. The role type refers in fact to the principal male role, which can be either a scholar, a military general, or any characterization in between.
2. Zhengyin huadan. The principal female role.
3. Xiaosheng. The supporting male role.
4. Erbanghua. The supporting female role.
5. Chousheng. The comic role.
6. Wusheng. Literally the "military" role, it is no longer restricted to warriors or generals in Cantonese opera. It is often the role for an antagonist to the principal male role.

In the play *The Magic Pearl*, the distribution of the six role types are as follows: Si Tingfong fills the principal male role, Lady Pearl fills the principal female role, Golden Scale fills the supporting male role, Little Bou fills the supporting female role, the God of Law fills the comic role, and the magistrate fills the military role.

Description of a performance

In order to give the reader some sense of the atmosphere of a performance, and in particular the role of music in the opera, it seems appropriate to offer a brief description of the beginning of the first act of *The Magic Pearl* as recorded on July 14, 1975.[12] Several minutes before the curtain rises the melodic ensemble begins an overture. This consists of a series of well-known tunes which are neither regarded as especially suitable for an overture nor specifically associated with this particular play; the instrumentalists simply agree on these tunes at the time and perform them without notation. In some performances today a taped recording may be used instead. When the play is about to begin, the percussion ensemble takes over and plays a *paizi* tune associated with the raising of the curtain. The sudden burst of the loud and brilliant *suona* (an oboe-like, double-reeded instrument) and percussion music alerts both the performers and the audience to the fact that the show is about to start. The specific *paizi* tune is neither named nor notated in the script because the instrumentalists know what it is without such aids.

Two men and two women, minor performers who play the townsfolk of Sei Jau, enter stage right; their stylized movements and the accompanying percussion pattern are those typically associated with stage entrances. When they reach the center of the stage they begin a dialogue in which they summarize the background of the story; their delivery involves a special style of speech and is accompanied by regular strokes on a woodblock. At the end of the scene they exit stage left, accompanied by a percussion pattern that is usually associated with stage exits. A performer's entrances and exits are almost always achieved through highly stylized movements and accompanied by percussion patterns.

When the God of Law enters stage right, he performs a set of forceful dance-like movements befitting his role type, the military official. The percussion music that accompanies his entrance is louder and more elaborate than that in the first scene. Such variations generally reflect the professional standing of the actor and the dramatic importance of his role in the opera rather than the social status of the character he portrays; for example, a principal performer in the role of a beggar will be given louder and more elaborate entrance music than a minor performer, even though the latter portrays a high-ranking general. When later the God of Earth enters he is not accompanied by any special percussion pattern because he is a minor actor in real life and his role in the opera is relatively unimportant.

The God of Law introduces himself and explains his mission by means of various songs and speech types, simultaneously executing additional stylized movements; his performance, both oral and kinetic, is generously accompanied by percussion music. The dialogue between the God of Law and the God of Earth is delivered in a mixture of speech and song and punctuated throughout by percussion music which draws attention to bodily movements and facial expressions and highlights the emotions that are expressed. The God of Law exits stage left accompanied by another flourish of percussion music; the exit of the God of Earth that immediately follows, like his entrance, has no such accompaniment.

As regards the aural aspect of performance the most distinctive feature, perhaps, is the prominence of percussion music throughout as an accompaniment to curtain-raising, entrances and exits, body movements, dance, speech, song, and other dramatic happenings. Besides the specific function which each kind of percussion music serves, its omnipresence helps to sustain a dramatic mood throughout the performance, reminding the audience that the show is on.

3 Musical instruments

Percussion instruments

While the number of instruments[1] in an ensemble may vary according to the size of the troupe, a "core" set of instruments is used in almost any performance, the most important among which are the three woodblocks. The largest of these, which we shall call the "large woodblock," is a hollow, rectangular wooden box roughly 2 inches by 4 inches by 8 inches (figure 3.1). Along each of the long sides of the box is a thin slit extending almost to the two

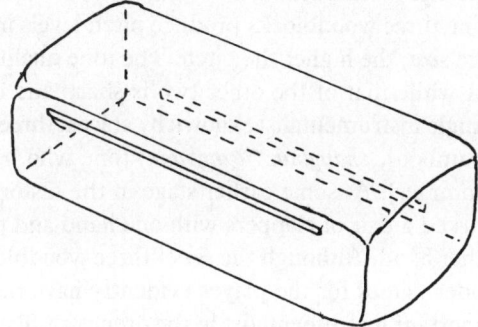

Figure 3.1 Large woodblock

ends. The woodblock is known to the musicians variously as *bangzi* (*bongji*), *mubang* (*mukbong*), *bukyü*, and *gokyü*. The first of these names, *bangzi*, is used in Northern China to refer to a different percussion instrument, consisting of two round sticks of hard wood struck against each other. The second name, *mubang*, is a variation of that same name. The third and fourth names are onomatopoeic in the Cantonese dialect; the romanization is in Cantonese pronunciation only.

The other two woodblocks are made in the same way as one another but differ only in size. The larger of the two, which we shall call the "medium woodblock," is known as *duk* and the smaller, which we shall call the "small woodblock," as *dik*. The names, romanized according to Cantonese pronunciation, are obviously onomatopoeic and have no written characters to represent them. Each is a solid block of hard wood roughly trapezoidal in shape. The dimensions of the medium woodblock are approximately 1½ inches by 1½ inches by 5 inches, with the base surface slightly larger than the top surface (figure 3.2); the smaller

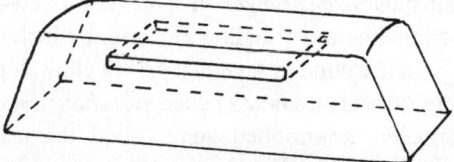

Figure 3.2 Medium woodblock

woodblock is about two-thirds that size. On one side near the top (smaller) surface is a thin slit cut through to the other side.

The large and small woodblocks are fastened onto two sides of a small wooden stand and protrude like leaves from a branch. The medium woodblock is fastened to a separate wooden stand that is placed to the left of the first stand (figure 3.3). To play the woodblocks one

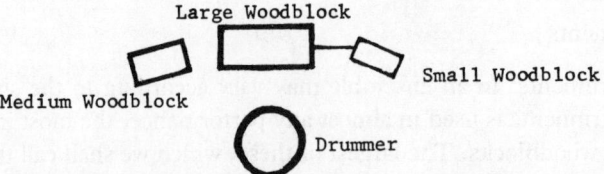

Figure 3.3 Placement of woodblocks

strikes them with two bamboo sticks, the large woodblock on the edge just above the slit, the medium and small on the top surface. The three woodblocks produce pitch levels inversely proportional to their sizes; the smaller the size, the higher the pitch. The tone quality of the large woodblock is mellow and resonant while that of the other two is sharp and crisp.

The set of woodblocks is played by a single instrumentalist, known by at least three names: the *zhazhu* (*jajuk*) [one who holds the bamboo], *zhangban* (*jeungbaan*) [one who holds the clappers], and the *dagulao* (*dagulou*) [drummer]. At some earlier stage in the history of the opera the same musician would have worked a pair of clappers with one hand and played a drum with a bamboo stick held in the other hand. Although the set of three woodblocks has since replaced those instruments, the older names for the player evidently have persisted.

The woodblock player is the most important instrumentalist in the orchestra. By beating the woodblocks he controls the tempo of the accompaniment to the singing passages, and by means of signals given with his hands and bamboo sticks he tells the other percussionists what percussion pattern to play and how to play it. Because the percussion music which he "directs" is indispensable to singing passages and dramatic moments alike, he is the only musician who must know every detail of the whole opera.

For certain kinds of singing he accompanies with another set of three or four woodblocks called *muyü* (*muk'yu*) [wooden fish]. These are hollowed, rounded woodblocks of a relatively soft wood; in shape they somewhat resemble a fish with a huge head and a tiny tail. Because of their different sizes, each of these woodblocks produces a different pitch. This shape and the kind of wood from which they are made give them a tone quality that is mellower than that of the small and medium woodblocks and less resonant than that of the large woodblock.

The three remaining instrumentalists in the percussion ensemble handle the rest of the core percussion instruments, which are divided into two sets: the Cantonese gongs and cymbals, and the Peking gongs and cymbals. The former comprise five major instruments. A large, flat (unknobbed) gong, called *wenchangluo* (*mancheunglo*) or *suluo* (*soulo*) [civil gong or tranquil gong], has a diameter of roughly 20 inches and a shallow rim about 1 inch in width. Played with a wooden stick whose padded head is wound in several layers of cloth, it produces a deep and mellow tone and is used during quieter moments called *wenchang* (*mancheung*) [tranquil scenes]. Its counterpart is a smaller, unknobbed gong called the *wuchangluo* (*moucheunglo*) [military gong] or *gaobianluo* (*goubinlo*) [high-rimmed gong], which has a diameter of about 12 inches and a relatively high rim of about 3 inches. Played with a wooden stick with an unpadded head, it produces a sharp, bright sound, and is used mainly to accompany stage action associated with battle scenes or with actors portraying military officers.

The two gongs are matched by two pairs of large cymbals, one called *wendabo* (*mandaaibat*) [large civil cymbals] used for quiet scenes, and the other called *wudabo* (*moudaaibat*) [large military cymbals] used for battle scenes. Usually each is paired with the gong of the corresponding name described above. The civil cymbals have a diameter of about 20 inches; the military cymbals are slightly smaller. The fifth instrument in this set is a pair of small, high-rimmed gongs called *danda* (*daanda*) [single stroke gong], which have a diameter of only 3 inches and a relatively high rim of about 1 inch. The two are tuned at a fraction of a tone apart so that, when struck simultaneously, as they almost always are, a "chord" of a distinctive and penetrating tone results. They are especially important in accompanying ritual plays such as *Minister of the Six States* and *Supreme Deity Holds Court*.

The set of Peking gongs and cymbals, as the name implies, are transplants from the Peking opera of Northern China. It comprises three instruments: *jingbo* (*gingbat*) [Peking cymbals] is a pair of small cymbals about 8 inches in diameter; *jingluo* (*ginglo*) [Peking gong] is an unknobbed gong about 12 inches in diameter; and *xiaoluo* (*siulo*) [small gong] is an unknobbed gong about 8 inches in diameter. The Peking gong is played with a wooden stick which has a padded head, the small with the edge of a thin, flat strip of wood; when struck, the former produces a distinctive downward-trailing tone, the latter an upward-trailing tone.

The three instrumentalists handle both sets of gongs and cymbals, which are usually not played at the same time. The Peking set is used mostly in quieter scenes, while the Cantonese set, which produces a much louder and richer sound, is mostly for battle scenes and spectacles that involve a large number of performers on stage, such as a trial or a wedding. The large military cymbals are especially prominent when used to accompany the entrance of famous performers. The three woodblocks (and occasionally the wooden fish) are used with either set of gongs and cymbals.

Besides the core instruments described above, two large drums are sometimes used for special effects. One of them, called the *zhangu* (*jingu*) [war drum], is barrel-shaped, about 1½ feet high, with a head 1 foot in diameter. It is suspended vertically on a wooden frame and is played with two wooden sticks with padded heads. The other, called *dagu* (*daaigu*) [big drum] or *wuyingu* (*ng'yamgu*) [five tone drum], is shaped somewhat like a giant goblet with a large drum head about 2 feet in diameter tapering to a narrow bottom of about half the size; it is approximately 2½ feet high, is suspended vertically on a wooden frame, and is played with two wooden sticks with padded heads. Together with the gongs and cymbals, these drums are used to accompany battle scenes and, occasionally, the entrance of famous performers.

Occasionally two of the percussion musicians also play a pair of wind instruments called *suona* (*sonaat*), oboe-like, double-reeded intruments with a wooden pipe and a flaring conical end made of metal. One large and one small, they cover two different pitch registers an octave apart, and are sometimes referred to respectively as *dadi* (*daaideik*) and *xiaodi* (*saideik*), literally "large pipe" and "small pipe." With an extraordinarily loud and brilliant sound, they are almost always played together with the other percussion instruments. Despite the fact that they are wind instruments, they are considered as part of the percussion ensemble, apparently because their dramatic functions coincide with those of the percussion rather than the melodic ensemble.

Percussion music and its dramatic functions

The four percussionists almost always play as a closely-knit unit. They exploit the different pitch levels, dynamic ranges, and timbres of the various instruments and, singly or in ensemble, generate formulaic patterns of sound from these instruments called *luogudian* (*logudin*) [percussion patterns]. Through the ages, a repertory of such patterns, each with a title, was established. In addition, certain patterns have come to be so closely associated with certain stage actions that they are mutually determinate; that is, an actor automatically performs certain actions on stage when he hears the pattern, and, vice versa, the instrumentalists automatically produce the pattern when they observe a certain action being performed on stage. Most patterns exhibit a certain degree of flexibility, both in themselves and in their relationship to stage action; this flexibility allows the instrumentalists and the actors some latitude for improvisation. The patterns range from a single stroke on a gong to complex juxtapositions of several instruments in a prescribed rhythm. Some of the patterns are relatively fixed in length, while others are sufficiently flexible and open-ended that they can be played at different tempos and may last as long as the stage action calls for.[2]

Percussion music has a broad range of functions in performance, the most basic of which is to serve as an accompaniment to movements on stage. Three different kinds of percussion patterns can be identified, each serving a different kind of stage action. The first is used to punctuate brief stage movements of various sorts, such as a jerk of the head, a flip of a hand, or a sudden roll of the eyeballs. The music in these cases, always simple and short to coincide with the movements, usually consists of no more than a single stroke on a woodblock or gong, or a combined stroke of the ensemble as a whole.

More complicated patterns are used to accompany certain action-sequences. In length and structure such patterns are relatively fixed in order to accommodate relatively inflexible sets of movements. Two examples of such action-sequences are the formal entrance of an actor in an important role, which involves a specific series of movements and gestures, and when an actor performs a preestablished set of stylized movements with his hands, arms and head to indicate puzzlement and anxiety.

The third type of percussion music accompanies a prolonged sequence of movements without a fixed length or structure, for example, a combat sequence. In such cases, the music consists of small, repetitive rhythmic figurations and is not necessarily in strict synchronization with the movement on stage, although the two are equal in duration. Only at the beginning and the ending of such a sequence of stage action are there fixed patterns which serve as terminal markers.

Percussion music is also used to suggest thoughts, emotions, and other kinds of dramatic expression that may not be visually obvious. For example, a gentle gong stroke in the middle of a monologue may suggest a sudden change in the actor's train of thought; a sudden crash on the large cymbals may underscore an actor's anger.

Occasionally certain sounds in nature are imitated by the percussion ensemble; for example, the rocking of a boat is represented by the rubbing of the pair of Peking cymbals to produce a sound suggesting of rippling water. In such cases the music exploits the distinctive timbre and color of individual instruments. The relationship between the instrumental sound and its natural counterpart is often one of conventionally accepted equivalence rather than exact imitation.

Musical instruments

Percussion music also serves as accompaniment to passages of speech and song. In speech passages simple and short patterns, such as a single stroke on the woodblock or the gong, are often used to accentuate important words or phrases. In the case of songs with a regular meter the woodblocks may be struck to mark time for the melodic ensemble and the singer as well as to provide a timbral accompaniment. The strokes may either coincide with the metrical strong beats, or depart from them to create irregular patterns and rhythmic tension. Many songs, particularly the so-called aria types, are preceded by special percussion patterns that function as preludes. Earlier in the history of the opera when opera scripts were not used, these percussion patterns served as signals to the melodic ensemble who otherwise would not know which song the actor was going to sing.

Percussion music is also used in ways that can be considered as peripheral to the strictly dramatic aspects of the performance. For example, special percussion patterns are used as punctuation signals minutes before a performance begins and at the moment it ends. Other percussion patterns are used during changes of scenes, which may or may not involve the lowering and raising of the curtain. If there is no curtain, and if the stage is simply bare of actors for a short moment between two scenes, the percussion music serves as a marker for the scene-change as well as an aural link to sustain interest from one scene to another.

The preceding summary of the many functions of percussion music should be sufficient to indicate its ubiquity and importance in opera performances. The most significant of the functions is to provide an aural counterpart to the movements and gestures on stage which, by accentuating them, enhances their dramatic significance. The story is more vividly and emphatically told as a result.[3]

A different kind of "percussion music" is provided by the two wind instruments in the percussion ensemble, the *suona*, which play a special repertory of tunes called *paizi* (*paaiji*), usually accompanied by the real percussion instruments in the ensemble. Compared to the other tunes in Cantonese opera, the *paizi* tunes have a more archaic flavor, and are generally accepted as borrowings from the Kunqu opera. They are further distinguished from the other tunes for their unusual texture produced by the extraordinarily loud and brilliant sound of the *suona*, gongs, and cymbals.

Each *paizi* tune is traditionally associated with, and used to accompany, a formulaic "scene," called *paichang* (*paaicheung*). In general, *paichang* scenes differ from ordinary scenes in that they are either great fanfares, such as the formal entrance of a king, a homecoming after victory, and a banquet, or ones with heightened dramatic tension, such as a suicide, a chase, a verdict of guilty after a court trial, and an execution. Some of these "scenes" concern specific actions such as rowing a boat, drinking wine, and the ritual kowtowing of the bride and groom in a wedding. *Paizi* tunes are also used for purposes quite apart from the drama, such as the signalling of the start of a play immediately before the raising of the curtain. Some *paizi* tunes may be fitted with words, sung as fixed tunes, and accompanied by the melodic ensemble.[4]

Melodic instruments

The melodic ensemble[5] consists of about a dozen instruments which can be categorized as bowed lutes, plucked lutes, struck zither, and wind instruments. The most important instrument is the two-string bowed lute called *erhu* (*yiwu*), or *yuehu* (*yutwu*), sometimes

Figure 3.4 *Erhu*

Figure 3.5 *Sanxian*

referred to in the West as a two-string fiddle (figure 3.4). The small cylindrical-shaped body that serves as the soundbox is about 4 inches long and 3 inches in diameter. The front end of the wooden frame is covered with boa or other snake skin and serves as the sound board; the back end is partially covered with decorative wooden lattice-work. The neck, a wooden rod about 2 feet in length, pierces the middle of the body diametrically. The player holds the fiddle vertically, with the lower half of the soundbox held tightly between the player's thighs, a position which dampens certain overtones and results in a mellow tone quality.

The two strings are fastened from two tuning pegs at the top of the neck, stretched along the neck and across the sounding board, and are then secured to the bottom of the body. The strings are tuned a fifth apart; the higher pitched string is a steel wire, the lower made either of nylon or of twisted silk. The strings are stopped with the fleshy part of the left-hand fingers; there is no fingerboard since the strings are suspended away from the neck. The bow, about the same length as the neck, is operated with the right hand. Placed in between the two strings, its horse hair rubs the underside of one string and the upperside of the other to produce resonance.

The *erhu* player is the leader and the most important musician of the melodic ensemble; he and the woodblock player are the only instrumentalists who read from an opera script during a performance. The other members of the melodic ensemble rely upon his signals for guidance on what tune to play and such aspects of execution as tempo and rhythmic nuances. His relationship to the principal singer is extremely close and, as a result, is critical to the success of a performance. An established singer always has an *erhu* player as his associate who is familiar with his style of singing and his idiosyncracies and who acts as his personal accompanist in all performances.

The construction of *yehu* (*yewu*) [coconut shell bowed lute], resembles that of the *erhu* except that the soundbox consists of half a coconut shell covered with a thin wooden board. The neck is slightly longer than that of *erhu*, resulting in a longer length for the strings. The instrument produces a mellower sound than the *erhu* and covers a lower pitch register.

The other bowed long-neck lutes are almost identical to the *erhu* in construction but are of successively larger sizes. They are the *zhonghu* (*jungwu*) [medium *hu*], the *dahu* (*daaiwu*) [large *hu*], and the *dihu* (*daiwu*) [low *hu*]. They are tuned like the *erhu*, but at a fourth, an

Musical instruments

octave, and two octaves lower respectively. Their relationship to the *erhu* in size and pitch register are somewhat like those of the viola, cello, and double bass to the violin. Although these instruments, which provide the low end of the pitch spectrum, were developed only in the last few decades, they are standard elements of today's orchestra.

In the plucked lute category the most important instrument is the long-necked *sanxian* (*saamyin*), which is often referred to in the West as a three-string "banjo" because of the similarity in shape and timbre to its Western namesake (figure 3.5). The body is a small, squarish soundbox with rounded corners, covered on both front and back with snakeskin. The box is pierced by a neck 3 feet in length which serves in its entirety as a fretless fingerboard. The three strings are made of nylon or twisted silk; the two outer strings are tuned an octave apart, with the middle string at a fourth or fifth higher from the lower string. The instrument is held almost horizontally with the soundbox resting on the player's right knee, and the strings are plucked with a small plectrum.

The *pipa* (*peipa*) is a short-necked plucked lute with a large pear-shaped wooden body some two feet in length (figure 3.6). The back is shallowly rounded and the front covered with a wooden sound board. Four strings, made of nylon or silk, are tuned so that the two outer strings are an octave apart, with the two inner ones at a fourth and a fifth from the lower string. The fingerboard in the neck area has four triangular-shaped frets, and ten or more thin bamboo frets stretch along the surface of the soundbox from the neck to the middle of the body. Held upright on the thigh, it is played with the nails of all five fingers on the right hand while the left hand stops the strings at various fret positions.

The *yueqin* (*yutkam*), another short-necked plucked lute, derives its popular English name of "moon guitar" due to the shape of its soundbox, which is a large, flat, wooden disk roughly 18 inches in diameter and 2 inches deep (figure 3.7). The short neck is about 6 inches long. Two sets of double strings of nylon or twisted silk are tuned a fifth apart. Ten frets line the neck and the body. The instrument is held almost vertically, and the strings are plucked with a plectrum.

The *qinqin* (*cheunkam*) is a long-necked plucked lute somewhat resembling a cross between the moon guitar and the three-string banjo. Like the former, it has a disk-shaped soundbox and a fretted neck; like the latter, it has three strings, a long neck, and a snake skin rather than a wooden covering on the surface of the disk. The strings are tuned at successive fifths (so that the outer strings have an interval of a ninth) and are plucked with a small plectrum.

The *yangqin* (*yeungkam*), a struck zither, is sometimes known in English as the "butterfly zither" from its colloquial Cantonese name *hudieqin* (*wudipkam*) (figure 3.8). It is a shallow box of symmetrically trapezoidal shape, roughly 2 feet by 3 feet. Approximately twenty sets of double or triple metal strings stretch horizontally across the surface of the box and over high, movable bridges. The strings are fixed to one side of the box and wound around tuning pegs at the other side. The player strikes the strings with two thin, supple bamboo hammers, one in each hand. The strings are tuned to the heptatonic scale used in Cantonese music. The zither player is generally considered the second most important melody instrumentalist of the ensemble. (This instrument is discussed further in chapter 10.)

The wind instruments include the *dizi* (*deikji*) or transverse flute, a short bamboo pipe (without any metal attachment) of about 1 foot in length, with one end open and the other closed, six finger-holes, a blow hole, two "string" holes, and an extra hole covered with a delicate membrane, usually a piece of onion skin. The membrane adds a distinctive nasal

30   Cantonese opera

Figure 3.6   *Pipa*

Figure 3.7   *Yueqin*

Figure 3.9   *Dizi*

Figure 3.8   *Yangqin*

timbre to the tone quality of the flute (figure 3.9). The *xiao* (*siu*), or *dongxiao* (*dungsiu*), is an endblown bamboo flute about 2 feet in length with six finger-holes and a blow hole at the end. The *guan* (*gun*), or *houguan* (*haugun*), is a double-reed, oboe-like instrument made of hard wood. Blown vertically, it is about 1½ feet long and has seven finger-holes and a 3-inch long double reed as a mouthpiece. The tone quality of the *xiao* is gentle and mellow, that of the *guan* loud and piercing.

The size of an orchestra varies depending upon the size of the opera troupe; the precise make-up of the ensemble is not critical to an opera. A full-sized troupe generally has about twelve melodic instrumentalists and four percussionists. Usually each musician plays a different instrument; occasionally two play the same kind of instruments. A smaller troupe would have a correspondingly smaller instrumental ensemble. The "core" set of instruments that even the smallest troupe should have includes all the core percussion instruments, and the *erhu*, the *yangqin*, the *sanxian*, and the *dizi*.

Occasionally certain Western instruments may be substituted for the melodic instruments: the violin, the saxophone, the electric guitar, the banjo, and the cello. For an explanation of this curious anomaly, one must look into the recent history of the opera. During the 1920s and 1930s the general influx of Western culture exerted a great influence over the performance practice of Cantonese opera, including the introduction of Western musical instruments.[6] For two or three decades traditional Chinese melodic instruments were completely replaced by Western ones. The 1950s restored all the traditional Chinese instruments to the stage. However, the Western instruments still occasionally appear today, especially in small opera troupes or in a large troupe under less formal performing conditions. For example, a cello was used in a performance of the play *Giving the Magic Pearl at Rainbow Bridge* in 1975 and a saxophone in a performance of *Sacrificial Offerings to Lady Wei* in 1973. There has been an effort by more purist-minded performers and audience members to eliminate these foreign elements.

During accompaniment of most vocal music, all the instruments join in and generally play the same melody as the vocal line in heterophony. For some songs, a special, traditionally determined, "orchestration" may be used. For example, in the narrative song called *Nanyin* (*Naamyam*) the accompaniment calls exclusively for instruments with a mellower timbre, such as the coconut shell bowed lute (*yehu*), the struck zither (*yangqin*), and the endblown flute (*xiao*). In recent years part-playing, in the Western sense, has been introduced into performances on occasion. The lower-pitched instruments in particular are likely to be given different melodic lines to play in counterpoint against the main melody.

4 *Social context*

Performances of Cantonese opera in Hong Kong during the 1970s can be grouped into two major categories in terms of social context: those mounted primarily as an important component of religious festivals to honor and please a deity (or deities), and those intended chiefly to entertain a paying public or a private (or semi-private) gathering. These two kinds of performance shared essentially the same repertory and performers but differed in their social function, source of financial support, physical location and set-up, and, to some degree, the kind of audience. Closely connected with these social and economic factors were certain differences in artistic standards and in aspects of performance practice.[1]

Secular performances

Performances as commercial ventures were of several kinds, among which the most important were those that drew attention to themselves by having the most renowned singers, charging expensive admissions, and involving relatively large budgets. These performances were generally initiated and organized by a *banzhu* [troupe head], who somewhat resembled an impresario or theatrical entrepreneur in the West. He hired actors, instrumentalists, and other personnel to form a temporary troupe which gave a series of performances and was then disbanded. The troupe would be identified by a name with an auspicious meaning, or one that reflected the names of the principal actors.[2] Sometimes such a troupe attained a semi-permanent status when the same set of people performed together under the same name and *banzhu* for an extended period of time. In the prosperous era of the 1920s and 1930s, such a troupe might remain in existence for several years, staging performances at regular intervals. In the 1970s, a troupe would stay together for a series of performances usually for some five to fifteen days in duration, at the end of which it would disband, and might not reform for several months. The members of the troupe could, of course, perform under a different *banzhu*, but in that case a different troupe-name was required.

Commercial performances were generally held in modern theaters in an urban environment. While permanent theaters are known to have existed in other parts of China as early as the tenth century,[3] incidental documents from the Canton area, such as county gazettes, do not mention such theaters but refer only to opera performances held in specially-built temporary structures of a type still used today in Hong Kong. From about the turn of the century permanent "opera houses" of modern style are known to have existed in urban centers such as Canton and Hong Kong. In the 1920s there were about ten opera houses in Canton.[4] In the 1930s the Taiping Theater and several other theaters in Hong Kong staged Cantonese operas twice a day throughout the year, from 12 noon to 5 pm and from 7 pm to midnight; on special occasions and certain Saturdays, the evening performance would be

Social context

followed by an all-night show. For a period during the 1930s, one new opera was produced each week at the Taiping Theater, as well as performances of many old operas.[5]

During the 1970s opera houses no longer existed in Hong Kong. A few modern theaters which showed films regularly might be rented occasionally to opera troupes for one- or two-week periods. The ticket prices had to be relatively high in order to cover the high rental fee for the theaters. Only the middle and upper-middle class could afford to, and did, attend. Top-ranking performers were usually hired in order to attract an audience large enough to cover expenses and show a profit. During the 1970s there were only about a dozen actors considered sufficiently prestigious to appear in these performances.

On average, there would be a total of about six or seven short performance-series in a year, each lasting one to two weeks, with afternoon and evening shows every day. (An exception was the first day, when there was no matinée.) Each show would consist of a single opera of about four hours in length. A new opera was generally written for such a performance-series and repeated every evening. In the afternoon performances old operas from the established repertory were presented, a different one each day. On the first evening the regular opera was always preceded by a ritualistic piece called *Liuguo Fengxiang* [*Minister of the Six States*]. On the first afternoon (which was the second day of the series), the regular opera was always preceded by another ritualistic piece called *Baxian Heshou* [*Birthday Greeting from the Eight Immortals*].

The kind of commercial performance described above was technically sophisticated and regarded as upholding the highest artistic standards. Innovations were more likely to be tried out in such a series than in other kinds of performances, and it was here that one could find experiments in adopting ideas and techniques from other theater forms of higher social status, for example, traditional Peking opera, the Revolutionary opera from Mainland China during the Cultural Revolution, and Western theater. The actors tended to be self-conscious about their role as "creative artists," talking of "reforms" and "improvements." The modern theaters were fitted out with state-of-the-art light and sound equipment and had comfortable seating for the audience.

Among the most celebrated and respected opera troupes of the last three decades was the Xianfengming troupe [Song of the Celestial Phoenix], active in the late 1950s and early 1960s. Aside from the exceptional talents and professionalism of its principal performers Ren Jianhui (Yam Gimfai in Cantonese), Bai Xueixian (Baak Syutsin), Liang Xingbo (Leung Singbo), and Jing Cibo (Laing Chibaak), playing the principal male, principal female, comic, and military roles respectively, the troupe's performances were known for being well-staged, meticulously rehearsed, and dramatically coherent. The greatest credit should probably go to its scriptwriter, Tang Disheng (Tong Diksang), who was highly educated and was familiar with the scripts of classical operas such as the Yuan *zaju* and Kunqu opera. Borrowing heavily from the vast operatic literature of the past, he produced new scripts that were dramatically well-constructed and a text that was highly refined.

Tang Disheng and the Xianfengming troupe were exceptions; despite the high respect they earned from the audience, the troupe did not become a model for the others to follow. The majority of the troupes catered to more popular tastes and a wider audience. At the other extreme of the spectrum from the Xianfengming were daily performances by small troupes in amusement parks. Two places in Hong Kong during the 1970s had such performances: the Lai Chi Kok Amusement Park and the Kai Tak Amusement Park. The two parks offered a potpourri of entertainment, including old movies, a few other kinds of Chinese opera (for example, the Peking opera, and less frequently, the Swatow opera), nightclubs, striptease shows, a zoo, a roller-skating rink, an ice-skating rink, pinball machines, many kinds of rides, game stalls, and a variety of eating places. They were not generally considered "reputable" places by upper-middle class city dwellers; naturally the opera performances held there were little esteemed. The troupes were generally smaller and the performers less well-known than those who performed in modern theaters. A different opera was staged each evening, all of them from the traditional repertory. The admission fee was low, and the quality was regarded by other professionals as relatively undistinguished. The audience tended to be drawn largely from the lower-middle class.

One performance context of recent origin is government-sponsored free entertainment, catering mainly to lower-class city dwellers. In the 1970s there was one such troupe in Hong Kong, sponsored officially by the Radio Television Hong Kong, a government enterprise. All the singers were amateurs in two senses: first, they were regular employees of Radio Television Hong Kong and performed in the opera only as an avocation; second, none of them (apparently) was trained and brought up in the professional operatic community but instead had learned to sing and perform by participating in the private music clubs (see below). Most of the instrumentalists, however, were professional musicians who might also work regularly in other opera troupes. The amateur singers, who were generally better educated than the professionals, approached the matter of performance with greater self-consciousness. For example, rehearsals were held on a regular basis – a rarity in the professional troupes – and the singers often learned their parts by studying opera scripts containing detailed musical notation. The professional performers generally did not hold the amateurs in very high esteem artistically. Being supported by the government, however, the troupe was financially secure and assured of regular performances.

This government-supported troupe gave approximately two or three performances a month. Each performance lasted two hours, during which two or three scenes were staged, each from a different play. This kind of programming resembles the performance of *zhezixi* [operatic excerpts] in Peking opera, but it is unusual in the Cantonese opera tradition. The troupe had its own repertory, and the texts of the scenes were written by its own scriptwriter. Performances were held in various playgrounds around the city, chiefly in the more congested low-income districts. A small temporary stage was set up with an open space in front for the spectators; no overhead cover or seating was provided. Since there was no admission charge and no real physical boundary to the "theater," the audience tended to wander in and out of the spectator area at random. Attendance was generally good, with audiences of between 200 and 400.

On rare occasions, secular performances were also held in private homes by wealthy patrons of the opera, small stages being set up for the purpose, sometimes permanently. Professional instrumentalists and singers would be hired to accompany amateur performers in the staging of scenes of operas. These performances would not be publicized; a small, private audience would be invited. On even rarer occasions, these performances were held in public theaters and admission was charged to benefit charity causes.

Social context   35

Ritual performances

The secular, commercial performances saw a gradual decline in popularity after the heyday of the 1930s. The number of troupes as well as the number of accomplished singers and musicians has gradually but noticeably decreased during the last several decades. Nevertheless the total number of opera performances has remained more or less constant because by far the largest proportion of operatic activities has always involved ritual performances.[6] Such performances, catering to popular taste rather than to that of an elite, have existed in China for many centuries, and were occasionally referred to in historical records.[7] First-hand accounts of performances of this kind from the early part of this century, however, are more readily available.[8]

Incidental documents from the nineteenth century and earlier refer to opera performances almost always in connection with some ritualistic occasion. Indeed such occasions constituted the most important milieu for the performance of regional operas in China for many centuries, particularly from the end of the Ming and beginning of the Qing dynasties, when regional operas began to flourish. As Tanaka Issei has pointed out, performances of regional operas during the late Ming and Qing dynasties played a role in a variety of ritual occasions: the celebration of divine birthdays, the propitiation of orphan souls, prayers for a good harvest or for the protection of the community from flood and drought, and such rites of passage as marriage, the coming of age of sons, success in the civil service examinations, and funerals.[9]

Although ritual performances were held throughout the Pearl River Delta, they were especially important in villages where commercial performances were not held. On the birthdays of major deities there would be general festivities of which operatic performances were an integral part. Most villages sponsored three or four performances a year for some of the following festivals:

> the Birthday of Guanyin [Goddess of Mercy] on the nineteenth day of the second month;
> the Birthday of Tianhou [Queen of Heaven] on the twenty-third day of the third month;
> the Birthday of Qijie [Seventh Heavenly Maiden] on the seventh day of the seventh month;
> the Yu Lan Festival, or Ghost Festival, sometimes also known as the Hungry Ghost Festival, on the fifteenth day of the seventh month;
> the Birthday of Huaguang [Patron deity of Cantonese opera] on the twenty-eighth day of the ninth month.

Performances also played an important role in major secular calendrical festivals such as the Lunar New Year and the Dragon Boat Festival on the fifth day of the fifth month.

A festival with opera performances was an "event" for a village and would attract people from neighboring communities. The number of performances per year was an indication of the economic condition of the district. Temporary structures of bamboo poles and palm leaf mats were erected as theaters, some of them able to hold between 2,000 and 3,000 spectators. *Panyu County Gazetteer* (1872) records a fire during an opera performance in such a temporary structure in which "about fourteen hundred people were killed . . . One thousand people escaped" (chapter 53, p. 38).

Opera troupes of all sizes, whether in the city or in the country, performed throughout the year with only two recesses, one for about ten days at the New Year, the other from the first to the eighteenth of the sixth month. The latter recess, which marked the end of the opera season, was known as *san ban* [dissolving the troupes] and was a time when there could be considerable reshuffling of performers from one troupe to another, and when contracts for the coming year were usually signed. During the season, the troupes travelled widely in the Delta region, either on boats or on foot.

Political and social changes on the Chinese Mainland have caused a sharp decline in such ritual-oriented performances in recent decades. In Hong Kong, however, ritual performances have always been more prominent than commercial ones and have played an extremely important social role. It is a well-documented fact that commercial performances have suffered a decline in attendance since their height of popularity in the 1920s and 1930s.[10] The various social and economic factors to which the decline has been attributed have evidently not affected the popularity of ritual performances,[11] which suggests that the two kinds of performance have different social functions and economic foundations. The following account of ritual performances in Hong Kong is based upon field work conducted during 1972–73 and 1974–75.

Performances were held in towns and villages throughout the New Territories and the outlying islands, and, less frequently, inside the city proper. The list of the major festivals involved is similar to that given above for the earlier part of the century:[12]

> the Lunar New Year;
> the Festival of Hong Sheng [Sage of Hong] on the third day of the second month;
> the Birthday of Guanyin [Goddess of Mercy] on the nineteenth day of the second month;
> the Birthday of Tianhou [Queen of Heaven] on the twenty-third day of the third month;
> the Festival of Beidi [Lord of the North] sometimes called the Bun Festival, held exclusively on the Cheung Jau island in Hong Kong sometime between the last day of the third month and the tenth day of the fourth month; the organizing committee determines the exact date by casting lots before the image of the god;
> the Dragon Boat Festival, on the fifth day of the fifth month;
> the Yu Lan Festival, or Ghost Festival, sometimes also known as the Hungry Ghost Festival, on the fifteenth day of the seventh month.

A festival usually lasted about five days, with one or two opera performances on each day. It was not important that the festival be held around the actual date of the divine birthday or the traditionally accepted date for such a festival. For practical reasons, such as the availability of the opera troupes, adjustments were frequently made. When a village or a city neighborhood decided to celebrate an occasion with an opera performance, money was solicited from local residents, especially from businessmen. A *jingli* [manager] was hired, who was responsible for organizing the show and engaging the performers.[13] The quality of the show (as gauged by the status of the leading actors, the total number of players in the troupe, and so forth) depended upon the amount of money that the community was able to raise. A process of bargaining between villagers and manager over the choice of the leading actors often preceded a final settlement. The performances were usually free of charge to everyone, especially if they were held in a remote area of the colony. If they were held in the city an admission fee was generally charged.

Performances were almost always held in temporary structures built especially for the occasion in empty lots. Giant sheds made of bamboo poles and aluminium sheets, these structures varied greatly in size, from a seating capacity of several hundred to one or two or three thousand. The audience area was not enclosed by walls, and spectators generally spilled out into the open lot outside of the shed. In densely populated or easily accessible areas, with a good troupe and well-known star performers, up to 4,000 people might be present at a time. Almost inevitably the shed was constructed in such a way that the stage faced the temple of the god being honored; if necessary, a temporary temple was built outside the theater shed and in the appropriate position.[14] In front and on either side of the big shed were food stalls and soft drink pedlars. Gambling tables and stalls, although officially not permitted, were sometimes set up around the audience area if the shed was situated in a remote area. These stalls were centers of continuous and lively activity before, after, and even during, the performances.

On the first day of the series of three to five days, only an evening performance was held, while on subsequent days there were both afternoon and evening performances. Each show consisted of a different four-hour long play from the established repertory; thus a five-day series involved nine different plays. In some villages, additional all-night performances were staged. Moreover, the ritualistic plays *Minister of the Six States* and *Birthday Greeting from the Eight Immortals* always preceded the first evening and first afternoon shows respectively.

In a village such a performance-series was, of course, an important occasion for the local residents. In some small villages, where such a series occurred only once or twice a year, a performance would attract essentially the entire population to the shed, leaving the rest of the village almost deserted for a few hours. Throughout the duration of the series, the whole place would resemble a carnival, drawing spectators from neighboring villages, neighboring islands, and permanent boat-dwellers. Even city residents would make a special trip to join the festivities.[15]

In both commercial and ritual-related performances the six leading actors and two or three leading instrumentalists in a troupe performed only in the evenings. The principal roles in the afternoon operas were taken by the second-rank actors who also performed minor roles in the evening operas, and the principal instrumental positions were taken by the second-rank instrumentalists. If there were all-night shows, the participants were actors and instrumentalists of still lower ranks. While Western instruments, such as the violin and saxophone, have completely disappeared from the evening performances in recent years, their use by the same instrumentalists in afternoon performances persisted in the 1970s.

Non-dramatic contexts

There was a long tradition, traceable to the last century, for vocal music of the opera to be performed and listened to under non-theatrical contexts. The renowned amateur singer Pan Xianda (Pun Yindaat), in reminiscences about the days of his youth around the turn of the century, remembered that there were four kinds of non-theatrical performance involving the music of the Cantonese opera: *bayin* (*baat'yam*) [eight tones or eight instruments], *guji* (*gugei*) [blind songstress], *nüling* (*neuiling*) [female entertainer], and *wanjia* (*waanga*) [amateur singers].[16] Only the tradition of the *wanjia* still existed in Hong Kong during the 1970s. In each of these traditions the music was performed without staging, make-up, or costumes and with a minimum of dramatic gesture – a mode comparable to concert performances of arias from Western operas. Usually only lyrical passages from the operas were performed with a minimum amount of dialogue. Since there was little movement or use of gesture, the singers concentrated on singing technique in a much more self-conscious way than did their stage counterparts, and thought themselves musically more sophisticated and artistically superior. A regular operatic orchestra usually accompanied the singing, but because of the lack of stage action the percussion part played a noticeably smaller role.

The term *bayin*, or "eight tones" refers to the music performed by a group of men, each of whom played an instrument and at the same time sang the part of one of the characters in a story. Though of a lower social status than those of opera, these Eight Tones groups had at one time served a social function similar to that of the opera troupes, performing chiefly in villages during religious and secular festivals. They also performed for private occasions on a smaller scale, such as birthday or wedding celebrations, and were usually cheaper to hire than the opera troupes. This mode of performance gradually disappeared in the early decades of the twentieth century.

Guji, or "blind songstress" refers to a class of blind female professional singers who were active in the early part of the century. They were hired to perform at a variety of public places of leisure including teahouses, opium houses, and gambling houses. They were also called upon to provide entertainment for special community-sponsored events on calendrical and religious festivals, such as the New Year and the birthday celebrations of gods and goddesses. Private households would also hire them for performances at home. Once popular in cities such as Canton and Hong Kong, these singers gradually disappeared during the 1920s and 1930s, and vanished from the scene completely by the middle of the century. They performed both operatic arias and popular narrative songs of the Canton area, accompanied by only one or two instrumentalists and often playing instruments themselves. This type of singer, which despite the name could include a small number of blind men, was probably on the lowest rung of the social ladder.[17]

Nüling, or "female entertainer" refers to "sighted" singers of operatic songs and popular narrative songs in public and private environments similar to those served by the "blind songstresses." According to an autobiographical account, sighted singers started to appear on the scene around 1920 to compete with blind singers, and soon thereafter replaced them as the most important entertainers in such environments.[18] Since the restaurants and brothels in which they sang were often housed in boats moored on the rivers of Canton, the music was sometimes referred to as *hediao* (*hodiu*) [river music].

The height of popularity of *nüling* was during the 1920s and 1930s. When Canton and Hong Kong were occupied by Japan in the late 1930s and early 1940s, such kind of entertainment suffered a sharp decline. Out of it there later developed, after the war, a related form called *getan* (*gotaan*) [song-platform] in Hong Kong, which were performances held usually in teahouses. In the 1960s, when opera performances in Hong Kong were at their lowest ebb, teahouse singing flourished; there were even performances in ordinary restaurants and nightclubs. The 1970s again saw a sharp decline in its popularity, and in 1975, only one such teahouse was known to exist.[19]

Wanjia, or "amateur singers," were non-professional but sometimes highly accomplished singers who performed operatic excerpts chiefly for their own and their friends' enjoyment.[20] They formed clubs and met regularly for singing sessions either at a member's house or at specially established clubhouses. A club might be organized by people of the same professional or social group, such as the Hong Kong Steer Slaughterers' Club, or by residents of the same neighbourhood, such as the Music Section of the East District Women's Club, or by members of the same clan, such as the Pan Family Club. Finally, clubs might be formed by people who simply shared an interest in singing and nothing else. Very often the music clubs became centers of social interaction for their members.

There were about thirty to fifty Cantonese opera clubs in Hong Kong in the 1970s. Members met about once a week for two to three hours, either in club houses or at members' homes. The number attending ranged from a dozen to over fifty. Most of the singers were amateurs from the fairly well-to-do and upper-middle classes. The instrumentalists were professionals, semi-professionals, or retired players invited by the singers but in general not paid in monetary terms. Their compensation seems to have taken the form of a meal after each gathering, gifts from the singers on festive occasions such as the New Year (which might in fact consist of money), and less tangible advantages such as contacts with economically and politically influential members of the society. Occasionally, a music club put on a more formal performance for personal friends, usually during a celebratory banquet of some kind or as a benefit performance for some worthy social cause.

A club usually met in a room of medium size, and although there was no real "audience" to speak of, nevertheless an amplification system was invariably provided for the singer. Each singer took his or her turn in front of the microphone while the others might either sit quietly listening or chat in another room, waiting for their turns. Although in repertory and style of singing the performances were similar to those of teahouse singers, most of the songs were specially written by amateur or professional scriptwriters on the basis of the established repertory. The text was neatly written out or mimeographed, and while the name of the singer for whom the song was written was often prominently inscribed on the pages, the scriptwriter's name might not appear at all. The singers guarded these texts with pride and secretiveness. When I asked one singer to let me make a photocopy of one of his songs, he agreed to it only with great reluctance.

The amateur singers' clubs had long been important and flourishing social institutions throughout China. They offered the educated and other respectable members of the society an opportunity to indulge in the singing of opera and popular narratives without the social stigma usually attached to such activities when performed professionally. The texts of the songs tended to be written in a more refined literary style, and emphasis was placed on instrumental playing as well as on the singing. Singers and instrumentalists alike tended on the whole to regard their activity self-consciously as "fine art." This attitude and the generally higher social standing and economic power of the singers were no doubt important factors in the continued success of the clubs in the ever-changing society of China in recent decades. When the commercial (although not ritualistic) performances of opera were struggling for survival, and when the other genres of non-dramatic performance had all but disappeared, the tradition of amateur singing was still actively practiced in the 1970s.

The many modes of performances of operatic music without staging described above are inclusively called Yuequ, or "Cantonese operatic songs." Even though the performance contexts have almost disappeared altogether (except for amateur singers), the operatic songs themselves have enjoyed great popularity among all walks of life during the last few decades through the medium of recording. This is attested not only by the large number of commercial recordings released during the 1960s and early 1970s, but also by the amount of airtime on radio stations, which matched any other type of popular music. During the summer of 1972, one of the Hong Kong television stations held a fund-raising show for the relief of the victims of a typhoon. Entertainers from many different media took part, including movie actors, nightclub singers, comedians, Western-style pop song singers – and Cantonese opera singers. Viewers called in, made pledges, and requested songs or other forms of entertainment from their favorite performers. After one evening, more than HK$ 800,000 was raised. Significantly, 90 per cent of the pledges were accompanied by requests for performances of operatic songs by Cantonese opera stars. The late 1970s, however, saw a decline in the popularity of these songs, most noticeably reflected in record stores and on radio.

A discussion of non-stage performances of the opera must include a mention of the medium of film. Throughout the decade of 1960, a huge number of Cantonese operatic films was produced in Hong Kong; almost every stage singer appeared in them. The majority of them simply transformed stage performance onto the screen without significant change except for reducing the duration to less than two hours. The 1970s saw a sudden and sharp decline of these films; almost none have been made since then.

One other major medium of performance which shares musical material with Cantonese opera to a large extent is the Cantonese rod-puppet theater, called *zhangtou mu'ouxi* (*zoengtau muk'ngauhei*) [theater of puppets on sticks], or, more commonly and colloquially, *mutou gungzaixi* (*muktau gungzaihei*) [theater of wooden dolls]. There is little documentation on this form of theater, possibly because of its extremely low social status.[21] Interviews with the few surviving puppeteers in Hong Kong suggest that the puppet theater must have had a long history and continued to be popular until the 1940s. It served similar social and ritual functions in the villages and cities as did opera but was much cheaper to hire. Although its popularity once matched that of the opera (though catering to a lower social class), today only a handful of puppeteers are left. The sole surviving troupe in Hong Kong still performs occasionally during religious festivals and, sponsored by a government recreation program, gives regular performances in public parks in the city.[22]

The rod puppets are about half life-size. The head is carved out of wood and often has movable eyes; the body consists of a wooden frame draped with an elaborate costume. The puppeteer operates the legless figure by holding a central rod connecting to the head in one hand, and manipulating the puppet's arms with the other hand; the puppeteer also provides the voice of the puppet in songs and speech. A diminutive orchestra provides the accompaniment. Since all the puppeteers are men, there is always an extra female singer backstage who supplies the voice for the female puppet roles.

The puppeteers operate behind a curtain of about 10 feet wide and 5½ feet high which separates as well as hides them from the audience. The puppets themselves appear over the top of the curtain, held above the puppeteers' heads. The instrumentalists sit at one corner behind the curtain. A backdrop separates the "stage" from a backstage area, where puppets used for the performance dangle from a rope hung across the backstage.

Although historical records are lacking, existing performance practices indicate that the rod-puppet theater and the Cantonese opera are, historically speaking, closely related. They share an almost identical repertory of stories, although the puppet theater appears to

Social context

emphasize those with fighting scenes. The physical appearance of the puppets, in terms of make-up, headgear, and costumes, is almost identical to that of the live actors, their movements often quite similar. Most importantly, in musical material – in singing and instrumental melodies, in percussion patterns, and in various speaking styles – the two theaters overlap extensively.

One important difference, however, is that the puppet theater has a smaller instrumental ensemble than does the opera: the performances I attended during the 1970s had only two percussionists and two melodic instrumentalists. Since the percussion instruments were identical in kind and number to those of opera, the musicians had to double up their duties in order to manage them all. The melodic ensemble consisted of only the *erhu* (two-string bowed lute) and the *guan* (oboe). This difference in size could well have an economic origin, since the opera has always catered to an audience that was slightly better-off financially.

Another difference between the two theaters is in the musical material used in performance. That of the puppet theater seem to have undergone considerably less change, preserving an older set of tunes and an older style of singing. Indeed, a comparison between recordings made of the puppet theater in the 1970s and recordings of opera from about forty or fifty years ago shows a great deal of similarity. The opera, on the other hand, has undergone a noticeable evolution in its musical material during the last half century.

5 The opera script

The script plays a critical role in the creative process of an opera. Since musical notation is seldom used either before or during a performance, the script acts as the sole fixed reference point for the coordination of scriptwriters, singers and instrumental accompanists, and as the basis for their creative process of the music.

During religious or secular festivals when the performance of opera is partly for ritualistic purposes, only old plays are staged; a series of performances, which usually lasts three to seven days, may include as many as a dozen or so plays. Some of the principal singers have to perform two plays in a single day throughout the series, others one play a day. Thus an enormous amount of material has to be memorized and performed within a short time. There is never any rehearsal; copies of the script are distributed among the principal singers one or two days before the performance.

Mai Bingrong, a renowned singer active from the 1940s to the late 70s, has stated that he usually did not look at the script until the day of the performance, and sometimes not until a few minutes before curtain-time. Since in most cases he had performed the particular play before, one quick reading was sufficient to refresh his memory of the text. He regarded exact recall as unnecessary so long as he had memorized the first sentence of a passage and its rhyme. The formulaic style of the scripts enables an experienced singer, like Mai, who knows the gist of the dramatic situation, to reconstruct the text to an adequate degree of accuracy.[1]

Not surprisingly, such performances are often quite flexible and freely improvised. While the outline of the story is not altered, the dialogue and the song text sometimes depart from the written script quite drastically. Occasionally the dramatic continuity is temporarily suspended when the singers, and even the instrumentalists, might exchange jokes on stage.

The situation is a little different when a major opera troupe produces a new play in a modern theater for commercial purposes. Both the performers and audience take a more serious attitude towards such performances than towards performances in ritualistic context. A somewhat different set of artistic criteria is in force, among which is an expectation that the opera script should possess a certain degree of literary refinement. The performers are expected to adhere to the script to a large extent, often undergoing a process of preparation and rehearsal. Improvisation which detracts from dramatic coherence is frowned upon.

The initiative to stage a new opera usually comes from the *banzhu* (*baanjyu*), the financial backer of the project.[2] He discusses the idea with the few leading singers whom he intends to hire, covering such topics as story outline, production plan, dates and place of performance, and salaries. When an agreement is reached, the *banzhu* hires a scriptwiter, the other singers, and the *erhu* and woodblock players for the orchestra. Minor performers such as dancers and acrobats are hired through a guild called the Society of the Eight Harmonies. Providing the rest of the instrumentalists is usually the responsibility of the *erhu* and woodblock players:

The opera script

each has his own regular cronies from among whom to form the melodic and percussion sections of the orchestra respectively.

The dates of the performances are set, and the theater in which the performances will take place is reserved. If this is the first time that the principal male and female performers are collaborating under the management of this particular *banzhu*, a new name for the troupe is usually invented. If they have worked together before under the same *banzhu*, they retain the old name of the troupe. Such a troupe is a rather fluid organization assembled for the occasion and dissolved after the series of performances has been completed. Nevertheless the principal singers and instrumentalists tend to perform together regularly over a period of several years, while minor performers are more likely to join different troupes whenever and wherever their services are called for.

The germ of the story may be created by one or more of the troupe members: the *banzhu*, the principal singers, or the scriptwriter. They generally collaborate in producing an outline of the story, and the scriptwriter will then work out the details of the scene-distribution and overall structure of the opera. He is also solely responsible for writing the script and designing the distribution of various types of speech and song and percussion patterns.

About one week before the opening, the scriptwriter will have completed the script and distributed mimeographed copies to the principal singers and instrumentalists and to the *banzhu*. A meeting is then called and held, usually in a private banquet room of a nightclub. This meeting, known as *jiangxi* (*gonghei*), literally "discussing the opera," involves the *banzhu*, the scriptwriter, a so-called *tichang* (*taicheung*) [prompter] whose role is somewhat similar to that of the stage manager of Western theater, the six principal singers, and the two principal instrumentalists (the woodblock player and the *erhu* player). The meeting usually begins around noon and may last until the early morning hours of the next day. During the first four or five hours, the dozen or so participants sit around a large round table, each with a script in front of him. The singers read and sing through the whole opera softly while the two instrumentalists supply, in vocalized form, all the necessary percussion patterns or melodic preludes and interludes that accompany the singing.

During such a session, the participants often stop to make comments, suggestions, and changes in the text. Although everyone takes part in the discussion it is the principal male performer who is usually the most vocal and the most influential. (During one such session which I visited, the principal male performer happened to be relatively young and inexperienced; the dominant voice then was that of the comic role performer, who was one of the most prominent performers of this role type in Hong Kong at the time.) The discussion might involve the choice of an oral delivery type in which a particular text passage is to be sung, changes in the text by addition, deletion, or modification, subtleties and refinements in the singing such as the execution of a melisma or the enunciation of a syllable, relationships between vocal line and accompaniment, and stage movements.

After supper, the meeting moves to a larger room. A few scenes which involve stage actions of several performers together are worked out with the movements added. There is no director; everyone adjusts himself to the overall situation, at the same time making comments and accepting (or rejecting) suggestions from others. This second phase of the meeting, in which gestures and movements are tested out, is sometimes omitted.

One or two days after the first meeting, the principal male performer and the principal female performer, who always have the largest share of the singing, will each meet privately with the *erhu* player to go through the singing passages. The script does not provide any musical notation but instead gives the titles of tunes according to which the text is to be sung. The singer, using the title and the text itself as guidelines, tries out various ways of singing the passages. These sessions are called *duqu* (*dok'kuk*) [measuring the song], which could be translated "realizing the song."

If the opera has complex group scenes involving dances or battles, they are rehearsed separately. A dance or acrobatics expert may be hired to supervise such a rehearsal, although very often it is the principal male performer who plays this role. Sometimes, however, there may be no preliminary rehearsal at all for such scenes, despite the fact that they may involve two dozen or more performers.

Usually a final rehearsal on stage for all performers and instrumentalists is held on the afternoon of the first evening performance; this allows the performers to go through the movements of group scenes such as dances or battles. Occasionally long passages of singing are also rehearsed. At times there may be two such stage rehearsals, at times none at all.

Normally the opening night's performance is the first time that the opera as a whole is put together. Reactions on the part of the audience as well as the troupe members themselves often affect what changes are made in subsequent performances. In the case of *The Magic Pearl*, the first performance lasted about five hours instead of the normal four hours; not surprisingly, it was cut down to the proper length during subsequent performances. Specific criticisms and changes may involve either major or minor modifications of the text, music, and stage movements. Such changes are made by the actors and the instrumentalists; it is not considered necessary to consult the scriptwriter.

A performance-series usually lasts from one to two weeks, during which time the new opera is performed every evening. Other old operas are staged during the matinée show, a different opera each day. The principal singers are expected to perform both the old opera in the day-time and the new opera in the evening. Although the total amount of material covered may not be as great as in a series of ritual performances, the pressure involved is often more intense because of the new opera in the evening performances.

A small number of copies of opera scripts are mimeographed with the text handwritten in large-size characters; its pages string-bound in a manner that has not changed for over sixty years. The scripts are distributed among the six principal singers and the two principal instrumentalists. Their chief content is, of course, the text of all the oral delivery; of equal importance, however, are the titles of the types of oral delivery that are placed immediately before a passage of text. These titles tell the singers how to treat the text and the instrumentalists how to accompany the singer. The script also provides, at appropriate places, the titles of the percussion patterns to be performed by the percussion orchestra, as well as a small number of instructions on stage movement.

In order to give a concrete illustration of the role that the script plays in the performance of an opera, the script of the first two-thirds of act 1 (henceforth referred to as act 1) of *The Magic Pearl* is translated and presented here. The original is a working copy of the script used by the performers.[3] Oral delivery types are italicized; percussion patterns are placed within quotation marks. "*Cont.*" (continue) denotes a continuation of the same oral delivery type as designated in the previous instruction.[4]

The opera script

Act 1 of *The Magic Pearl*
[Line]

(Percussion pattern and *paizi* for the raising of the curtain.)
(Percussion pattern "Moth on the Lamp" accompanying the entrance of two men and two women onto the stage. They gaze at the scenery.)

Woman A (*Patter Speech*):
5   ᵃPeach blossoms red, apricot blossoms red, ten thousand flowers dance in the breeze;
ᵇAround the town of Sei Jau a sea of flowers, Rainbow Bridge spans from east to west.

Man A (*cont.*):
10   ᵃUnderneath Rainbow Bridge is Lake Hung Jaak, whose beauty poets all praised;
ᵇUnfortunately the good days are no longer here, I lament over the difference between then and now.

Woman B (*cont.*):
ᵃFormerly, beside the Rainbow Bridge was Ching Yeung Market;
15   ᵇDuring market days, what a crowd there used to be.
ᵃUnfortunately in recent years, there has been great flooding;
ᵇThe water took our lives, our property, and our food.

Man B (*cont.*):
ᵃMagistrate Gong has prayed to Heaven, but what's the use!
20   ᵇThe floods keep coming, there must be a demon living in the lake. (He looks into the lake.)

Man A, Women A, B (quickly stop him, *Plain Speech*): Be careful what you say. The demon might hear you . . . (They look frightened.)

Man B (scared, *cont.*): There it is, Rainbow Bridge, where we used to stroll. But now we
25   had better go to Bin River instead. (All agree and exit stage left.)
(Instrumental music. A cloud of good omen flies across the sky.)
(Percussion patterns "The Rushing Wind" and "The Four Beats.")

Wai To, God of Law (enters with a series of stylized movements, *Poetic Speech* at stage front):
30   ᵃDelivering human beings to Nirvana, I demonstrate magic power,
ᵇI accumulate merits, ten thousand-fold;
ᶜIn my hand the diamond demon-subduing club,
ᵈDemons, devils, with one sweep, vanish.
(He performs more dance movements, *Percussion Speech*):
35   I am
The Purple Bamboo Forest's God of Law, Wai To, that I am.
Because Hung Jaak Lake overflows,
Magistrate Gong of Sei Jau
Made offerings to Gods in Heaven,
40   Moving the all-merciful Goddess of Mercy.
In order to save the multitude of lives
She has asked me, Wai To, to come
To make an investigation.

Should there really be demons causing trouble,
45 Huh! huh! I, Wai To, surely shall deal with them.
(*Gwanfa* lower line):
ᵇI am here to save men from demons, they shall do no more harm.
ᵃWith my magic power, I clap my hands and summon
(*Plain Speech*): Where is the God of Earth? Where is he? Where?
50 Earth (enters dressed in rags, *cont.*): Greetings to Wai, the God of Law.
Wai (*cont.*): Ugh! I, the God of Law, have summoned for the God of Earth. Who is this poor lost soul?
Earth (*cont.*): God of Law, I am not a lost soul; I *am* the very God of Earth.
Wai (*cont.*): You are the God of Earth?
55 (*Muk'yu*):
ᵃThe God of Earth should be rich with offerings from human beings,
(*Plain Speech*): How is it you are in such a sorry state?
Earth (*Muk'yu*):
ᵇMy temple is empty, I only have the Northwest wind to fill my stomach.
60 Wai (*Plain Speech*): The Earth Temple by Rainbow Bridge used to receive endless offerings,
(*Muk'yu*):
ᶜYou mean you've lost your supernatural power, and no one respects you any more?
Earth (*Plain Speech*): No, that is not so.
65 (*Muk'yu*):
ᵈMy poverty simply comes from bad fortune.
Wai (*Plain Speech*): How is it since you took over the place, the temple has become deserted?
Mmmm.
70 (*Muk'yu*):
ᵃCould it be even a God can sometimes fall into hard times?
Earth (*Plain Speech*): There are good reasons why people no longer come to make offerings.
Wai (*cont.*): Yes? Why?
75 Earth (*cont.*): The people are afraid to come to Rainbow Bridge,
(*Muk'yu*):
ᵇBecause there is a water demon living in the lake.
Wai (*Plain Speech*): Oh! So there really is a water demon in there. No wonder Magistrate Gong said in his prayer:
80 (*Muk'yu*):
ᶜFor no apparent reason, the water overflows from the lake.
Earth (*cont.*):
ᵈThat's what reduced this poor God of Earth into a helpless worm.
Wai (*Plain Speech*): How annoying!
85 (*Gwanfa* lower line):
ᵇThat cursed demon dares to cause trouble here; I, the God of Law, shall have no mercy.
ᵃI'll crash into that Water Palace ("One Stroke"), and catch the devil ("One Stroke"), that'll teach it a lesson. (He exits.)

The opera script

90   Earth (quickly stops him, *Plain Speech*): God of Law, this Water Demon is no ordinary demon. She has cultivated herself for a thousand years, and can evade all harm from heaven and earth. She even possesses a magic pearl that can repel water.

Wai (*Rhymed Speech*):

^aSo she has a magic pearl! ("One Stroke") A magic pearl has the essence of the sun,
95   the essence of the moon, and the essence of the demon's own black power. So she has the protection of that precious object! No wonder she is so reckless.

Earth (*cont.*):

^bTo make it worse, the young dragon son of Bin River admires the beauty of this demon, and often comes to visit her. Every time he comes, he too stirs up high
100   waves.

Wai (*cont.*):

^cHa! ha! The Old Dragon of Bin River, why doesn't he discipline his son? Some day I shall report to the Heavenly Court; he'll be punished for letting his son run wild.

Earth (*cont.*):
105   ^dYou surely can blame the overflow of Lake Hung Jaak on both of them: the Water Demon and the Dragon Prince. One is a demon, the other a god. All the same, it is I, the Old Earth, that have to suffer the consequences.

Wai (*Plain Speech*): So be it!

(*Faaidim* lower line):
110   ^bI'll set up a trap by the Rainbow Bridge,

(*Gwanfa*):

^aI, the God of Law ("One Stroke") will disguise myself as a boatman, and set a bait in waiting. ("The Four Beats." He exits.)

Earth (*Plain Speech*): Gods are made of nothing but wood; only incense-burners are
115   true copper! (He exits. Sound of wind. "The Seven Strokes.")

Golden Scale (enters, *Faaidim* lower line):

^bThe wind obeys the tiger; the waves obey the dragon.

^aTen thousand miles of river; one thousand surging waves.

^bBin River and Lake Hung Jaak are but one body of water.
120   (*Gwanfa*):

^aThe Prince of Bin River visits the Rainbow Bridge; he is infatuated with a rare beauty. (*Plain Speech*): I, Prince Golden Scale, while touring the rivers and lakes, met the water demon, who has developed into a human form, and calls herself Lady Pearl. She is truly beautiful and has captured this Prince's heart. I often come to visit
125   her; but the proud Lady Pearl has never responded to my love. Hmph! Here I am, a bona fide god; while she is only a well-seasoned demon. How can she resist me? I think she is just pretending to be indifferent; actually she is simply shy. That is why I am here again looking for her. But neither Lady Pearl nor her maid Little Bou are at home. They must be roaming somewhere.
130   Let me go and find them.

(*Gwanfa* lower line):

^bI look everywhere in search of the beautiful girl; I hope to catch a glimpse of her on the other side of Rainbow Bridge.

^aSuch earthly Spring, such fragrant flowers, how can I stop the love-chords in me
135   from singing? (He exits.)

(Flute music of *Prelude to Dainty Steps*.)

Pearl (enters with her maid Little Bou; their dance-like movements are accompanied by percussion patterns. *Dainty Steps*):

Youthful hair, red dress, gauze sleeves flowing like clouds,

140　Jade willow, flying mist, spring air everywhere.

Bou (*cont.*):

Ten thousand peach branches in the wind swaying.

Pearl (*cont.*):

Green willows on river banks send forth sweet fragrances.

145　Swallows dashing among the flower beds in search of sweet dreams.

Bou (*cont.*):

My love and my yearning, to whom are they sent?

Pearl (*cont.*):

Deep in the sea palace, I live alone,

150　My sorrows are lasting.

Bou (*Gwanfa* lower line):

  [b]How colorful it is here on land; how black and murky under the water.

  [a]No wonder people say: better to be a pair of mandarin ducks than a lone god; ("One Stroke," she slowly looks at Lady Pearl, and understands;) she is taking this stroll

155　because she yearns for love.

Pearl (*Supported Speech*): Nonsense. We are taking this stroll purely to kill time. I am in no mood for love.

Bou (*cont.*): If that is so, then I was wrong. See the green hills over there. Shall we go and take a look?

160　Pearl (*cont.*): No, no.

Bou (*cont.*): Look, there is a crowd over on that side. Let us go and join the fun.

Pearl (*cont.*): No, no.

Bou (*cont.*): You are interested in neither a quiet place nor a bustling place. ("One Stroke")

165　Oh! No wonder she does not want to leave. Now I also do not want to leave.

Pearl (*cont.*): Why do you say that?

Bou (*cont.*): A young man of scholarly looks is walking this way. You only want to see whether he is handsome or not.

Pearl (*Gwanfa* lower line):

170　[b]She has said what's on my mind; how embarrassing! My cheeks are turning pink.

  [a]Let me hide in that bush of flowers, ("Three Strokes") and inspect the young man. (She exits, followed by Little Bou.)

Si Tingfong (enters, sings *Prelude to Naamyam*):

A thousand green branches gently swaying in the breeze,

175　Unsteadily in all directions;

The nightingales sing of love in the willow trees;

The spring wind has melted the winter cold.

Leisurely I stroll by the lake,

Enjoying the delicate beauty.

180　The water reflects a sheet of silky green,

The opera script

An arch of rainbow sits in the sky.
(*Plain Speech*): How beautiful is Lake Hung Jaak! What a shame.
(*Gwanfa* lower line without prelude):
ᵇThe dazzling lake and colorful hill detain my horse not; lanterns and flowers of the wedding beckon me on.
ᵃTravelling a thousand miles I search for my dear one; to prostrate at the Jade Hall, to join my beautiful phoenix.
(*Plain Speech*): How vast is Lake Hung Jaak; on the other side lies my inlaws' home. Let me hire a boat. (He looks around.) Why is there not a single boat on the lake?
Wai (backstage, *Plain Speech*): You there, sir, do you want to hire a boat?
Si (*cont.*): Yes.
Wai (*cont.*): Here I come.
(He enters disguised as a boatman, with rowing gestures; *Rowing a Boat*):
The moonlight is my bed, the spring breeze is my pillow;
I have lived half my life among the reeds.
The waves are like scattered jade and pearls.
Row, row, the light boat glides over the water;
I hide my true face, that of the God of Law.
(*Plain Speech*): Who calls for a boat?
Si (*cont.*): Mr. Boatman, here I am. How much do you charge for taking me across the lake?
Wai (*cont.*): One hundred copper coins.
Si (*cont.*): That is fair enough.
Wai (*cont.*): Sir, please come aboard this way. (He helps Si to board the boat.)
Si (performs gestures of boarding a boat, *cont.*): Why is there only one boat on the whole lake?
Wai (*cont.*): The wind and the waves are rough. No one dares to be on the water. Would the gentleman please sit tight.
(They perform dance movements to indicate boat rocking in rough water.)
Pearl, Bou (enter, *Plain Speech*): Would the boatman please wait!
Wai (*cont.*): Well! Aren't you the two de . . . (coughing to hide his near slip of tongue, nodding.)
Bou (*cont.*): Yes, we are two travelers who want to cross the lake. But we can't find any boat on the lake. Would you please let us share your boat?
Wai (*cont.*): You two want to get in the boat? That's exactly what I had hoped.
(*Gwanfa* lower line):
ᵇI have been waiting for a whole day. Finally ("One Stroke") an honorable customer has come to this lake.
ᵃSince you two ("One Stroke") are not human . . . ("One Stroke")
Bou (*Plain Speech*): I beg your pardon! What do you mean, my mistress and I are not human?
Wai (*cont.*): Well, uh . . .
(*cont.*) what I mean is, you two are not my customer's relatives. ("One Stroke") You see, I already have this customer, and since you are not related to him, I'm afraid, that . . .

50   Cantonese opera

(*Gwanfa*):
One boat cannot be hired out to two parties.
Bou (*Plain Speech*): But we have an emergency.
Si (*cont.*): Since the ladies have an emergency, why don't you take them across first, and
230   then come back to take me?
Bou (*cont.*): But that is not necessary.
(*Gwanfa* lower line):
ᵇBig-hearted people are always ready to help others, especially since we are all going the same way.
235   ᵃThough the boat is small ("One Stroke"), it can hold three people ("One Stroke"), let us all go together.
Wai (*Plain Speech*): Well?
Si (*cont.*): Since there is no other boat in sight, I don't object to this arrangement.
Wai (*cont.*): Are you also willing to pay the hundred copper coins?
240   Bou (*cont.*): Of course.
Wai (*cont.*): Well, since you all consent to it, then please come aboard. (He helps them aboard.) Here we go.
(*Prelude to Bongji Maanbaan*. They perform dance movements imitating riding a boat.)
245   Pearl (*Bongji Maanbaan* lower line):
ᵇI am most grateful for your help; I truly appreciate your kindness and your tolerance of our rude intrusion.
(*Supported Speech*): This humble woman begs for forgiveness. (She bows low in formal greeting.)
250   Si (*cont.*): It is really nothing. May the lady please not stand on ceremony. (Hurriedly he helps her up.)
Wai (*cont.*): Hey, the boat is too small and the waves are too rough for all this ceremonious bowing. You'll all get dumped into the water!
Bou (*Bongji Maanbaan*):
255   ᵃHaving formally met, yet not knowing his name; I shall investigate. Men and women are supposed to keep their distance; but then I am, of course, ignorant of the proper human etiquette.
(*Supported Speech*): An encounter like this must be predestined; it is only proper and polite that we ask each other's name. Surely you don't need me to teach you that.
260   Si (*cont.*): Thank you for reminding me, my lady. This unworthy man Si Tingfong extends his greetings . . . (he bows in formal greeting.)
Wai (*cont.*): Hey, now it's your turn to rock the boat! Please sit tight!
Pearl (*cont.*): Please, sir, do not stand on formality.
Si (*cont.*): May I ask the lady what her honorable name is?
265   Pearl (*cont.*): Uh . . .
Bou (*cont.*): My master's last name is Baak, the young lady is called Pearl. My name is Little Bou.
Pearl (*cont.*): May I ask the young gentleman, are you passing through here on your way to the city to take the examination?
270   Si (*cont.*): No.

The opera script

(*Bongji Maanbaan* lower line):
ᵇHumbly dressed, ashamed, I amount to nothing;
plainly cloaked, I cannot pick the red cassia;
by the window, studying hard, I am still a struggling student at school.

275 Wai (*cont.*):
ᵃA scholar, with high ideals; no wonder he looks serious and respectful.
(*Plain Speech*): But in these days there are lots of evil things around. Beware of licentious temptations, or you will be doomed. Take note, take note!
Pearl (*Chatjiching* lower line):
280 ᵇIt is destined that our paths should cross;
ᵃI had not expected to have an escort on this boat trip.
ᵇIt stirs up my countless heavy thoughts;
ᵃLife is like a spring dream,
ᵇMeetings and partings happen all too swiftly.
285 Bou (*cont.*):
ᵃHas the young gentleman understood the meaning of her words? (Ends line with a melisma.)
Si: Uh . . .
Wai (*The Monk Dreams of a Wife*):
290   The words you have heard;
    The meaning you seem not to have understood.
    This boatman surely knows what she means:
    She is willing to marry him,
    For she cannot tolerate cold blankets at night.
295 Bou (*cont.*):
    She's in love with a scholar . . .
    How handsome and elegant he is.
Si (*cont.*):
    I am already engaged to the Moon Goddess;
300   I have to decline this true love.
Pearl (*cont.*):
    Lament for this fragile, drifting flower!
    I hope the warm East wind will come and dispel the cold frost.
Si (*cont.*):
305   I bewail my evil fate;
    I am unable to offer a marriage contract.
Pearl (*cont.*):
    My wish and longing have turned to emptiness.
Bou (*cont.*):
310   She wants to fulfil her wish;
    But her seed of love has been planted in the wrong soil.
Pearl (*cont.*):
    Such is love; such is fate.
    A trip together on the boat is nothing but a dream. (She looks sorrowful.)
315 Wai (*Plain Speech*): Sir, I know it is none of my business. Such a beautiful and virtuous

girl you could not find anywhere else. Yet you do not want her! I'm afraid that after you leave this boat you'll regret it, and then it will be too late. This boatman feels that you two are indeed a good match.
(*Long Gwanfa* lower line without prelude):
320 ᵇOne is a true beauty, the other is a perfect lover, she sends her love through her bewitching eyes, he is anticipating love under the moon. As the saying goes: "To be in the same boat, each of you need to prepare yourself through one lifetime; to sleep on the same pillow, each of you needs to prepare yourself through three lifetimes."
ᵃLet this boatman be your matchmaker ("One Stroke"), young lady, the pearl
325 around your neck ("One Stroke") will make a good betrothal present.
Pearl ("One Stroke"; she caresses her pearl; *Gwanfa* lower line):
ᵇOld boatman ("One Stroke"), if you are willing to be the matchmaker, I shall obediently offer this betrothal present. (She starts to take off her pearl.)
Bou (quickly stops her, *Plain Speech*): My Lady, this is the magic pearl. Please do not
330 be rash.
Pearl (*Gwanfa*):
ᵃLittle Bou, a priceless gem is easy to obtain ("One Stroke"), when compared to true love ("One Stroke"); I am willing to offer my pearl. (She takes off the pearl.)
Si (quickly stops her, *Plain Speech*): Young lady, this is a priceless pearl. I do not dare
335 accept it . . . and I cannot accept it.
(*Long Yiwong* lower line):
ᵇMy marriage contract was determined when I was a child; the six rites and the three documents of marriage have been offered to the Gong family. ("One Stroke")
Wai (*Plain Speech*): The only family near Rainbow Bridge named Gong is the
340 Magistrate. Is the gentleman the future son-in-law of the Magistrate?
Si (*cont.*): That is right.
(Continue lower line of *Long Yiwong*):
But how the world has changed in ten years' time. My future father-in-law has since gained promotion, fortune, and high status. But my own father has been
345 demoted and lost all his wealth.
ᵃThe purpose of my visit to Rainbow Bridge today
Is but an attempt to renew the relationship.
Pearl (*Plain Speech*): Now I understand.
(*When the Petals Fall*):
350 The lute strings have broken,
And my longing heart feels the pain.
Bou (*cont.*):
Like floating duckweed, we drift, now together, now apart.
Si (*cont.*):
355 I am indebted to their infinite love,
I lament over the unfortunate consequences of fate.
Pearl (*cont.*):
From now the lute will be stained with tear drops,
Never will I find true love again.
360 Bou (*cont.*):

The opera script

But true and constant love will bring the two together again.
Si (*cont.*):
I am waiting for another rendezvous at the other side of Rainbow Bridge.
Bou (*Plain Speech*): Since the young gentleman is already bound by a marriage
contract, we understand. But since the two of you have met according to fate, you can still be true friends. The young gentleman is welcome to visit my mistress in the future.
Si (*cont.*): If I should be free some day, I surely would pay you a visit. But I wonder where the young lady lives?
Bou (*cont.*): My mistress lives below the Rainbow Bridge.
Si (*cont.*): But below the bridge is Lake Hung Jaak. How can anyone live there?
Pearl (*cont.*): Please don't pay attention to Little Bou's nonsense.
Bou (*cont.*): What I mean is . . . beyond the Rainbow Bridge.
Wai (*Gwanfa* lower line):
ᵇThe light boat glides along on the water like a leaf; the stone bridge appears ahead like a rainbow.
ᵃLife is just like a ferry boat crossing; as you reach the other side, you say farewell and never meet again. (The boat touches shore.)
Wai (*Plain Speech*): All ashore, please.
Si (*cont.*): Old sir, I want to go to the home of the Magistrate. Being a stranger here, I don't know whether to head east or west.
Wai (*cont.*): It is right over there. Since I have earned my two hundred copper coins today, I want to go to the village to buy some wine and meat. Let me accompany you.
Si (*cont.*): Thank you, old sir.
Bou (*cont.*): My mistress wants to . . .
Pearl (*cont.*): Young sir . . .
Si (*cont.*): My lady, after I meet Magistrate Gong, I shall come and visit you. But you said you live beyond the Rainbow Bridge . . .?
Pearl (*cont.*): We are the only household beyond the bridge.
Si (*cont.*): I will keep my appointment soon. (Si and Wai exit.)
Bou (*cont.*): My lady . . . my lady, they are already out of sight!
Pearl (*Gwanfa* lower line):
ᵇI pity myself for being more unfortunate than the peach blossoms; bowing my head, I don't dare to blame the East wind that brought us together,
ᵃMy name has not been registered on the rock of marriage, I am left to live with empty dreams.

Besides the text of the opera itself, the script contains two other kinds of information, collectively known as *jiekou* (*gaaihau*). *Jie*, a technical term which first appeared in the scripts of *nanxi* of the Song dynasty, refers to instructions on the actors' gestures and movements; since such gestures and movements are almost always accompanied by percussion music, *jie* instructions are therefore addressed to percussionists as well as singers. *Kou* [mouth, or voice] are instructions to singers on how the text is to be orally delivered.

Included in the *jie* instructions are the names of percussion patterns such as "Moth on the

Lamp" (line 2), "The Rushing Wind" (line 27), "The Four Beats" (line 27), "One Stroke" (line 83), and so forth. These patterns are drawn from a traditionally established repertory and are shared by all plays. They may be used repeatedly in one play, chosen by the scriptwriter for various reasons. "The Rushing Wind," for example, is chosen out of dramatic considerations, being an appropriate prelude to signal the arrival of a heroic character, the God of Law; "The Four Beats" is formulaically used as an accompaniment for the stylized movements of a formal entrance; "Moth on the Lamp" is the conventional percussion prelude for the speech type *Patter Speech*; "One Stroke" is used in many places to accentuate parts of speech or gestures.

Some of the percussion patterns are specified in the script not only to instruct the instumentalists but also to suggest to the actors certain gestures and movements that are formulaically associated with these patterns. Conversely, some stage directions, such as "they gaze at the scenery" (line 3), "they look frightened" (line 23), and the like, suggest specific percussion patterns to the instrumentalists. The relationship between certain percussion patterns and stage movements is so close that a direction pertaining to one may often imply a direction pertaining to the other.

Nevertheless, much of the percussion music in a performance is not specified in the script. As a rule, actors improvise movements and gestures on stage; alert and experienced instrumentalists automatically provide the appropriate percussion accompaniment. If one listens to a recording and follows the script at the same time, one hears much more percussion music than is indicated in the script. The titles of percussion pattern given in the script prescribes only the bare essentials; the instrumentalists are expected to fill in the appropriate details in the course of the performance. The details, which include the specific combination of instruments, the elaborateness of the pattern, and loudness, depend upon the role type, the status of the actor in real life, as well as the dramatic situation.

The *kou* part of *jiekou*, a term which includes both speech and song types, is placed in parenthesis immediately before a passage of text. *Patter Speech* (line 4), *Plain Speech* (line 22), and *Percussion Speech* (line 34) are examples of speech types. *Gwanfa* (line 46), *Faaidim* (line 109), and *Bongji Maanbaan* (line 245) are examples of aria types. *Dainty Steps* (line 138), *Rowing a Boat* (line 193), and *The Monk Dreams of a Wife* (line 289) are examples of fixed tunes. *Muk'yu* (line 55) and *Naamyam* (line 173) are examples of narrative songs. The scriptwriter is responsible for choosing the appropriate oral delivery types and composing the text, which is considered well-written if it fits the dramatic context, if it is good poetry in its own right, and if its verse structure matches the musical elements defined by the type.

During a performance, a singer often exercises a certain degree of freedom in the execution of these oral delivery types: his version of a tune (or speech type) may vary from versions of the same tune performed either by himself or by other singers, either in the same play or in different plays. The degree of difference among the versions depends on many factors: the particular oral delivery type in question, the prosodic structure of the text, the dramatic context of the passage, and the individual style of the singer. Thus although the musical material of all plays is drawn from a common stock of preexistent material, it does not follow that music in Cantonese opera is necessarily repetitious: the "same" tune heard in two different plays (or sung with different texts in the same play) may sound quite different. The identity of a tune and range of its variation are important issues in the study of Cantonese opera.

The opera script

Some oral delivery types can vary so extensively from version to version that each type may more accurately be considered as no more than a set of rules or patterns that the singer must follow when delivering the text. These rules or patterns involve both the verse structure of the text and such musical elements as melody, rhythm, meter, tonal mode, and the nature of the instrumental accompaniment. The complexity and rigidity of the rules vary from type to type. For example, the *Patter Speech*, one of the simpler types, demands that the singer deliver the text using a speaking voice and inflection without any prescribed tonal pattern, but following a regular beat and a prescribed metrical pattern.

Most oral delivery types are associatively linked with varying degrees of rigidity to different dramatic situations or narrative functions. The *Patter Speech*, for example, is used mostly with texts that are essentially narrative rather than lyrical or dramatic in nature. The aria type named *Faaidim* is used during dramatically tense moments. The different fixed tunes, on the other hand, are usually used in lyrical sections of the opera.

In general no musical notation is provided in the script, nor is it necessary; the rules and patterns implied by the titles of oral delivery types are sufficient to guide the singer in performing a passage of text. In one sense, the titles are an extremely condensed and abstract form of musical notation. The singer's talent and expertise through years of performing experience allow him to transform literary titles into oral expression.

The inexplicitness inherent in this form of notation has been criticized as a sign of its inadequacy since the notation has little control over the details of the performance. This criticism is based upon the assumption that such control is necessary and desirable. In Cantonese opera, however, the performer is permitted, certainly not discouraged, to express himself freely and individually. A performer is trained with that end in view, and the use of literary titles and the absence of notation allows him the necessary scope of flexibility. On rare occasions a scriptwriter puts down musical notation alongside the text if he feels that the tune he chooses may not be known to the singer or the instrumentalists. In the above translation, musical notation is provided only for the fixed tune *Dainty Steps* in the original script.

The degree of flexibility varies according to the oral delivery type; for example, the performers are most free in improvising on *Plain Speech*, evidenced by a comparison of the translation above (based chiefly upon the written script) and the recording of the actual performance. The degree of flexibility also depends upon the role type; the Comic Role, represented by the God of Law in *The Magic Pearl*, improvises more than the other characters. For example, immediately following line 242, the God of Law, disguised as the boatman, playfully flirted with Little Bou to provide comic relief, all of which was not in the script.

As mentioned earlier in this chapter, changes on the script are often made before a performance, and are marked into the script for the various performers. The copy of the script of *The Magic Pearl* which I possess (the working copy of the scriptwriter) has many markings scribbled on it. The translation above, when compared with the recording, offers some concrete examples. The recording was made at the seventh and last performance of the series; some material was deleted in this performance because the original script was too long. For example, the fixed tune *When the Petals Fall* (line 349) was deleted altogether in this performance. The aria type *Chatjiching* sung by Lady Pearl (lines 279–284) originally has five lines; for this performance, lines two and three were skipped by the singer.

While the use of opera scripts has been standard practice in the past fifty years, older performers remember that, in the early part of the century, new operas were sometimes staged without the benefit of a script. In such cases the creative process took the following form. The deviser of the story, called *jiangxi shiye* (*gonghei siye*) [master of story-telling], first orally briefed the performers about the story a day or two before the performance. On the day of the performance he wrote an outline of the plot on a large placard and had it pasted backstage near the stage entrance. The outline listed the act divisions, the entrances and exits of the characters, and some of the oral delivery types a particular character should use in a particular act. Known as *tigang* (*taigong*) [outline], the placard reminded the performer when he was supposed to go on stage and what he was supposed to do when he was there.

In such a performance the performer extemporaneously composed the text and music himself according to the dramatic situation and the suggested oral delivery type. Sometimes he was left to choose an oral delivery type himself. In order to communicate to the instrumental ensemble which oral delivery type he was going to use, a performer flashed an established set of hand and finger signals called *shouying* (*sauying*) [hand shadows]. The ensemble then provided the proper instrumental prelude and accompaniment to the singing. Each signal referred to a specific oral delivery type; for example, sticking out the thumb and the index finger at right angles to each other, with the other three fingers curled against the palm denoted the aria type called *Yiwong Maanbaan* (short for *Jingsin Sapji Yiwong Maanbaan*, see p. 154).

The creative process outlined above underscores the importance of improvisation in both text and music on the part of the performers. Today, despite the existence and reliance on a script, it is not uncommon for a performer to depart from the written text while on stage.[5] The *tigang* is still routinely drawn and pasted near the stage entrance backstage, mainly for the benefit of a large number of performers who are not given a script.

6 *Speech types*

Despite their lack of musical tones, the speech types are important vehicles of musical expression in Cantonese opera. They differ from one another in metrical and rhythmical patterns, verse structure, and patterns of instrumental accompaniment. Each type is also traditionally associated with particular dramatic situations. The scriptwriter chooses a speech type that he considers as appropriate to the dramatic situation and then composes the text in accordance with certain rules and guidelines on the verse structure prescribed by that speech type. The performer then delivers the text accordingly. For example, in one type each phrase must end with a rhymed syllable; another type must be delivered with a regular beat; yet another is inseparable from a particular kind of gong-accompaniment. The rules and guidelines are not rigid however; a certain degree of flexibility is allowed during a performance.

This chapter will identify the rules and guidelines of the major speech types as a way of understanding the musical nature of speech in Cantonese opera and of the creative process of the speech types. Before proceeding, the reader is advised to read appendix 1 for an introduction to the Cantonese dialect and appendix 2 for notes on transcription symbols.

The major speech types

Seven speech types are commonly used in Cantonese opera:

1. *Baak* [*Plain Speech*]
2. *Tokbaak* [*Supported Speech*]
3. *Wanbaak* [*Comic Rhymed Speech*]
4. *Logubaak* [*Percussion Speech*]
5. *Sibaak* [*Poetic Speech*]
6. *Haugu* [*Rhymed Speech*]
7. *Baaklaam* [*Patter Speech*]

(Examples of all these speech types, except for *Comic Speech*, are to be found in the script in chapter 5.)

Among the seven speech types, *Plain Speech* is the closest to the vernacular Cantonese heard on the street. The text is in prose form with no formalized manner of delivery. There are, nevertheless, some differences between *Plain Speech* on stage and vernacular Cantonese on the street. First, the prose style of *Plain Speech* is not always vernacular; if the character in the drama delivering the text is a scholar or a government official, the text may be written in the literary style, either classical or contemporary, in order to reflect his learned background. Second, even without any prescribed rhythmic pattern, spoken Chinese lends itself easily to the grouping of syllables into various simple units of beats, resulting in fairly distinct rhythmic patterns. This kind of rhythmic pattern is sometimes noticeable even in ordinary speech. When the actor delivers in *Plain Speech* on stage, he exaggerates this rhythmic pattern to bring out the syntactic groupings.¹ Third, the performer often exaggerates the melodic contour formed by the sequence of liguistic tones, not unlike the style of delivery known as *Sprechstimme* in Schoenberg's *Pierrot Lunaire*. Finally, in the case of most women roles, the actresses generally speak in falsetto, further distancing *Plain Speech* from street dialect. All the above characteristics tend to enhance the dramatic impact and effectiveness of this speech type.

Supported Speech is identical to *Plain Speech* except that the melodic instrumental ensemble constantly accompanies the spoken words. It is also called *Longleuibaak*, meaning literally "speech in the waves." The term is probably a verbal play on a familiar term *longleuibaaktiu*, or literally "the white ribbon in the waves," a nickname given to a fictional character Zhang Shun in the famous Ming dynasty novel *All Men are Brothers* because Zhang is an expert swimmer. Since the word *Baak* can mean either "white" or "speech," the truncated form of *longleuibaaktiu* cleverly implies that the speaking voice is to be perceived as weaving in and out of the accompaniment like a swimmer.

Supported Speech is used for lyrical and tender moments in the drama, and often occurs in the middle of a singing passage, where the performers may insert a segment of dialogue or monologue. The accompaniment usually consists of repetitions of a short melodic motif based upon a fragment of the accompaniment used during the singing. In *The Magic Pearl* act 1 lines 248–253 and lines 258–270, the instrumental accompaniment to the speech is an extension of the instrumental interlude for the preceding oral delivery type called *Bongji Maanbaan*. Occasionally *Supported Speech* is accompanied by an independent tune, as in lines 156–168.

Comic Rhymed Speech is characterized by a particular verse structure in which the last syllable of each line must be rhymed. The rhymed syllables almost always belong to the Entering Tone category of short syllables that end abruptly with one of the three consonants /-p, /-t, and /-k. The lines do not have a poetic meter or a prescribed length, although they usually tend to be short or of medium length (less than ten syllables). When delivered, the text is spoken like plain speech with no particular rhythmic pattern except for a slight slowing down at the end of each line, which adds emphasis to the rhymed syllable. Furthermore, the rhymed syllables are often accompanied by light taps on the small woodblock, which has a sharp, high-pitched sound.

The aural effect produced by *Comic Rhymed Speech* is of a string of chatty lines, now long and now short, without metrical flow but always ending suddenly in rhyme – the suddenness being accentuated by the abrupt sound of the Entering Tone syllables and by the woodblock accompaniment. The total effect is light-hearted if not comical. Indeed *Comic Rhymed Speech* is used mostly by comic roles, or by any role during light-hearted moments of the drama. Since there is no example of this speech type in *The Magic Pearl*, one from another opera, *Dinühua* [*The Royal Beauty*], is given in figure 6.1. The rhyme in this example is "/-ik," which occurs at the end of every line.

       Jeung Chin, jan siu sik a, yik wak ga siu s$\overset{x}{\text{i}}$k(R) a?
       Jeung Chin, is this news true or false, would you say?

       Man dou dai neui wui sang ngo jau sam chik ch$\overset{x}{\text{i}}$k(R).
       Hearing that the princess is alive, my heart goes pitter-patter.

Speech types

Mei dou em tong jau gang fei hon si̊k(R).
We haven't reached the temple, it isn't even the festival of Hon Sik.

Je si waan wan si mei dong, em tong na yau gwai deui ji̊k(R)?
How can she come back alive? How can there be a ghost in the temple?

Ngo deui fu gwai bat mong, deui gung jyu cheung seung yi̊k(R).
I can't give up fame and fortune; yet I can't forget the princess either.

Jeung Chin a Jeung Chin, nei yau mou ying cho yan, yik wak tai cho si̊k(R)?
Jeung Chin, oh, Jeung Chin, are you sure you have seen the right person?

Transcription notes

R = rhymed syllable
x = a tap on the woodblock

Figure 6.1 *Comic Rhymed Speech*

The syllable "a" added after the rhymed syllable in the first line is known as a grammatical particle. It is meaningless in itself, but affects the mood and subtle nuances of the sentence as a whole. Commonly used in daily street talk, such particles are frequently found in other speech types with ending rhymes, such as *Rhymed Speech*, *Patter Speech*, and *Poetic Speech*. With the grammatical particle, the rhyming is partially hidden, which makes it more difficult for the novice to hear the structural pattern. Nevertheless the very subtlety of this device is what appeals to the experienced ear.

Percussion Speech is also called *Yinghungbaak* [*Heroic Speech*], a name that reflects its usual dramatic function. Its text consists of a sequence of short lines, each of which is built around a four-syllable nuclear phrase. Additional syllables may be added to complete the line grammatically. The delivery of the four-syllable nuclei is slightly slower, more deliberate and accented than that of the rest and is in regular pulses. A simple percussion pattern is used as a punctuation mark at the end of each line, most commonly a single beat on the medium woodblock followed immediately by a stroke on the Peking gong combined with a clash of the Peking cymbals. At the end of a passage the percussion pattern is generally more elaborate.

Percussion Speech is used mostly for military roles, and for any other male role during emotionally tense moments. In *The Magic Pearl* act 1, an example can be found in line 34, transcribed and translated in figure 6.2. It consists of eleven lines, most of which contain one or more such four-syllable nuclei, marked in the example by single quotation marks. The percussion patterns are shown in square brackets and are placed at the points where they occur.

Poetic Speech, also called *Ninbaak* [*Recitation*], has a relatively rigid verse structure. A complete unit has four lines; each line has the same number of syllables as the others in the unit, either five or seven. According to the syntactic structure, the line is broken into smaller segments of two or three syllables. A five-syllable line has a segmentation of 2 + 3; a seven-syllable line has a segmentation of 2 + 2 + 3. The three-syllable group is further divisible into either 1 + 2 or 2 + 1 depending on the syntactic structure. Relatively rigid rules also govern the rhyming and the choice of linguistic tones for certain syllables. The final

Cantonese opera

              [c G]
Wu naai

I am

                         [bb . . . bb]   [bbgG]
'Ji juk lam jung' 'wu faat tin jyun' 'Wai To si ya'.
The Purple Bamboo Forest's God of Law Wai To, that I am.

                   [b G]
'Ji yan Hung Jaak' 'wu seui faan laan',
Because Hung Jaak lake overflows,

          [b G]
Sei Jau Gong taai sau
Magistrate Gong of Sei Jau

          [b G]
'Seung jau tin ting'
Made offerings to Gods in Heaven

                             [b G]
Ging dung lieu 'daai ci daai bei' Gun Sai Yam pou saat.
Moving the all-merciful Goddess of Mercy.

                [b G]
Wai ching gau 'baat sing chong sang',
In order to save the multitude of lives,

              [b G]
'Jau chi ming an' 'Wai To chin loi'
She has asked me, Wai To, to come,

      [b G]
'Cha taam yat faan'.
To make an investigation

          [b G]
'Yeuk yin jan yau' 'yiu mat wai hoi',
Should there be really demons causing trouble,

                 [bbb . . .gG] [bbb . . .gGcccGc c G]
Ha! ha! an, Wai To, ding jau 'ba ta cheui heui'.
Ha! ha! I, Wai To, surely shall deal with them.

Transcription notes
Percussion accompaniment is indicated in square brackets. The instruments are represented by the following letters: b = medium woodblock, c = Peking cymbals, g = small gong, G = Peking gong and Peking cymbals together. Dots refer to an indefinite number of repetitions of the preceding symbol (sound).

Figure 6.2 *Percussion Speech*

Speech types

syllable of lines one, two and four must rhyme and must belong to one of the even tone categories; the final syllable of line three must not rhyme and must belong to one of the oblique tone categories. This verse structure resembles that of the Chinese poetic genre called *jueju* (*jütgeui*), sometimes translated as the "quatrain," although the rules are not as rigidly observed in *Poetic Speech* as in poetry composition.[2] Figure 6.3 summarizes the verse structure for *Poetic Speech* with seven syllable lines (for an explanation of the symbols, see appendix 2).

	P1	P2	P3
L1	_ _,	_ _,	_ _±R;
L2	_ _,	_ _,	_ _±R;
L3	_ _,	_ _,	_ _x;
L4	_ _,	_ _,	_ _±R.

Figure 6.3 Verse structure of *Poetic Speech*

The performance of *Poetic Speech* can be described as speech recitation with a pattern of pauses within the verse structure which varies quite freely from performance to performance. The non-metrical rhythm further adds to the difficulty of notating such a performance. The pattern of pauses deducted from a large number of performances from different operas is shown in figure 6.4 (applied to *The Magic Pearl* act 1 line 30) with a new notational system that uses slashes to indicate two different, though related, sets of information. The greater the number of slashes between syllables, the longer the pause between them, and the greater the likelihood that such a pause will occur in any performance. The penultimate syllable "a" in the last line is a nonsense syllable added to emphasize the pause before the last syllable.

This notational system therefore indicates the probability of occurrence of a musical feature besides being a descriptive symbol. It also assumes that the length of a pause and the probability of its occurrence are correlated. The performances, of course, vary from one to

1	2	3	4	5	6	7
Pou	dou/	jung	sang//	hin/	san	[b G] tung(R)///
Jik	ha	gung	dak//	maan/	maan	[b G] chung(R)///
Sau	seung	gam	gong/	hong//	mo	[b G] chyu///
Yiu	mo	gwai	[c G] gwaai///	yat	[bbb...............bb g G] sou a///	hung(R)

Delivering human beings to Nirvana, I demonstrate magic power,
I accumulate merits, ten thousand-fold;
In my hand the diamond demon-subduing club,
Demons, devils, with one sweep, vanish.

Figure 6.4 *Poetic Speech*

another; the relative duration of the pause may change, and pauses may be added or deleted. In some performances, for example, the long pause that usually occurs between syllables six and seven of the last line falls instead between syllables five and six, regardless of the syntactic structure of the text.

Poetic Speech is always accompanied by percussion patterns, which occur at five places: during the pauses after each line, and in the middle of the last line. The specific patterns and the instrumentation may vary depending upon the role type that is performing. For example, in the case of a military role the Peking gong is generally used; in the case of a scholar role a small gong will be used. Figure 6.4 includes percussion patterns in square brackets.

Poetic Speech is used most often as the opening utterance of a major character when he appears on stage for the first time in the play. The content of the text can vary widely, ranging from description of scenery to the expression of a thought, mood, or feeling. *Poetic Speech* is generally followed immediately by a formal self-introduction. Because of this particular usage, it is sometimes also called *Yanbaak* [*Introductory Speech*]. In the first act of *The Magic Pearl*, the God of Law appears on stage and recites a passage of *Poetic Speech*, followed immediately by a self-introduction delivered in *Percussion Speech*.

Rhymed Speech follows a verse structure in which the unit is a couplet with two phrases in each line. There is no rule prescribing the number of syllables in a phrase, but each phrase should be of roughly equal length. The model verse structure for rhyming and linguistic tones in a complete couplet is shown in figure 6.5.

```
         P1                    P2
L1    _ _ . . . _ ±,        _ _ . . . _ xR;
L2    _ _ . . . _ x,        _ _ . . . _ ±R.
```

Figure 6.5   Verse structure of *Rhymed Speech*

Many scriptwriters impose an additional linguistic tonal pattern: when there are two or more couplets in succession, the final syllables in each couplet may alternate between the upper and lower kinds of Even Tones. The basic unit that repeats itself therefore becomes a quatrain rather than a couplet (Upper Even Tone is represented by the symbol "+`", Lower Even Tone is represented by the symbol "+\"):

```
L1    . . . . x
L2    . . . . +`
L3    . . . . x
L4    . . . . +\
```

Figure 6.6 is a transcription of *Rhymed Speech* with two couplets from *The Magic Pearl* act 1, lines 94–107. The rhyme and the linguistic tones of the ending syllables of each phrase and line are marked. A comparison with the model verse structure in figure 6.5 shows that the example departs from the model in two ways. First, the final syllables of the second line, *tou*, does not rhyme with the other three final syllables: *hung*, *jung*, and *gung*. Such irregularity appears to be tolerated by performers and listeners in this speech type, being found elsewhere

Speech types

		WAI TO:
(Line 1)	(P1)	A, Yun loi na seui yiu lin jau yat fo fan seui dik yun jyu a; fan seui yun jyu naai si yiu mat kap cheui yat yut jing wa, gang ga yi yun gung sau lin, keui yun loi yau chi bou mat pong san(+),
	(P2)	Naan gwaai keui yau chi mou hung(xR) a.

So she has a magic pearl! A magic pearl has the essence of the sun, the essence of the moon, and the essence of the demon's own black power. So she has the protection of that precious object! No wonder she is so reckless.

		EARTH:
(Line 2)	(P1)	Waan yau a, yan wai bin seui siu lung seui yin seui mou mei sik, si seung dou loi taam fong(x),
	(P2)	Mui loi yat chi, jau gang hing hei bo long tou tou(+R) a.

To make it worse, the young dragon son of Bin River admires the beauty of this demon, and often comes to visit her; every time he comes, he too stirs up high waves.

		WAI TO:
(Line 3)	(P1)	Ha! Ha! bin seui lou lung wai ho bat ba ta yi ji gun gaau ne? Hou, doi bun wu faat wui tin seung jau ji si(+),
	(P2)	Yat ding ching faat na lou lung jeung yi ji fong jung(xR) ding la.

Ha! Ha! The Old Dragon of Bin River, why doesn't he discipline his son? Some day I will report to the Heavenly Court; he'll be punished for letting his son run wild.

		EARTH:
(Line 4)	(P1)	Kei sat hung jaak wu seui faan laam, yau yu seui mou lin jyu so ji, yik yan bin seui siu lung yi hei(x),
	(P2)	Yat che yat jing, choi hoi fu liu ngo ni go tou dei gung gung(+R) a.

You surely can blame the overflow of Lake Hung Jaak on both of them: the Water Demon and the Dragon Prince. One is a demon, the other a god. All the same, it is I, the Old Earth, that have to suffer the consequences.

Figure 6.6   *Rhymed Speech*

in the script; it indicates that rhyme schemes can be rather flexible. Second, a string of several phrases replaces the first of the model verse structure in each line, a deviation not uncommonly found for this speech type in this and other operas.

A performer often deviates extemporaneously from the written text during a performance. One type of improvisation for *Rhymed Speech* is the adding of grammatical particles to the end of a line. In the above example, syllables that appear after the rhymes: "a" in lines 1, 2 and 4, and "ding la" in line 3, are such examples.

Rhymed Speech is most often used for dialogue: the lines of couplet are divided between the two speakers, each taking an alternate line. The text is delivered in a manner close to that of *Plain Speech*, except that the rhymed syllables at the end of lines are given extra emphasis. This is achieved by slowing down the preceding several syllables and by adding a strong stress to the rhymed syllable.

The last speech type, *Patter Speech*, has a relatively elaborate verse structure with a basic unit consisting of two lines of two phrases each (figure 6.7). Each phrase has seven syllables, with an internal syntactic division of 4+3. Both lines must end with a rhymed syllable. The

Opening couplet:

L1 ___,__+R,   _____+R;
L2 _____x,   _____+R.

Subsequent couplets:

L1 _____±,   _____xR;
L2 _____x,   _____+R.

Figure 6.7 Verse structure of *Patter Speech*

first phrase of the first line and the second phrase of the second line must end with a syllable with Even Tone, while the other two phrases must end with a syllable with Oblique Tone. The first line of the opening couplet observes a different set of rules: its first phrase has six syllables instead of seven, divided into 3+3, and ends on a rhymed syllable with Even Tone. Its second phrase has seven syllables and ends on a rhymed syllable with another Even Tone. A passage may consist of any number of couplets.

A further rule which some scriptwriters observe is that the second line of alternate couplets are to end in Upper Even Tone and Lower Even Tone syllables respectively. The result is a quatrain structure rather than a couplet structure. Another variation is that the number of syllables may be five instead of seven in each phrase of a couplet.

Patter Speech is the only speech type that has a relatively well-defined rhythmic pattern. The syllables are delivered according to a constant stream of steady beats, produced by repeated strokes on the large woodblock. The beats do not contrast in dynamics; in other words, there is no apparent metrical grouping. Occasionally, however, there may be local regular patterns of simple duple or triple meter resulting from the syntactic structure of the text and the singer's manner of delivery. Figure 6.8 shows an example of *Patter Speech* taken from lines 5–20 of *The Magic Pearl* act 1. Note that this version consists of both seven-syllable phrases (first two couplets) and five-syllable phrases (last three couplets). The meter correspondingly changes from a duple pattern to a triple pattern. Notice also the irregularity in rhythm at the very last line of the passage through the repetition of the last three syllables. This is a formulaic ending that all *Patter Speech* follows.

Study of a large number of different versions of *Patter Speech* shows that the delivery is not always as consistent in its metrical structure as that shown in figure 6.8. It often happens that there is a shift of metrical pattern from duple to triple, or vice versa, in the middle of a couplet, sometimes even in the middle of a line. Performers are also known to ad-lib on stage and insert extra syllables in a line, thus changing the meter.

Patter Speech is used most often when a long narrative passage is involved. Typically it occurs at the beginning of an opera (as in *The Magic Pearl*) where a summary of the background of the story is given prior to the main action on stage.

Flexibility of speech types

The names of the speech types change from time to time, and name variants sometimes coexist. As already noted, *Supported Speech* is sometimes called *Speech in the Waves*, and *Percussion Speech* is also known as *Heroic Speech*. Multiple names do not disrupt

Speech types

L1 Tou fa hung, heng fa hung(+R),   maan fa gam sau mou cheun fung(+R);

Peach blossoms red, apricot blossoms red, ten thousand flowers dance in the breeze;

L2 Sei Jau sing ngoi fa yu hoi(x),   Hung Kiu yat jo kwa sai dung(+R).

Around the town of Sei Jau a sea of flowers, Rainbow Bridge spans from east to west.

L1 Hung Kiu ji ha hai Hung Jaak wu(+),   sou yan mak haak gaai si jung(xR);

Underneath Rainbow Bridge is Lake Hung Jaak, whose beauty poets all praised;

L2 Ho sik gam si mou sing fong(x),   yik sik fu gam taan bat tung(+R).

Unfortunately the good days are no longer here, I lament over the difference between then and now.

L1 Yi chin Hung Kiu bin (+),   si Ching Yeung si jaap yung(xR);

Formerly, beside the Rainbow Bridge was Ching Yeung Market;

L2 Yat dou heui kei yat(x),   seui sit dou ya bat tung(+R).

During market days, what a crowd there used to be.

L1 Ho sik gan nin loi(+),   Hung seui faan laan yung(xR);

Unfortunately in recent years, there has been great flooding;

L2 Seung yan wo hoi ming(x),   wo mat yau seung nung(+R).

The water took our lives, our property, and our food.

L1 Gong taai sau jai tin(+),   ying yin hai mou jok yung(xR);

Magistrate Gong has prayed to Heaven, but what's the use!

L2 Hung seui yi yin yau(x),   yat ding yau gwaai mat joi kei jung, joi kei jung(+R).

The floods keep coming, there must be a demon living in the lake.

Figure 6.8 *Patter Speech*

communication among musicians so long as the performers, the scriptwriters and the audience all recognize the basic structural features and the dramatic functions of each type, whatever it is called.

The structural features of each speech type are also liable to change or modification. For example, in the opera *Shenyuan Chunmeng* [*Spring Dreams in the Chen Garden*], *Poetic Speech*, normally delivered without instrumental accompaniment, is accompanied throughout, making it a combination of *Poetic Speech* and *Supported Speech*. Other speech types besides *Percussion Speech* may be accompanied by percussion music, as one finds in most examples given in this chapter. Every once in a while the audience is pleasantly surprised by such creative manipulation of musical structure to achieve new musical and dramatic effects.

Three of the seven speech types have fixed forms. *Poetic Speech* is almost always in quatrain form; in rare instances, it may appear in couplet form, in which case only the last two lines of the quatrain are used. *Rhymed Speech* and *Patter Speech* always exist in the couplet form (or quatrain form if the Upper–Lower alternations of Even Tones are observed among the couplets). *Poetic Speech* never occurs for longer than one quatrain at one passage, while the *Rhymed Speech* and *Patter Speech* can continue indefinitely as a string of couplets (or quatrains). The speech types that do not have fixed forms in theory have no limit to the length of their occurrence. *Rhymed Speech* and *Patter Speech* have another characteristic in common: they allow interruptions by other oral delivery types – most often *Plain Speech*. The other speech types always exist as closed entities.

Because of the structural flexibility of the speech types, each type can be considered as a set of rules or guidelines according to which the scriptwriter composes the text and the singer delivers it. The degree of flexibility in the rules varies from one type to another. For example, *Poetic Speech* has a relatively rigid verse structure, while *Patter Speech* has a relatively rigid rhythmic structure. *Plain Speech* is the most flexible of all the types because it is not governed by any explicit rule. This does not, of course, mean that it is delivered totally without regard to aesthetic norms. According to the prominent opera singer Mai Bingrong, *Plain Speech* is the most difficult oral delivery type to perform properly and effectively for the very reason that its guidelines are not spelled out.[3]

7 Aria types

Aria types, or *bongwong* (*banghuang* in Peking dialect), are the most important category of songs in Cantonese opera for several reasons. First, from the historical point of view, they were the only songs sung in Cantonese opera until the early decades of the twentieth century, when other tunes were introduced. Second, all *bongwong* songs share several basic structural features which bind them with a stylistic coherency. Third, there are only a small number of preexistent tunes upon which the *bongwong* songs are based – about thirty[1] – and they are repeatedly used in a play and are, of course, shared by all plays. Consequently *bongwong* songs are the most familiar ones to the audience.

Bongwong songs are important from the musicological point of view because of their structural features and how they are performed and transmitted. One characteristic is that *bongwong* tunes, when sung to different sets of text, almost always have distinctly different melodic contours; versions of the same "tune" may sound quite different from one another. For this reason, a tune is better described as a tune "type" to include the many variant forms. *Bongwong* tunes are used exclusively in the theater, always sung to words, and many of the tunes have traditionally-established dramatic associations. Thus, *bongwong* songs are called "arias" to emphasize their dramatic significance. These are the reasons why *bongwong* songs are translated as "aria types."[2]

Through repeated use in different plays over an extended period of time and through many generations of performance and transmission, a tune in a particular regional opera undergoes drastic and lasting changes in different aspects, most often in metrical and rhythmic structures. A single tune develops into two or more versions, each of which in time sufficiently differentiates itself from the others so as to establish its own identity, name, and dramatic function. Although these tunes share certain tonal, modal, and large structural features, they tend to differ from each other in metrical, rhythmic, and melodic details. Such tunes can best be described as forming a "tune family," a term which not only indicates the shared features, but also points to the fact that the tunes have developed from a single tune through the passage of time. To extend the analogy further, one could speak of a family of "offspring tunes" having evolved from a "mother tune," and their names often testify to the genetic relationship.

The thirty or so aria types in Cantonese opera belong to two "families"; they are "offspring tunes" which bear the names of either *bongji* or *yiwong*, the two "mother tunes" out of which they evolved (thus *bongwong*). *Bongji* and *yiwong* are two families of tunes among several that developed in northern and eastern China and became very popular in many parts of the country during the seventeenth and eighteenth centuries. Known under different names for the many regional variations, these two styles form the core of musical material for many of today's regional operas. For example, the two families of tunes which form the core of musical material in Peking opera, the *xipi* and the *erhuang*, are believed to have developed from the same roots as *bongji* and *yiwong* respectively in Cantonese opera.

Structurally, all aria types consist of two short lines of melody (or their variant forms) sung to two lines of text. The two lines of melody may be repeated any number of times in a song passage, depending upon the number of couplets of text. The same aria type may also appear at several different points in the play when called for by dramatic and structural situations. Aria types are accompanied by an instrumental ensemble; the nature of the accompaniment and its relationship to the vocal melody may differ from one aria type to another.

The aria types are associated with certain dramatic moods at different degrees of specificity. In general the tunes in the *bongji* family are associated with a brighter outlook, brisker dramatic action, and lighter mood, while the tunes in the *yiwong* family have the opposite effect. Of course, the individual tunes within a family, owing to their different musical features, differ in their dramatic associations. For example, an aria type called *Faaidim* (belonging to the *bongji* family) which has a fast tempo and an irregular meter, suggests extreme agitation, while another called *Faansin Yiwong*, which is slow and melismatic, induces a mood of melancholy. The scriptwriter chooses an aria type in part to fit the dramatic requirements of the story. During a performance, the audience appreciates the aria types both for their musical appeal and for their dramatic effectiveness.

Two versions of the same aria type, because they are sung to different sets of text, almost always differ in melodic contour. In addition, a singer may exercise a certain degree of freedom in the execution of an aria type and thus produce a version that varies from other versions. Thus, although only a limited number of aria types is used in all the plays, the music is not necessarily repetitious: the "same" tune heard in two different plays (or sung to different sets of text in the same play) can sound quite different. The degree to which the versions differ depends on many factors: the particular aria type in question, the text and its verse structure, the dramatic context of the passage, and the individual style of the singer.

Take, for example, the two versions (A and B) of an aria type called *Chatjiching* (belonging to the *bongji* family) shown in figure 7.1. They have quite different melodic contours, yet they

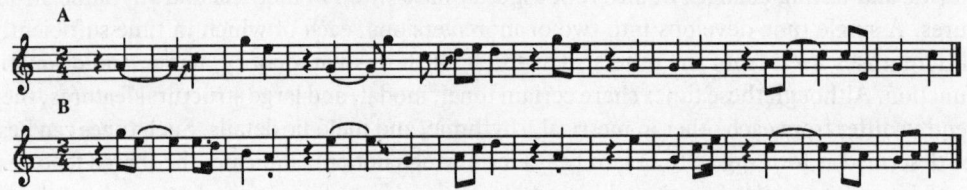

Figure 7.1 Two versions of *Chatjiching*

are considered to be the same aria type. It is obvious that the identity of the *Chatjiching* does not depend on a specific melodic contour. Some structural features in these versions must be invariable to allow a listener to recognize that a song passage is one aria type and not another. Such recognition is critical to the effectivenes of a performance because of the important dramatic functions that aria types play in the opera. It also goes without saying that musical identification is basic to the appreciation and enjoyment of music.

Aria types 69

Identity and anatomy of an aria type

The invariable features can be abstracted by a comparative study of several versions of an aria type. Nine versions of the *Chatjiching* sung by the male role are transcribed and aligned in figure 7.2 to facilitate easy examination and comparison.

Based upon the versions in figure 7.2, the structural features that appear to be invariable, or nearly invariable, are abstracted and summarized below (for an explanation of the symbols, see appendices 1 and 2). They are assumed to contribute to the identity of the aria type.

Figure 7.2   Nine versions of *Chatjiching*

1 Verse structure of text

The text of a particular aria type follows certain structural regularities in regard to the number of syllables (words) in a line, the caesura pattern, and in the rhyme and linguistic tonal patterns. For the *Chatjiching,* each line of text has seven syllables with a caesura after the fourth syllable, separating the line into two phrases. The last syllable of each phrase follows certain rules governing linguistic tones; the last syllable of each line must rhyme. The verse structure of one couplet of text for the *Chatjiching* is shown in figure 7.3.

```
        P1          P2
L1     ___+,      __xR;
L2     ___x,      __+R.
```

Figure 7.3   Verse structure of *Chatjiching*

In practice, the number of syllables in a line is somewhat flexible. Extra syllables are quite frequently either written into the script by the scriptwriter or ad-libbed by the performer on stage. Generally called "padding syllables," these extra syllables may clarify the meaning of the text or add rhythmic interest to the tune. Padding syllables will be discussed in chapter 9.

2 Metrical pattern and syllable placement

Most aria types have a well-defined metrical pattern in terms of repeated units of strong and weak beats.[3] The two lines of melody have a fixed number of such metrical units. The most commonly found metrical patterns are: one strong beat followed by three weak beats, an alternation of strong and weak beats, and a series of strong beats. Each of the metrical units has duple subdivisions in between the strong and weak beats. In *Chatjiching*, the metrical pattern is an alternation of strong and weak beats, and the two lines of melody comprise twelve metrical units, or measures. The transcription uses a duple meter and assigns the first quarter note as the strong beat and the second quarter note as the weak beat.

The syllables of the text in the nine versions of *Chatjiching* in figure 7.2 are similarly distributed within the framework of twelve measures. The pattern is abstracted and shown in figure 7.4.

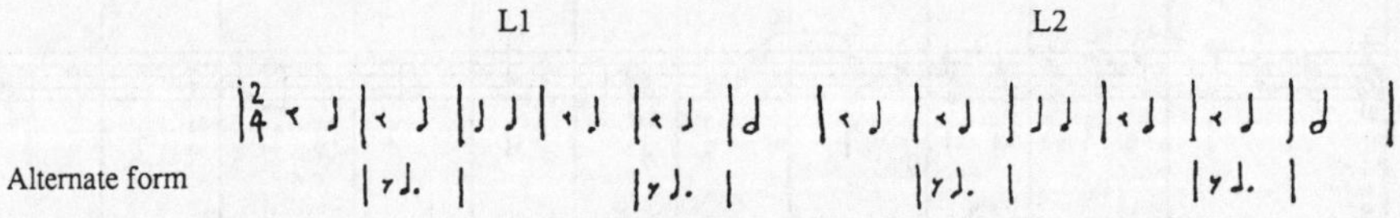

Figure 7.4   Syllable placement of *Chatjiching*

3 Sin

"*Sin*" is a tonal feature or a set of tonal rules which, on the simplest level, may be understood as somewhat equivalent to a "scale." But on other levels, it may be equated with the concepts of "key" and "mode". All aria types belong to one of three *sin*s called *jingsin* [regular *sin*], *faansin* [reverse *sin*], and *yifaansin* ("*yi*" and "*faan*" are the name of the two pitches in the Chinese heptatonic scale). While the issue of *sin* will be treated in full in chapter 10, it suffices to mention here that, in essence, aria types in a particular *sin* emphasize five of the seven pitches in the Cantonese heptatonic scale (see chapter 2 on the heptatonic scale); these five will be called principal pitches. *Chatjiching* belongs to *jingsin*, which has the following set of principal pitches shown in figure 7.5.

Aria types

Figure 7.5 Principal pitches of *jingsin*

4 Line-ending pitches

The different versions of *Chatjiching* adhere to the same line-ending pitches of D and C for the two lines of melody respectively. For some aria types, the final note at the end of phrases in the middle of a line also adheres to prescribed pitches, although there is generally more flexibility in the choice of phrase-ending pitches than line-ending pitches. The line-ending pitches may vary according to the tune family, to the *sin*, and to the role type.

5 Instrumental accompaniment

As a general rule, the melodic ensemble accompanies the vocal line by playing the same tune heterophonically throughout, and the woodblocks further accompany by accentuating certain beats. Individual aria types are often distinguished from one another by special sorts of accompaniment unique to the aria type. The special interplay between vocal line and instrumental accompaniment produces a distinctive overall musical texture for certain aria types. In the *Chatjiching*, for example, a steady stroke of the large woodblock on every strong beat (not shown in the transcription) and the absence of the voice on many of these same beats (measures 1, 2, 4, 5, 7, 8, 10, 11) create a unique texture. Most aria types are also identified by their individual instrumental preludes and interludes. For some the prelude is in two parts, the first one consisting of a percussion pattern, the second one a short tune played by the melodic instruments. The interludes are short melodic fragments played between two lines or two phrases of the vocal line. The *Chatjiching* does not have such a prelude or such interludes.

Aria type as a structure and as a process

The above analysis shows that what identifies and categorizes an aria type is not the melodic contour, which may vary widely from one version to another, but some other structural features that remain invariable. One may view these structural features as a set of rules, upon which the creation of aria types is based. To understand this point, one begins with Harold Powers' observation on the term "mode": "[Mode] has always been used to designate classes of melodies, and in this century to designate certain kinds of norm or model for composition or improvisation as well."[4] Note that this definition treats the concept of mode from two opposing perspectives. On the one hand, mode is considered as a system for the classification of existing tunes as if they were material objects. On the other hand, mode is considered as a model or a set of rules which guides the process by which new musical material is composed. Powers' statement, with its dual approach to the understanding of mode, can be generalized into a discussion of categories of melodies in general, and can conveniently be applied to the understanding of aria types in Cantonese opera.

On the one hand a particular aria type can be understood as a subfamily of tunes within the large family of aria types. These tunes belong to the same subfamily because they share certain textual and musical features which enable an experienced listener to identify the aria type and to associate it with its traditionally-established dramatic meanings. He may or may not know the aria type by name; more likely than not, he is not aware of the analytical features of the tune that enable him to make the identification.

On the other hand, an aria type is a norm or a model for composition or improvisation by the scriptwriter and the singer. The scriptwriter first chooses an aria type, identified by a name, from a pool of aria types. His reasons for making a particular choice may be either dramatic or structural, or both. Once the choice is made, the specific aria type defines certain textual and musical rules which the scriptwriter and the singer must follow. Some flexibility is allowed in the application of some of these rules. The scriptwriter composes a set of verses that fulfills the textual rules of the aria type and the dramatic requirements of the opera. The name of the aria type, which is written into the script, guides the singer to perform the verses according to that type's designated musical rules.

The shared features of the aria type from the listener's point of view are, of course, equivalent to the rules for creating the aria type from the scriptwriter's and the singer's point of view. From one point of view the music is regarded as structure, from the other, as a process.[5]

Consider the aria type named *Jingsin Sapji Bongji Jungbaan* [Regular *Sin*, Ten Syllable, *Bongji*, Medium *Baan*]. Usually abbreviated to simply *Jungbaan*, its name reflects certain textual, metrical, rhythmic, and melodic features of the text and tune that all versions of this aria type share, or rules that all scriptwriters and singers must follow in the writing and performing of the aria type. The term *sapji*, which mean "ten syllables," refers to the number of syllables in a line of text, and further implies certain patterns of rhyming and of linguistic tones within the line. Furthermore, these structural features or rules governing the text imply certain metrical and melodic rules governing the tune. "Ten syllable" line is one of the two most commonly used line-lengths, the other being "seven syllable," or *chatji*. Thus, an aria type that is closely related to *Jingsin Sapji Bongji Jungbaan* [Regular *Sin*, Ten Syllable, *Bongji*, Medium *Baan*] is *Jingsin Chatji Bongji Jungbaan* [Regular *Sin*, Seven Syllable, *Bongji*, Medium *Baan*].

The term *jungbaan* [medium *baan*] refers in part to the tempo of the tune. More importantly, it refers to the metrical pattern of strong and weak beats, rhythmical features in the placement of syllables of the text, and the degree of melismaticness of the aria type. The other commonly-used *baan* in addition to *jungbaan* are *maanbaan* [slow *baan*], *faaijungbaan* [fast medium *baan*], and *saanbaan* [non-metrical *baan*]. Thus, an aria type that is closely related to *Jingsin Sapji Bongji Jungbaan* [Regular *Sin*, Ten Syllable, *Bongji*, Medium *Baan*] is *Jingsin Sapji Bongji Maanbaan* [Regular *Sin*, Ten Syllable, *Bongji*, Slow *Baan*].

The term *jingsin* refers to the *sin* in which the aria type is sung. As mentioned earlier, there are three *sins* in the music of Cantonese opera: *jingsin* [regular *sin*], *faansin* [reverse *sin*], and *yifaansin* (always abbreviated to simply *yifaan*). Thus *Jingsin Sapji Bongji Jungbaan* [Regular *Sin*, Ten Syllable, *Bongji*, Medium *Baan*] is related to two other aria types: *Faansin Sapji Bongji Jungbaan* [Reverse *Sin*, Ten Syllable, *Bongji*, Medium *Baan*] and *Yifaan Sapji Bongji Jungbaan* [*Yifaan Sin*, Ten Syllable, *Bongji*, Medium *Baan*].

Finally, the term *bongji* refers to the name of the tune family to which this aria type belongs. Aria types in the same tune family, with few exceptions, share certain melodic features, and, more specifically, the line-ending and phrase-ending pitches at critical junctures of the tune. Thus, an aria type that belongs to the *yiwong* family but is otherwise related to *Jingsin Sapji Bongji Maanbaan* [Regular *Sin*, Ten Syllable, *Bongji*, Slow *Baan*] is *Jingsin Sapji Yiwong Maanbaan* [Regular *Sin*, Ten Syllable, *Yiwong*, Slow *Baan*].

The term "feature" is used with the intention of suggesting a possible analogy with the concept of "feature" in phonetics, according to which a "phonetic representation" of speech

Aria types

is characterized by the degree of intensity with which a given feature is present in a particular speech segment. One particular segment may be voiced, with affrication, without stopping or complete closure of the vocal tract, while another may be nasal, voiced, "acute." The array of features by which the sounds of speech are differentiated appears in large measure to be shared by all human languages, and the features themselves have been cited as examples of "linguistic universals."[6]

One may similarly consider an aria type as a "musical segment" characterized by its values with respect to a number of largely independent properties or features. This interpretation is supported by the fact that sometimes the names of aria types, such as *Jingsin Sapji Bongji Jungbaan* [Regular *Sin*, Ten Syllable, *Bongji*, Medium *Baan*], explicitly identify these features and their specific values. The *sin*, the number of syllables in a line, the tune family, and the *baan* constitute the structural features of an aria type, or, from the scriptwriter's and singer's point of view, the rules governing its compositional process. Through permutations, these features or rules yield the thirty or so aria types in common use today. Obviously not all the permutations are realized as aria types, otherwise the number would be greatly in excess of thirty. For example, the *yiwong* family of tunes does not have a "medium tempo" category; in both *bongji* and *yiwong* families the "slow tempo" category does not exist for seven-syllable lines, and so forth. Some permutations may come into vogue at one time or another, others may go out of fashion. The repertory of aria types is known to change through the ages.

The names of aria types do not necessarily specify all the distinguishing features. For example, the name *Jingsin Sapji Bongji Jungbaan* is often abbreviated to simply *Jungbaan* [Medium *Baan*] because, unless otherwise specified, the other three features are automatically assumed to be what they are. The name is expanded to *Chatji Jungbaan* [Seven Syllable, Medium *Baan*] if a seven syllable line is involved, and to *Faansin Chatji Jungbaan* [Reverse *Sin*, Seven Syllable, Medium *Baan*] if, in addition, the aria type is sung in reverse *sin*. Some aria types developed names which, in whole or part, appear to be unrelated to their structural features. For example, *Chatji Jungbaan* is frequently called *Chatjiching* instead; in this usage, the origin and meaning of the character *ching* is obscure.

The names do not specify explicitly the nature of instrumental accompaniment, but prescribe it by convention. Thus one of the most distinctive features of *Chatjiching* – the woodblock sharply accentuating the strong beats at which points the voice is mostly silent – is uniquely associated with this aria type, and is recognized by the audience and followed by the performers. There is no clearly-defined distinction among the variety of accompaniments, some of which will be described in the next section.

For some aria types, the tessituras, line-ending pitches, and degree of melismaticness may vary depending upon the role type of the performer. Thus one may consider role type as another differentiating factor for aria types, contributing yet another set of rules. This factor is known among musicians as *hau*, a term which literally means "throat," and which may be translated as "voice types." According to Chen Zhuoying, nine different voice types were recognized in the early part of the century.[7] Today there are only three voice types: the *sanghau* [male voice], the *daanhau* [female voice], and the *daaihau* ["big" voice]. The last refers to the voice type for characters of heroic stature, such as generals or gods.

With few exceptions, each of the six major role types is consistently associated with a specific voice type in all plays, as is shown in figure 7.6.

The first difference among versions of the same aria types sung by different voice types is in the tessitura of the tune: generally between E below middle C to G above middle C for the

Civil-military role	male voice
Young male role	male voice
Comic role	male voice
Principal female role	female voice
Supporting female role	female voice
Military role	"big" voice

Figure 7.6   Role types and voice types

male voice type, one octave higher for the female voice type, about a fifth higher for the "big" voice type.[8] The second difference is that voice type changes the line-ending pitches for some aria types but not for others. The third difference is in the degree of melismaticness of the tune–text relationship; in general, the male and female voice types are more melismatic while the "big" voice type is more syllabic. The last difference is in the voice quality: the "big" voice, partly because it sings at a higher tessitura, is more forceful and strained than the male voice type. It goes without saying that male and female voice qualities are different.

The different versions of an aria type which result from differences in voice type are not generally considered to constitute "different" aria types. Voice types are not specified in the name of an aria type because it is clear from the script which character, and thus which role type and voice type, is singing. In recent years, however, the relationships between role types and voice types have not always been consistently observed. Historically, the Military Role is often characterized with a fiery temper, with which versions of aria types characterized by the "big" voice type are naturally associated. It follows that other male roles, in order to express a heroic stature and fiery temper, will also use the "big" voice version of an aria type. An example is found in act 1 of *The Magic Pearl* (line 116): Golden Scale sings the aria type *Faaidim* in the "big" voice style, obviously a means to enhance his tempestuous character.

A summary of the features and rules that make up an aria type follows:

1. Tune family: A. *bongji*, B. *yiwong*;
2. Verse structure: A. *chatji* [seven syllables], B. *sapji* [ten syllables], C. others;
3. *Baan*: A. *maanbaan* [slow *baan*], B. *jungbaan* [medium *baan*], C. *faaibaan* [fast *baan*], D. *saanbaan* [non-metrical *baan*], and some variants within each category;
4. *Sin*: A. *jingsin* [regular *sin*], B. *faansin* [reverse *sin*], C. *yifaan*;
5. Instrumental accompaniment;
6. Voice types: A. male voice, B. female voice, C. "big" voice.

Major aria types

For comparison with *Chatjiching*, five other aria types in the *bongji* family are examined below. The first three belong to the *jungbaan* category. The fourth one is in *maanbaan*. The fifth one has a *saanbaan*, or non-metrical, rhythmic pattern.

1 *Faansin Jungbaan* (widely-used abbreviation for *Faansin Sapji Bongji Jungbaan*) Several examples of this aria type are transcribed in chapter 10 (in reference to discussion of *sin*) – ten lower lines and seven upper lines in figure 10.5. As the name indicates, this type belongs to the category of *faansin*, the text has ten syllables (*sapji*) per line, it is part of the *bongji* family, and it has "medium *baan*" (*jungbaan*). Its verse structure is shown in figure

Aria types

7.7. Note that this verse structure is shared by other kinds of *jungbaan* and *maanbaan* which have ten syllables per line. Its metrical pattern and syllable placement are shown in figure 7.8.

	P1	P2	P3	P4
L1	_ _+,	_ _x,	_+,	_xR;
L2	_ _+,	_ _x,	_ x,	_+R.

Figure 7.7 Verse structure of *Faansin Jungbaan*

L1 and L2 |2/4 ♪ ♩ | ♪ ♩ | ♩ ♪ | ♪ ♩ | ♫ ♪ | ♩ ♩ | ♪ ♩ | ♩ ♪ |

Figure 7.8 Syllable placement of *Faansin Jungbaan*

It should be noted that examples shown in figure 10.5 do not exactly follow the verse structure and syllable placement presented here because they consist of a large number of padding syllables (additional text that are either written into the script or improvised by the singer on stage).

Line-ending pitches for an aria type, with few exceptions, follow these rules: they depend upon the tune family, the *sin*, and the voice type, but do not depend upon verse structure and *baan*. Figure 7.9 summarizes all the line-ending pitches (upper line, lower line) for the aria types in the *bongji* family. (One exception to these rules is the aria type *Gaamji Fuyung*, to be discussed later in this chapter.)

	jingsin	faansin	yifaansin
Male voice	D, C	D, G'	C, G'
Female voice	C, G'	D, G'	C, G'
"Big" voice	G", C	*	F or C, G'

* "Big" voice is seldom used in faansin.

Figure 7.9 Line-ending pitches for the *bongji* family of tunes

Faansin Jungbaan belongs to the *bongji* family, and its *sin* is *faansin*. All the examples shown in figure 10.5 have line ending notes of D (for upper line) and G' (for lower line), verifying the table given above.

In so far as the instrumental accompaniment is concerned, the ensemble plays the same tune as the vocal line. The aria type has several versions of an instrumental prelude, one of which is given in figure 7.10.

Figure 7.10 Instrumental prelude of *Faansin Jungbaan*

76   Cantonese opera

2 *Faaidim* (literally "fast beats," a variant form of *Jingsin Chatji Bongji Jungbaan*) Its full name indicates that its *sin* is *jingsin*, it has a verse structure of seven syllables (*chatji*) per line, it belongs to the *bongji* family, and has "medium *baan*" (*jungbaan*).[9] Figure 7.11 shows an example of *Faaidim* transcribed from *The Magic Pearl* (act 1, lines 117–119; see chapter 5).

Figure 7.11   Three lines of *Faaidim*

Faaidim has an identical verse structure to *Chatjiching*. Despite the designation of "medium tempo," *Faaidim* has a metrical pattern of a series of strong beats (*baan*). A distinctive feature is that each musical line occupies seven strong beats, or measures in staff notation; no other aria type has this odd-numbered metrical structure. A passage usually lasts for two couplets, beginning with L2, the last line of which stretches out to four extra measures. Figure 7.12 shows the syllable placement for such a two-couplet unit. Note that the

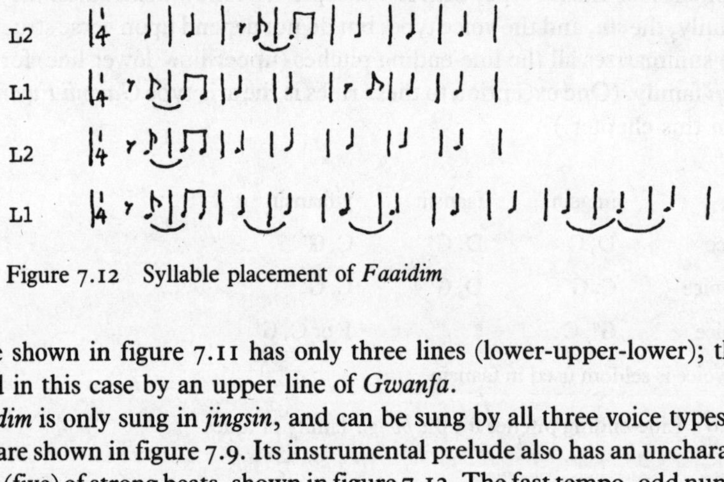

Figure 7.12   Syllable placement of *Faaidim*

example shown in figure 7.11 has only three lines (lower-upper-lower); the fourth line is replaced in this case by an upper line of *Gwanfa*.

Faaidim is only sung in *jingsin*, and can be sung by all three voice types. Its line-ending pitches are shown in figure 7.9. Its instrumental prelude also has an uncharacteristically odd number (five) of strong beats, shown in figure 7.13. The fast tempo, odd number of measures

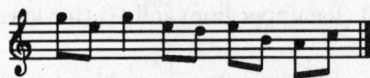

Figure 7.13   Instrumental prelude of *Faaidim*

in a musical line, and the many syncopations in the syllable placement render the *Faaidim* particularly appropriate for use during dramatic moments of extreme agitation.

Aria types

3 *Gaamji Fuyung* (literally "short hibiscus," a variant form of *Jingsin Sapji Bongji Jungbaan*)

Its full name indicates that its *sin* is *jingsin*, it belongs to the *bongji* family, and it has "medium baan" (*jungbaan*). The number of syllables in each line is ten (*sapji*) with an unusual internal structure of 5 + 5. The origin of the name "hibiscus" is obscure; but the aria type is one of a group of about five aria types all of which carry the word "hibiscus," among which "short hibiscus" is most widely used. Figure 7.14 gives four couplets of *Gaamji Fuyung* including

Figure 7.14   Four couplets of *Gaamji Fuyung*

instrumental accompaniment. Its verse structure and syllable placement are given in figures 7.15 and 7.16 respectively. Note that the example in figure 7.14 has many padding syllables.

```
           P1              P2
L1      _ _ _ _ +,       _ _ _ _ xR;
L2      _ _ _ _ x,       _ _ _ _ +R.
```
Figure 7.15   Verse structure of *Gaamji Fuyung*

Figure 7.16   Syllable placement of *Gaamji Fuyung*

The example in figure 7.14 shows that its line-ending pitches are D for the upper lines and G' for the lower lines. This is an example of how line-ending pitches do not follow the general rules given in figure 7.9: even though the example in figure 7.14 is sung in *jingsin*, its line-ending pitches follow that of *faansin*. The line-ending pitches for the female voice and "big" voice are the same as that for the male voice. This aria type is seldom sung in any other *sin* but *jingsin*.

78   Cantonese opera

Gaamji Fuyung has a rather peculiar melodic characteristic: in each couplet, the tessitura of the last phrase is lower than that of the first three phrases. (This point will be discussed further in chapter 8.) It also has a distinctive instrumental accompaniment. As illustrated in figure 7.14, the melodic ensemble is largely quiet during the singing; only the large woodblock and the small woodblock play a relatively fixed pattern marking the beats (not shown in the transcription). When the voice rests, the melodic ensemble plays two fixed interludes, one after each of the two phrases. Each of the two interludes has its own melodic figure which does not change from one version to another. The interludes also overlap slightly with the preceding vocal line. This aria type is known to project the text particularly clearly because the voice is largely uncluttered by accompaniment.

4 *Bongji Maanbaan* (widely-used abbreviation for *Jingsin Sapji Bongji Maanbaan*) Its full name indicates that it is in *jingsin*, it has ten syllables (*sapji*) in each line, it belongs to the *bongji* family, and it has "slow *baan*" (*maanbaan*). Several examples of this aria type are transcribed and discussed in chapter 9. *Bongji Maanbaan* has an identical verse structure as that of *Faansin Sapji Bongji Jungbaan* (the first aria type in this list, see figure 7.7). Its metrical pattern and syllable placement are shown in figure 7.17.

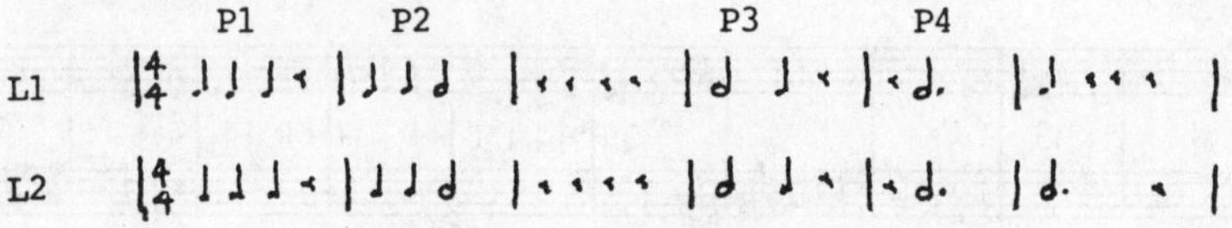

Figure 7.17   Syllable placement of *Bongji Maanbaan*

Figure 7.18   Instrumental prelude of *Bongji Maanbaan*

5 *Gwanfa*

This is the most frequently used aria type today. Its traditional verse structure, with seven syllables per line, is identical to that of *Chatjiching* (figure 7.3). However, a large number of padding syllables are routinely used today so that, more often than not, a line has fourteen syllables with seven syllables in each phrase. In other words, the caesura pattern for each line is 7+7 instead of 4+3. Figure 7.19 shows three versions of *Gwanfa* transcribed from act 1 of *The Magic Pearl*: version A (lines 132–135) is sung by the male voice, version B (lines 152–155) is sung by the female voice, and version C (lines 47–48) is sung by the "big" voice. Instrumental accompaniment is included in the transcription.

The most distinctive feature of *Gwanfa* is its rhythm, which does not have a regular pulse. It therefore does not have any representable syllable placement. The transcription in figure 7.19 attempts to suggest its rhythmic feature by assigning durational values to each note, but Western staff notation is clearly inadequate in this case.

Aria types

Figure 7.19 Three couplets of *Gwanfa*

The *Gwanfa* is the widely-used abbreviation for *Bongji Gwanfa*; a similar aria type also exists in the *yiwong* family. *Gwanfa* can be sung in *jingsin* and in *yifaansin*; the line-ending pitches in each *sin* are shown in figure 7.9. A particular feature of *Gwanfa* is the interplay between the voice and the accompaniment. The instrumental ensemble is in general silent during the singing but fills the pause between two lines of singing with an interlude. Occasionally the instrumental line enters before the vocal line ends, producing an overlapping structure.[10]

The instrumental interludes consist of formulaic melodic figures; for *jingsin*, the three most commonly used figures are as shown in figure 7.20. Notice that the three interludes end

Figure 7.20 Instrumental interludes of *Gwanfa* (*bongji, jingsin*)

on the pitches C, D, and G respectively. An interlude is chosen so that its line-ending pitch is the same as that of the preceding vocal line. In other words, if a vocal line ends on the pitch C, the interlude with a C-ending will be used at the subsequent pause of the voice.

There are only two interludes for the *yifaansin*: one ending on C and one ending on G. They are shown in figure 7.21.

Figure 7.21 Instrumental interludes of *Gwanfa* (*bongji, yifaansin*)

The two families of tunes: *bongji* and *yiwong*

There are approximately fifteen major aria types in the *bongji* family. The exact number depends upon whether one considers some tunes as different aria types or as merely versions of the same aria type. The criterion I use to arrive at the number fifteen is nomenclature: an

80 Cantonese opera

aria type is considered to have its own identity if it is specified by a distinctive title in the opera script. Thus different voice types do not result in different aria types even though the tessitura and the line-ending pitches are different. Besides the fifteen, there are another six or seven minor aria types which are used less frequently.[11]

The other major family, *yiwong*, has approximately the same number of aria types as *bongji*; the features that distinguish aria types in the family (*sin*, *baan*, number of syllables in a line, and so forth) are also similar to that of *bongji*. As in *bongji*, for example, there are also three *sin*s: *jingsin*, *faansin*, and *yifaansin*; but there are four major *baan*: *maanbaan* [slow *baan*], *jungbaan* [medium *baan*], *lauseuibaan* [literally "flowing water *baan*," or fast *baan*], and *saanbaan* [non-metrical *baan*]. The verse structure of the text also involves mainly seven-syllable lines and ten-syllable lines. However, one particularly complex aria type called *Cheunggeui Yiwong* [Long *Yiwong*] has a verse structure that involves nine phrases and twenty-eight syllables in a line, with a corresponding melodic line extending to ten measures. The *lauseuibaan* is syllabic in its text–melody relation and has a brisk tempo; it is comparable to the fast version of *jungbaan* [medium *baan*] in the *bongji* family.

The two families of tunes, *bongji* and *yiwong*, have different historical origins and without doubt at one time exhibited different melodic and modal characteristics. After being adopted into Cantonese opera, they gradually evolved and went through a regionalization process which might be called "Cantonization": a transformation of melodic and modal features that catered to the aesthetic tastes of the Cantonese audience. The linguistic tones of the Cantonese dialect undoubtedly played a significant role in shaping melodic characteristics (see chapter 8). The tunes probably lost much of their original melodic and modal distinctions, although the differences in line-ending pitches are retained. For example, the *Jingsin Sapji Bongji Maanbaan* (male voice) has line-ending pitches of D and C for the upper and lower lines respectively, while *Jingsin Sapji Yiwong Maanbaan* (male voice) has line-ending pitches of C and D.

Despite the blurring of distinctions between the two families of aria types, certain differences are still retained, as can be seen by a comparison of three pairs of instrumental interludes for the aria type *Gwanfa*, shown in figure 7.22. The comparison supports the

Figure 7.22 Comparison of *Gwanfa* instrumental interludes (in *bongji* and *yiwong*)

following observations, all of which are equally applicable to other such pairs of *bongji* and *yiwong* aria types, especially in their instrumental preludes and interludes:

1. The *yiwong* interludes generally have a lower tessitura;
2. A slightly greater emphasis is placed on the pitches D and B+ in *yiwong*.

A more subtle difference is that *yiwong* aria types are in general a little more melismatic than *bongji* aria types. Consequently, *yiwong* tunes appear to move more languidly than *bongji*

Aria types

tunes. Furthermore, the *sin* called *yifaansin* is more often used in *yiwong* than in *bongji*. All these differences underscore the distinction in dramatic function between the two families of aria types: *yiwong* is associated more closely with the lyrical and the melancholic and *bongji* with the dramatic and the sanguine. It must be remembered, however, that the aria types within each family exhibit a great range of dramatic functions, determined to a large extent by *sin* and *baan*.

8 Linguistic tones

Cantonese opera uses a limited number of tunes for its aria types; these are used repeatedly in the same play as well as in different plays. Chapter 7 shows that when sung to different texts, the "same" aria type can sound quite different in its many versions. Nine versions of *Chatjiching* are used as examples for the study of the identity of an aria type; while they differ from each other in melodic contour, the focus of the analysis is on their similarities. The question asked is: what structural elements do not change from version to version? These invariant elements are assumed to contribute to the identity of the *Chatjiching*.

In this chapter, the same nine versions will be used but the focus of the analysis will be on the *differences* in their melodic contour. Since there is no composer and no musical notation to guide the singers, how and why do they sing as they do? How and why do they produce such a variety of versions? The answers to these questions are undoubtedly complex, and may well involve factors that go beyond the scope of musicological study. Nevertheless, since the different versions are sung to different texts, part of the answer to the above questions may lie in the relationship between the text and the music.

The general relationship between word and music in songs has long been of concern to composers and a subject of study for musicologists. In a tonal language such as Chinese, the specific relationship between the tones of the syllables of the text and the tones of the melody has interested several scholars.[1] A tonal language is one in which pitch is used not only as intonation for speech, but also as a syllable-differentiating agent, serving the same distinctive function as vowels or consonants: the relative pitch levels, the contour of pitch movement, and the duration of pitch, may all be phonemically significant. The term "linguistic tone" refers to these pitch properties of a spoken syllable.

In Chinese vocal music, the specific relationship between linguistic tones and musical tones in a song can differ from dialect to dialect, and also among musical genres within a single dialectal region. In Cantonese opera, linguistic tones play a major and critical role in the creative process of the melodic contour of the aria types. In order to understand this role, one must first examine the structural relationship between the linguistic tones of the text and the corresponding melodic contour. Three features of the linguistic tones will be examined: tonal inflection, duration, and pitch level. Each of these features will be compared to the melodic behaviour of the musical line. A model of the creative process will then be constructed.

Transcriptions for the nine versions of *Chatjiching* are given in chapter 7, figure 7.2, which show the vocal line and linguistic tone symbols for each syllable of the text. The 136 syllables in the 9 versions are distributed among the 9 tonal categories as shown in figure 8.1 (see appendix 1 for a discussion on the linguistic tones of the Cantonese dialect). The 136 syllables are supplemented by 13 nonsense syllables (represented by the symbol "l" in the transcriptions), meaningless vocalizations that the singer adds extemporaneously during the performance to carry the pitches of the melody (see chapter 9).

Linguistic tones

Upper Even	Lower Even	Upper Rising	Lower Rising	Upper Going	Lower Going	Upper Entering	Middle Entering	Lower Entering
31	40	7	12	11	18	8	2	7

Figure 8.1 Distribution of 136 syllables among 9 tonal categories

Tonal inflection

With respect to tonal inflections, some linguistic tones have level contours, some rising contours, and some falling contours; nonsense syllables do not have specific linguistic tones. *Chatjiching* is a relatively syllabic aria type: a simple count indicates that 101 of the 136 sung syllables, about 74 per cent, involve a single pitch for each syllable (nonsense syllables are not counted). The rest are sung to two-pitch or three-pitch figures. A syllable sung to a single pitch normally exhibits a level melodic contour; however, some of these syllables are preceded by an ornamental upward glide (version C, measure 6 in figure 7.2; version will henceforth be abbreviated to v., measure to m.) or followed by an ornamental downward glide (v. C, m. 1). The two- and three-pitch figures can have either a rising contour (v. A, m. 6), a falling contour (v. A, m. 4), or, occasionally, a combination of rising and falling (v. B, m. 6). The question is whether the melodic contour of the tune is in any way related to the pitch contour of the linguistic tones of the text.

An examination of figure 7.2 shows that, in general, the pitch contours of the linguistic tones of the text and the corresponding melodic contour appear to match. Most syllables with level linguistic contours are sung to a single pitch, that is, a level melodic contour. Syllables with rising and falling linguistic contours are sung either to a single pitch preceded by an ornamental glide or to two- and three-pitch figures which reflect the contour of the linguistic tone.

There are exceptions to this general rule of matching. Occasionally two- and three-pitch figures are sung to a syllable with a flat linguistic contour. These apparent mismatches occur only three times in the nine versions: once in the middle of a line (v. C, m. 2), and twice at the end of a line (v. A, m. 6; v. G, m. 6). In the former case, the notes A and G, because of their long–short rhythmic relationship, do not function as a figure; rather, the note G serves as a passing note between the notes A and E. The reason for the mismatch at the line-end in versions A and G is quite different. The two- and three-pitch figures that consistently occur at the end of lines can be considered a special musical characteristic of this aria type, independent of the linguistic tones of the text. In chapter 7 it was noted that one of the features that identifies *Chatjiching* is the invariance of line-ending pitches: the upper line must end on D and the lower line on C. This particular rule appears to be invariant; the melodic contour therefore must adjust to it.

In version A, measure 6, for example, the syllable belongs to Lower Going Tone, which has a level contour, but it is sung to a figure of three pitches. Each of the three pitches can be explained. The third pitch is determined by the rule governing line-ending pitch in *Chatjiching*; the first pitch is relatively low because the Lower Going Tone has a relatively low pitch in the speech spectrum; and the second pitch serves as a passing note. In this particular case, therefore, the pitch contour of the melody is unrelated to the pitch contour of the linguistic tone. Other mismatches involving two- and three-pitch figures at the end of a line can be similarly explained.

Syllables with rising tonal contour are matched either by a figure with a rising contour of two or more pitches (v. D, m. 6; v. H, m. 6), or by a single pitch with an ornamental upward glide preceding the note (v. C, m. 6 and 10). A few instances where only one pitch is sung to the syllable without an ornamental upward glide preceding the note can be explained by the fact that the duration of the note is relatively short (an eighth note); presumably the singer does not have enough time to produce the appropriate tonal fluctuation in the melody (v. A, m. 1; v. B, m. 1). Apparent mismatches occurring at the end of a line (v. B, m. 6; v. F, m. 6) where a three-pitch figure first rises and then falls can again be explained by the *Chatjiching*'s rule on line-ending pitches.

Syllables with a falling tonal contour are generally sung by a two- or three-pitch figure with a falling tonal contour (v. A, m. 4 and 7). However, there are also cases in which the corresponding music is only one single pitch, that is, a level contour. There are several possible explanations for this apparent mismatch. First, the single pitch may be followed by a downward ornamental glide (v. C, m. 1), an imitation of the falling contour. Second, the very next sung syllable may be of a lower pitch than the one in question, thus producing the illusion of a falling contour (v. A, m. 3). Third, the relatively short duration of the pitch may not allow the singer enough time to produce the appropriate tonal inflection in the melody (v. B, m. 4). Fourth, the level contours may be considered as confirmation of the theory that the contours of both the Upper Even Tone and the Lower Even Tone can be either flat or falling (see appendix 1).

Finally one should consider the anomalies that occur in version A, measure 11 and version H, measure 8 in which a syllable with a falling contour is apparently sung to a rising melodic contour. The explanation is that both the note G in the first case and the note A in the second case serve as passing notes for the upward sweep of the melodic line.

This brief analysis shows that the linguistic tonal inflections of the text are generally retained in the singer's musical delivery; in other words, the singer follows what shall be called the rule of contour matching between linguistic tonal inflection and melodic contour. The singer, however, may depart from this rule because he must first follow the more important rule on line-ending pitches for the retention of the identity of the aria type. The rule of contour matching is also bypassed when the duration of the note is too short, and when the melody has to move in the opposite direction because of the pitch level of the following note. The singer also uses ornamental glides to reproduce linguistic tonal inflections.

Duration

With respect to duration, it may be recalled that there are two kinds of linguistic tones: those of relatively long duration without abrupt endings, and those of relatively short duration with abrupt endings of -p, -t, -k. The musical examples show that syllables with such short, abrupt endings are almost always sung to a staccato note (v. A, m. 5), or to a note immediately followed by a break in the voice (v. A, m. 10). Thus the melody consistently reflects the temporal element of the linguistic tone. The singer follows what may be called the rule of duration matching.

Pitch level

With respect to pitch level, a comparison of the linguistic tones of the text and the corresponding melodic contour shows that they match closely. An examination of the first five syllables of version A serves as an example. The sequence of linguistic tones exhibits the following pitch fluctuations: medium high–medium low–medium low–high–low. The corresponding melodic line has the following sequence of pitches: C–B–A–E–G. The rest of this version and the other versions confirm that this matching is quite consistent in all the performances, and can be generalized into what may be called the rule of pitch matching.

A question arises as to whether there is a one-to-one correspondence between individual linguistic tones and individual pitches (scale degrees) throughout an aria type, to be called "consistent pitch matching," or a matching that involves different sets of pitches (scale degrees) at different parts of the song, to be called "localized pitch matching." The question can be answered by a more systematic counting of the number of occurrences of a particular pitch in correspondence to a particular linguistic tonal category. If all the syllables of a particular linguistic tonal category are consistently sung to a single pitch, then one concludes that the matching is "consistent."

The counting is simplified for the most part by the fact that the singing is syllabic; in other words, only one pitch is sung per syllable in most instances. In cases where two or three pitches are sung to a syllable (v. A, m. 4 and 6), one has to devise a special way of counting. The assumption, in such cases, is that one of the pitches is the principal pitch and the other (or others) ornamental. The distinction between principal pitches and ornamental pitches is based upon the following assumptions and arguments.

First, in the case of Upper Even Tones, examples involving more than one pitch to a syllable consist mostly of two-pitch figures with falling contour (v. A, m. 4 and 7; v. B, m. 3 and 5). According to Kao in her study of contour behaviour in Cantonese speech,[2] when the Upper Even Tone assumes a falling contour, "this tone starts with initial stress at the high register, from which it falls to middle register accompanied by a gradual decay of the voice during the fall." Since in the spoken language the voice decays as it falls, it seems reasonable to assume that, in singing, the second and lower of the two pitches in such cases is an ornamental pitch. Therefore, the first pitch, the higher one, will always be considered as the principal pitch.

Second, in the case of Lower Even Tones, examples involving more than one pitch to a syllable similarly consist chiefly of two-pitch figures with a falling contour (v. F, m. 11; v. G, m. 11; v. H, m. 3). Kao states: "The voice starts from below the middle register and falls to low, then becomes drawn out at the bottom pitch."[3] The fact that the voice "becomes drawn out at the bottom pitch," leads one to conclude that, in singing, the second and lower pitch of a two-pitch figure is in such cases the principal pitch and the first and higher pitch is the ornamental pitch.

Third, in the case of Rising Tones in which the corresponding melodic figures are two- or three-pitch figures with a rising contour (v. B, m. 6; v. D, m. 6), Kao's description of the spoken language does not offer any clue as to which pitch should be considered as the principal one. For the purpose of the present study, the singer's performance is used as criteria for the determination of the principal pitch. In the case of syllables with Rising Tone that are sung to a single pitch (v. A, m. 1; v. B, m. 1; v. C, m. 6 and 10) the pitch is often preceded – but never followed – by an ornamental upward glide. In other words, the glide comes before the metrical beat rather than after the metrical beat. Furthermore, the end of a glide has a more stable and distinctive pitch than the beginning. These observations suggest that, for a syllable with a rising contour, the end of the contour is more stable than the beginning. Thus, in the case of two- or three-pitch figures with a rising contour, the last and highest pitch can reasonably be identified as the principal pitch.

Rule of pitch matching

The result of the counting is shown in the set of nine graphs in figure 8.2. Each graph corresponds to one tonal category. Graph A shows the result of the counting for the thirty-one syllables belonging to the Upper Even Tone: seven are sung to the pitch G, twenty-one to the pitch E, and three to the pitch D. Thus, the preferred musical pitch for syllables in the Upper Even Tone is E. The other eight graphs are read in similar fashion.

The graphs show that certain pitches and certain linguistic tonal categories have definite affinities, although the degree of affinity varies from one tonal category to another. The matching is particularly striking for the Upper and Lower Going Tones (graphs D and G) and for the Middle and Lower Entering Tones (graphs E and H),[4] slightly less so for the two Even Tones (graphs A and I) and the Lower Rising Tone (graph F). Such affinities strongly suggest a consistent matching between the linguistic tones and musical pitches.

Additional evidence for consistent matching can be found in the numbers assigned by linguists to the linguistic tones to indicate pitch levels. For example, the Upper Going Tone is "33," the Middle Entering Tone is "3," and the Lower Rising Tone is "23" (for which the principal level has been shown to be "3"). They share the same linguistic tonal level of "3." Graphs D, E, and F show that syllables belonging to these categories also share the same musical pitch of C.

This observation indicates first, that the linguists regard the pitch levels of the tonal categories as consistently related; and second, that the relationships between linguistic tones proposed by linguists are to a great extent preserved in the singing of aria types. Indeed, based upon the numbers assigned to the linguistic tonal categories, the nine tonal categories can be classified into four groups. The first group corresponds to the pitch level of "5" and includes the Upper Even Tone "53," the Upper Entering Tone "5," and the Upper Rising Tone "35." The second group corresponds to the pitch level "3" and includes the Upper Going Tone "33," the Middle Entering Tone "3," and the Lower Rising Tone "23." The third group corresponds to the pitch level "2" and includes the Lower Going Tone "22" and the Lower Entering Tone "2." The last group corresponds to the pitch level "1" and includes the Lower Even Tone.

While in actual speech, speakers of Cantonese use a variety of pitch levels for a given linguistic tone depending upon sex, age, the meaning of the words, and the speaker's emotional state, strong pitch relationships still exist among the linguistic tones. It is not surprising that singers easily translate these indeterminate pitch levels into fixed musical pitches so that the corresponding musical pitches retain the same relationships exhibited by the original linguistic tones.

Nevertheless there are many anomalous situations, instances in which different pitches are

Linguistic tones

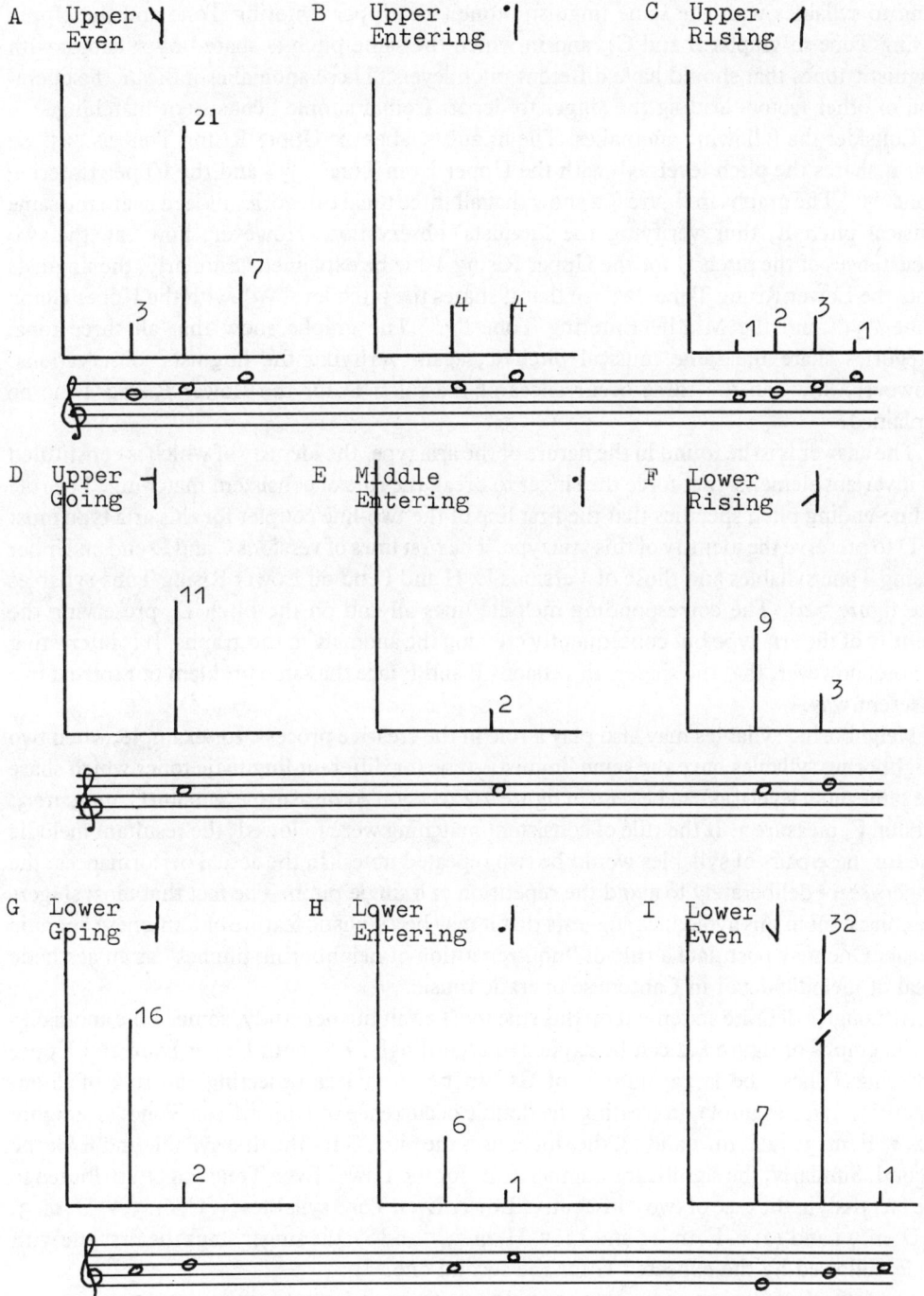

Figure 8.2 Frequency of occurrence for pitches

sung to syllables with the same linguistic tone (the Upper Entering Tone and the Upper Rising Tone in graphs B and C), and in which the same pitch is shared by syllables with linguistic tones that should have different pitch levels. These anomalies indicate the operation of other factors leading the singer to depart from a simple "consistent matching."

Consider the following anomalies. The linguists label the Upper Rising Tone as "35" so that it shares the pitch level "5" with the Upper Even Tone "53" and the Upper Entering Tone "5." The graphs in figure 8.2 show that all three tonal categories indeed share the same musical pitch E, thus verifying the linguists' observation. However, how can the two occurrences of the pitch D for the Upper Rising Tone be explained? Similarly, the linguists label the Lower Rising Tone "23" so that it shares the pitch level "3" with the Upper Going Tone "33" and the Middle Entering Tone "3." The graphs show that all three tonal categories share the same musical pitch C, again verifying the linguists' observations. However, how can the three occurrences of the pitch D for the Lower Rising Tone be explained?

The answer is to be found in the nature of the aria type, the identity of which is constituted by invariant elements that force the singer to break the rule of consistent matching. The rule of line-ending pitch specifies that the first line of the two-line couplet for this aria type must be D to preserve the identity of this aria type. The first lines of versions C and D end on Upper Rising Tone syllables and those of Versions E, H and I end on Lower Rising Tone syllables (see figure 7.2). The corresponding melodic lines all end on the pitch D, preserving the identity of the aria type but consequently creating the anomaly in the graphs. It is interesting to note, however, that the singers in versions B and F face the same problem but solve it in a different way.

Neighboring syllables may also play a role in the creative process, for example, when two neighboring syllables have the same linguistic tone (or different linguistic tones which share the same pitch level), as can be seen in figure 7.2: version A, measure 2; version C, measure 3; version F, measure 3. If the rule of consistent matching were followed, the resultant melodic line for these pairs of syllables would be two repeated notes. In the actual performances, the singers seem deliberately to avoid the repetition of a single pitch. The fact that most singers are consistent in this avoidance suggests that it may be a stylistic feature of Cantonese operatic music. One may postulate a rule of "non-repetition of neighboring pitches" as an aesthetic ideal of melodic detail in Cantonese operatic music.[5]

Although a definite statement on this rule must await further study, some of the anomalies in the graphs of figure 8.2 can be explained accordingly. For both Upper Even and Upper Entering Tones, the large number of Gs can be viewed as reflecting the rule of "non-repetition"; for example, in treating the double occurrence of Upper Even Tones (see figure 7.2, v. F, m. 3; v. G, m. 1 and 2), the singer uses the pitch G for the first syllable and E for the second. Similarly, the significant number of Es for the Lower Even Tone can be attributed to the fact that, in the case of two consecutive Lower Even Tone syllables (v. C, m. 3; v. D, m. 3; v. D, m. 11 and 12; v. F, m. 11 and 12; v. H, m. 3, 7 and 8), the singer sings the first one with an E, followed by the expected G for the second one.

Once the factors that cause the anomalies in the matching are taken into account, the relationships between the four groups of linguistic tones and four sets of pitches in *Chatjiching* can be represented by a table of pitch matching shown in figure 8.3.

Such relationships can be deduced for other aria types as well. For example, most aria

Linguistic tones

Figure 8.3 Table of pitch matching

types belong to *jingsin* and sung by *sanghau* (male voice) and *daanhau* (female voice) exhibit relationships shown in figure 8.2. However, the same aria types sung by *daaihau* ("big" voice) has a different table of matching, reflecting its tessitura and melodic characteristics (figure 8.4).

Figure 8.4 Table of pitch matching for "big" voice

The aria type called *Gaamji Fuyong* ("short hibiscus," see chapter 7) exhibits the peculiar melodic feature whereby the first three of its four phrases follow the table of matching shown in figure 8.3, while its last phrase has a different table of matching (figure 8.5). The difference reflects the melodic structure of *Gaamji Fuyung*, in which the last phrase drops in tessitura by an interval of about a fourth. Tables (or rules) of pitch matching are, therefore, another way of identifying and classifying aria types.

Figure 8.5 Table of pitch matching for *Gaamji Fuyung* (last phrase)

A model of creative process

A singer of Cantonese opera is often called upon to sing a different opera each day for five consecutive days, and occasionally two different operas in a single day. He may have performed some of the operas before, but others may be new to him. Usually he is given a script only a few days before the performance, for which "rehearsals" in the Western sense do not exist.[6] Thus the singer must memorize at very short notice the texts of full-length operas, perhaps two in one day. He also has to sing a great quantity of music on stage without the aid of musical notation or of rehearsal. In other words, he has to "compose" spontaneously as he performs.

The above observation and analysis suggest that, as the singer spontaneously "composes" a melody, firstly he follows a rule of consistent pitch matching between linguistic tones and melodic contour and secondly he also follows other rules, including ones that define the identity of an aria type and others that define the style of Cantonese music, which may undercut the rule of pitch matching. Based upon these rules, a three-level model is proposed.

On the first level, names of aria types provided in the script specify invariant elements of the music which the singer will have learned through training and performance experience. These elements form the skeletal structure of the music of the aria type. On this lowest level, an aria type, to the singer, is but a set of rules to follow, and to the listener, a set of abstract patterns. The dramatic function of the aria type is effectively served when its identity is preserved.

On the second level, the singer uses, within the constraints of the skeletal structure and following the rule of pitch matching, the relatively less-defined pitches of the text's linguistic tones as a guide in creating a series of well-defined musical pitches to form the melodic line. In other words, this second level of the creative process allows the skeleton to be fleshed-out in actual music sound. The singer barely has time before a performance to learn the text, and during the performance he certainly does not have time to consider and consciously choose the pitches for each syllable. The experience he has gained through many years of listening and singing guides him to substitute certain pitches for certain linguistic tones. This ability to transform linguistic tones into musical pitches becomes second nature to him, just as speaking the dialect with the proper tones becomes second nature to every Cantonese speaker. From the listener's point of view, the retention of the essential characteristics of the linguistic tones projects the identity of the text accurately and unambiguously; the dramatic content of the performance is therefore properly communicated.

The role of linguistic tones in the creative process proves to be nothing more than a rough guide. While the second level alone could theoretically produce a version of the aria type, it is not rigidly determinative of the melodic contour. The melodic and rhythmic possibilities offer many alternative realizations in which the linguistic tones could be preserved in a performance. In addition, various rules that define the identity of an aria type and the Cantonese musical style may result in conflicts with the rule of pitch matching which the singer must resolve. Other factors that may affect the melodic realization include the meaning of a word or a phrase, the dramatic situation of the story, the idiosyncracies of an individual singer, and other stylistic features of the music of Cantonese opera. These factors must await a future study. The operations of all these rules constitute the third level of the creative process, the level that yields different "physical appearances" to the versions of the aria type.

From the singer's point of view, it is on the third level that he is permitted to exercise his individual creative power. From the listener's point of view, the third level is what differentiates a great performance from one that is merely adequate. Different speakers of the same language use the same basic vocabulary and the same syntactic structures; yet in expressing the same ideas one person can be a dull and matter-of-fact speaker while another is a moving orator. So it is with an opera performer: he can be an automatic converter of speech to passable Cantonese opera melodies, or he can be a truly great singer.

The role of linguistic tone

The present investigation focuses on the *Chatjiching*, which is among the more syllabic of the aria types. (However, it may sometimes be sung melismatically; see p. 153.) In more melismatic ones, the creative process may involve different and additional factors. The role of linguistic tones in the text remain powerful however, and the three-level model is probably still valid, although the contribution that each level makes to the total creative process may well be different.

While the importance of linguistic tones in the generation of the music has been amply illustrated, the question of why it is so important deserves some attention. One obvious explanation is the need for textual intelligibility. In other dialectal regions of China, however, the linguistic tones in vocal music do not play as large a role as in Cantonese opera[7] – a fact which suggests that ease of linguistic communication is not necessarily the only, or even the most important, explanation for this phenomenon.

Another reason may be aesthetic. Because there are only approximately thirty aria types in the total repertory of Cantonese opera, the material may seem rather limited and restricted. The present study has shown that, because of differences in the text, the same aria type is realized in performance through many different melodic contours. The aesthetic requirement of variety is met by this use of linguistic tones in the creative process. On the other hand, the fact that the Cantonese opera draws its melodic material from such a limited source could be viewed as a consequence of the creative process rather than its cause: since the melodic contour varies automatically according to the text, there is no need for a large number of aria types. Whichever way the argument goes, one fact is clear: the musical structure and the creative process of Cantonese opera are closely related to the use of a limited body of preexistent musical material.

A third reason might simply be considerations of convenience and expediency. Since performance practice demands that singers sing a large quantity of music in a short time without rehearsal and without the aid of musical notation, the singers use the linguistic tones as a guide to aid them in their difficult task. However, the opposite argument might again be advanced: the use of the linguistic tones might be regarded as the root of the creative process, freeing the singer from the necessity of notation and rehearsal. In either case, this study has shown that musical structure, creative process, and performance practice are closely linked and that linguistic tones play a vital role in the complex relationship.

9 *Padding syllables*

The text of aria types in Cantonese opera has to observe prescribed verse structures that involve, among other features, a certain number of syllables per line (pattern of line-lengths). In an actual performance the singer very often sings a greater number of syllables per line than are prescribed. For example, several versions of the aria type *Chatjiching* shown in figure 7.2 have more than the prescribed fourteen syllables in each couplet. The extra syllables are called *chenzi*, or padding syllables, and can be either written into the script by the scriptwriter or added extemporaneously by the singer.

The addition of padding syllables in a performance does not merely alter the text; because of the close relationship between text and music, the padding syllables unavoidably affect the melodic behavior, in particular the metrical and rhythmic structure of the aria type. The adding of padding syllables is also one way in which the singer exerts his individual creativity during a performance. This chapter investigates this creative process by focusing on the following questions. How much flexibility is there in the textual and musical structure of the various aria types and in the relation of text to music? In other words, how much flexibility does the singer have during a performance? How does a singer treat padding syllables and how does the treatment reflect his creative process?

The rules governing the pattern of line-lengths for aria types are recapitulated as follows (see chapter 7):

1. The basic unit of the text is a couplet, with an upper line L1 and a lower line L2.
2. The same number of syllables should be used in each line of a couplet and for all couplets in a section. In most of the aria types of Cantonese opera and in most of the other Chinese narrative and dramatic genres, the number is either seven or ten.
3. The seven or ten syllables of a line observe certain internal groupings according to the syntactic structure, the most common of which are 2+2+3 for a seven-syllable line, and 3+3+4 (or 3+3+2+2) for a ten-syllable line. The internal groupings are labeled P1, P2, and P3, where P stands for "phrase."

An examination of either written opera scripts or transcriptions of actual performances shows that the text of aria types usually has a larger number of syllables per line than is prescribed by the verse structure. The number of padding syllables and the frequency of their occurrence depend upon individual aria types. The *Chatjiching* is relatively unmodified: of the nine versions given in figure 7.2, only four have padding syllables, and not more than two are added to each line. An example of the other extreme is the aria type called *Bongji Maanbaan*, which has a prescribed line-length of ten syllables; but by far the majority of its versions sung today exceed that limit, sometimes containing twenty syllables or more.

Padding syllables

One might question the validity of a basic verse structure that in practice is almost never observed. There are two reasons for positing the existence of such an underlying structure. First, the texts of *Bongji Maanbaan* published in the 1930s and 1940s show very few padding syllables. While this fact does not necessarily reflect what happened during actual performances (since the performers were very likely to extemporize on stage as they often do today), it shows at least that the concept of such a basic pattern existed. Second, all the scriptwriters and performers interviewed today are conscious of the existence of the ten-syllable pattern and consider the longer lines to be a modification of the basic pattern.

Padding syllables are found in many genres of Chinese opera and poetry where specific line-lengths are prescribed. One of the major interests of scholars in Chinese poetry has been to distinguish padding syllables (*chenzi* in Peking dialect) from the so-called base syllables (*zhengzi*) in lines of verse. As Dale Johnson writes in his study of Yuan *zaju*: "The isolation of base syllables is important since they embody the metric structure of the verse; the key to the anatomy of the verse is its internal structure."[1] It is generally accepted that base syllables are "vital" syllables which provide the essence of the meaning of the text. Padding syllables, on the other hand, serve to clarify or elaborate; their presence or absence does not substantially alter the meaning.

Most studies of padding syllables have concerned the Yuan *zaju*, approached from the literary point of view; they focus on the identification of padding syllables based primarily upon the meaning of the text so that a "correct" reading results.[2] Some scholars recognize that the study of padding syllables must take into account the music to which the text is sung.[3] Generally speaking, however, their studies are based on the written text alone because the actual performance tradition in question has long been lost. One of the few exceptions is Yu Huiyong's study of the Shandong Drumsongs (a genre of narrative songs from Shangdong Province) in which the discussion of padding syllables is based upon actual performance practice.[4] The present investigation takes a similar approach in considering how the text is handled musically in actual performances. The aria type *Bongji Maanbaan* will be used as the paradigm.

Verse structure and syllable placement

Chapter 7 has shown that the identity of an aria type depends upon the prescribed verse structure of the text and the syllable placement of the tune. For *Bongji Maanbaan*, the verse structure and the syllable placement have already been given in chapter 7, but are reproduced here in figures 9.1 and 9.2 for convenience.

	P1	P2	P3	P4
L1	__+,	__x,	_+,	_xR;
L2	__+,	__x,	_x,	_+R.

Figure 9.1   Verse structure of *Bongji Maanbaan*

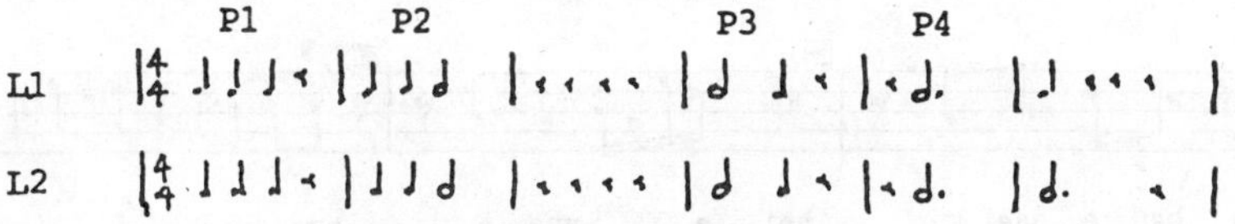

Figure 9.2   Syllable placement of *Bongji Maanbaan*

94 Cantonese opera

Not surprisingly, the phrase grouping of the text and the syllable placement of the tune correspond closely. Indeed, the syllable placement of a tune can be considered as a sequence of temporal slots into which the syllables of the text are to be fitted, one to each slot. In the case of *Bongji Maanbaan* there are ten temporal slots, into which fit ten syllables. If the text contains the exact number of syllables per line prescribed by the verse structure, then the singer's task of fitting syllables to slots is relatively easy. When there are more than ten syllables, whether written into the text by the scriptwriter or extemporaneously added by the singer on stage, it is usually the singer's task to accommodate them to the available slots. He will assign some syllables to the prescribed temporal slots, squeeze others by twos or threes into a single slot, and leave still others outside of the slot altogether. Because syllable placement constitutes one of the important structural features that determine and preserve the identity of the aria type, those syllables sung within the prescribed temporal slots are assumed to receive special emphasis from the singer and will be considered as "base" syllables. All others are considered to be padding syllables. How a singer adjusts the syllables to fit the slots reflects his evaluation of their relative importance. Thus, the singer's handling of padding syllables reveals his understanding of the text.

Different singers, or the same singer on different occasions, may perform the same text differently, in which case the distinction between padding syllables and base syllables may itself be different. The method of identifying padding syllables proposed here depends upon individual performances rather than the internal structure and meaning of the printed text. The ultimate purpose of this approach is not to determine which are the padding syllables and which are the base syllables; rather, through the analysis of padding syllables, it aims to investigate the degree of flexibility in the textual and melodic structure of the songs, the degree of freedom the singer enjoys, and the factors influencing his particular choices. Thus it is an investigation of the creative process of the singer on stage.

On the basis of structural relationships between text and syllable placement in actual performances, six kinds of padding syllables are defined. Each kind embodies a particular solution to the singer's problems in adjusting the text to the syllable placement. Various versions of *Bongji Maanbaan* are used to illustrate the analysis, which can be applied to other aria types. Musical examples transcribed from actual performances are presented as data.

Added phrase

The first kind of padding syllable is illustrated in figure 9.3, a transcription of an upper line of *Bongji Maanbaan*. The text consists of fourteen syllables, excluding the meaningless non-

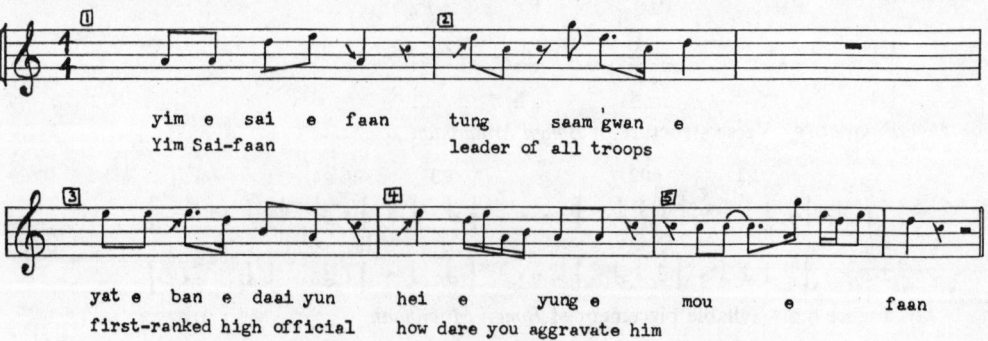

Figure 9.3 An upper line of *Bongji Maanbaan* with an added phrase

Padding syllables

sense syllables "e" repeatedly added by the singer (to be discussed in a later section in this chapter). The syllable placement abstracted from the performance is given in figure 9.4; the prescribed syllable placement is placed below it for easy comparison. The comparison shows two discrepancies: the rhythmic variation in measure 2 and the additional melodic phrase in

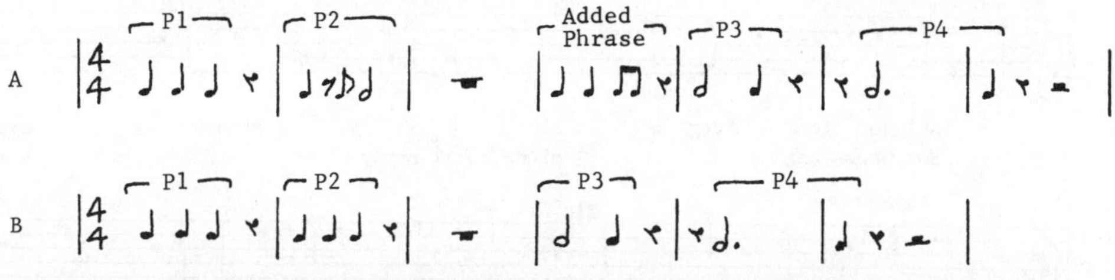

Figure 9.4 Comparison of (A) syllable placement of an actual performance transcribed in figure 9.3 with (B) prescribed syllable placement, showing an added phrase

measure 4. The rhythmic variation in measure 2 is commonly found in *Bongji Maanbaan* and is unrelated to padding syllables. The additional melodic phrase in measure 4, however, is added to the original tune to accommodate the four extra syllables. Padding syllables of this kind may be defined as syllables sung to an additional, independent melodic phrase and will be called "added phrase." The resultant melodic line shows an increase in the total number of metrical units.

The added phrase in *Bongji Maanbaan* is always in the form of a four-syllable, syntactically independent phrase. It only occurs between P2 and P3 after the measure of rests, and may appear in both L1 and L2 of the couplet. The syllable placement of this phrase is always

Added phrases that result in the lengthening of the melodic line are common in the narrative songs in northern China, such as the Peking Drumsong and Shandong Drumsong, in which syllable placement is also an important structural feature.[5] In these northern genres, the syntactic structure of the added phrase is usually an imitation of a portion of the original text (most often a unit of three to five syllables), and such phrases almost always occur in series, one immediately following another. For this reason, they are generally known as *duoju*, or "stacked phrases." The resultant melodic line is thus expanded by several rhythmically similar melodic phrases. Because the stacked phrases occur together and all share identical syntactic structure, they are easily distinguished from the rest of the text and cannot be treated by the singer as padding syllables of another sort. In *Bongji Maanbaan*, however, an additional phrase may be treated by a singer at his discretion as base syllables or as other kinds of padding syllables. That is why, in Cantonese opera, one cannot always parse the text of an aria type without actually hearing it performed.

Today the great majority of the versions of *Bongji Maanbaan* have an added phrase. As a result, the standard melody for each line of the couplet has seven measures instead of six and the line itself might be more appropriately called a fourteen-syllable than a ten-syllable line. Nevertheless, the *Bongji Maanbaan* should probably still be considered as having ten syllables per line of text and six measures per line of music because performers today still consider the longer versions to be variants of the shorter. Furthermore, a small but significant number of versions performed today retain the old pattern without the added phrase.

Phrase leader syllables

The second kind of padding syllable will be called a "phrase leader syllable," illustrated in figure 9.5 by the transcription of a lower line of *Bongji Maanbaan*. The syllable placement of the twelve syllables in this line is compared to the prescribed syllable placement in figure 9.6.

Figure 9.5 A lower line of *Bongji Maanbaan* showing phrase leader syllables

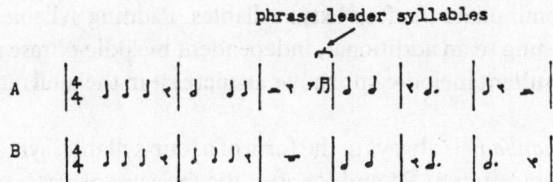

Figure 9.6 Comparison of (A) syllable placement of an actual performance transcribed in figure 9.5 with (B) prescribed syllable placement, showing phrase leader syllables

The syllables *keui keui*, sung to two sixteenth notes in the third measure, are classified as phrase leader syllables. They are set to an extra melodic fragment preceding the base melodic phrase. (Hence the extra melodic fragment may be called a phrase leader melody.) Since most base melodic phrases begin on a strong beat, the phrase leader melody in most cases naturally begins on an upbeat immediately preceding the strong beat. In effect, it is an anacrusis to the base melodic phrase.

From the textual point of view, many of the phrase leader syllables are semantically less important than the base syllables and are grammatically dispensable. In the above example, the term *keui keui* [mere] is a modifier used to emphasize the lowliness of the rank of the official post, and is less important than the syllables *ng ban*, meaning "fifth rank."

Occasionally a singer treats syllables that are semantically fairly important or grammatically not dispensable as phrase leader syllables. Figure 9.7 is a transcription of P1 and P2 of a line of *Bongji Maanbaan*. Each phrase has seven syllables (disregarding, for the moment, the

Figure 9.7 Two phrases of *Bongji Maanbaan*

Padding syllables

meaningless syllable "a" in phrase 2), four syllables more than the prescribed number; the two phrases also have parallel grammatical structures. The two syllables *piu ling* [drifting alone] in P1 and *chaam daam* [sad pale] in P2 are equally important in their respective phrases. However, the singer treats the latter as phrase leader syllables but not the former.

One reason for his choice may have been purely musical: to avoid the choppiness of two successive phrases each of which begins on the strong first beat of the measure. If the second phrase is given an anacrusis, the two lines exhibit superior rhythmic continuity. Another reason could be the singer's concern for the linguistic tones of the text. The two syllables *piu ling* in the first phrase belong to Upper Even Tone and Lower Even Tone respectively; the two syllables *chaam daam* in the second phrase belong to Upper Rising Tone and Lower Going Tone respectively. In Chinese phonology, syllables in the even tone categories are considered to project a sense of stability and resolution, while the oblique tone categories are considered to project a sense of instability and tension. Such considerations may have prompted the singer to place the two even tone syllables on a strong beat and the two oblique tone syllables on a weak beat. This example shows that phrase leader syllables may result from either musical or textual considerations or both. It also illustrates the extent of the freedom given to the singer during an actual performance.

To illustrate further the flexibility enjoyed by the singer in his handling of the text, two different performances of the same text by the same singer are compared. Figure 9.8a gives

Figure 9.8a Transcription of two versions of *Bongji Maanbaan*

the transcription of two versions of P1 and P2 of *Bongji Maanbaan*; figure 9.8b compares the text of the two versions with each other and with the printed script.[6]

The script consists of a total of fourteen syllables for the two phrases. Excluding the syllables transcribed as "a" which will be treated in later sections, the number of syllables in version A is fifteen and that in version B is eighteen. In version A, the singer treats the two syllables *ching saam* [black cloak, or humbly-dressed] of P1 as phrase leader syllables and adds extemporaneously the syllables *ngo* [I] in the beginning of the phrase; in P2, he sings the two syllables *bou yi* [cloth gown, or plainly cloaked] as phrase leader syllables. In version B, he treats no part of the original text as phrase leader syllables, but he extemporaneously adds

P1	ngo (I,)	ching humbly	saam dressed,	ji ashamed	a	kwai	bat amount	sing to nothing)	a	choi,
Version A	x	x	x	x	x	x	x	x	x	x
Version B	x	x	x	x		x	x	x	x	x
Script		x	x		x		x	x		x

P2	taan (Alas!)	yat	geui	bou plainly	yi cloaked,	mei	nang I cannot	paan pick	daan the red	gwai cassia)	a.
Version A				x	x	x	x	x	x	x	x
Version B	x	x	x	x	x	x	x	x	x	x	x
Script				x	x	x	x	x	x	x	

Figure 9.8b Comparison of the text of the two versions and the script

some phrase leader syllables of his own for each phrase: *ngo* [I] and *taan yat geui* [Alas] respectively for the two phrases.

The two renditions reflect different solutions to the conflict between textual and musical considerations. From the textual point of view, when the syllables are sung as phrase leader syllables, that is, to weak beats as anacrusis, they are given relatively less emphasis than if they were sung on a strong beat. From the musical point of view, singing the beginning syllables of a line of text as phrase leader syllables adds an anacrusis to the melodic line, which is a common form of melodic variation in aria types.

Figures 9.8a and 9.8b also illustrate the singer's freedom to add his own phrase leader syllables (and other kinds of padding syllables). In most cases, the purpose of such addition is to clarify the sometimes highly compressed and literary text by prefacing it with colloquial expressions. In figure 9.8b the addition of the syllable *ngo* [I] in the beginning of P1 is a case in point.

The phrase leader syllables are in many ways similar to what Dale Johnson calls verse leader *chenzi* in Yuan *zaju*, and to what Yu Huiyong calls *jiamao* [adding a hat] in Shangdong Drumsongs. Both writers describe these padding syllables as always preceding the base syllables and as being grammatically superfluous or of lesser importance than the base syllables. In methodology, Johnson's padding syllables are determined only from the written text, while Yu takes actual performances into account. In Cantonese opera, the phrase leader syllables defined above are recognized as such only when performed.

Multiplets

The third kind of padding syllable involves an internal modification of the syllable placement. When there is no padding syllable, each base syllable may be looked upon as occupying a single temporal slot along the melodic line. In most arias, a base melodic phrase is usually formed by two or more of these slots plus the rests. In *Bongji Maanbaan*, for example, the first phrase of L1 consists of three slots. When there are padding syllables, the singer sometimes accommodates them in the base melodic phrase by squeezing several syllables into the slot originally intended for one syllable.

In figure 9.7, four syllables, *piu ling yau chi*, are squeezed into the first slot (of a quarter note's duration) originally intended for one syllable. The next two syllables, *tyun pung*, occupy the space of the second slot, also intended for only one syllable. Thus the first and second syllables of the original three-syllable phrase seem to have multiplied into clusters of

Padding syllables

four and two syllables respectively. The duration of each slot does not change and the larger metrical structure is not disturbed; the syllables are simply sung to notes of shorter time value. When padding syllables are treated in this way by the singer, the clustered syllables that occupy one durational slot can be called "multiplets."

Thus the phrase *piu ling yau chi tyun pung syun* [drifting alone like a broken-sailed boat] from figure 9.7 may be viewed as a set of two multiplets and a single syllable: the first slot occupied by a four-syllable multiplet *piu ling yau chi* [drifting alone like a], the second slot by a two-syllable multiplet *tyun pung* [broken-sailed], and the third slot by a single syllable *syun* [boat]. Figure 9.9 compares the prescribed syllable placement with that of the actual performance, with the multiplets noted.

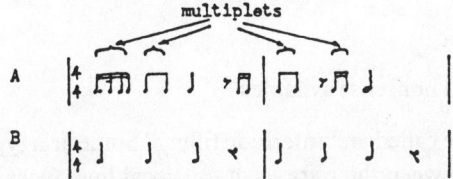

Figure 9.9 Comparison of (A) syllable placement of an actual performance transcribed in figure 9.7 with (B) prescribed syllable placement, showing multiplets

Some of the multiplets can be better understood when one realizes that in the Chinese language a two-syllable compound such as *tyun pung* is grammatically equivalent to, and therefore mutually exchangeable with, many monosyllabic words on the one hand, or three- or even four-syllable compounds on the other. Thus the phrase *tyun pung syun* [broken-sailed boat] could have been replaced, for example, by *baak syun* [white boat]. Because the multiplet *tyun pung* [broken-sailed] effectively discharges the function of a single syllable, the singer justifiably places it in one slot. For multiplets, the two or more syllables within a slot are all considered to be padding syllables; as a whole they play the role of one single base syllable.

The singer may also treat his text in such a way that syllables within a multiplet are not closely related to each other grammatically. Consider the phrase *tai leui huk cha am* [with tears he mourns in the tea hut] sung as P1 of L2 of *Bongji Maanbaan* in an actual performance of the opera *The Royal Beauty* (figure 9.10). The word *tai leui* [tears] forms a two-syllable compound,

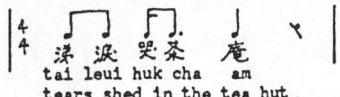

Figure 9.10 Syllable placement of one phrase from *The Royal Beauty*

and *cha am* [tea hut] forms another two-syllable compound; the single syllable *huk* [mourns] stands by itself. Thus this five-syllable phrase is grouped grammatically as 2+1+2, a pattern which one would expect to fit into the three temporal slots in P1 of L2 in *Bongji Maanbaan* as shown in figure 9.11. The syllable placement in the actual performance (figure 9.10), however, shows that the actual multiplet structure is 2+2+1. In this rendition, the second multiplet consists of two syllables which are grammatically not closely related. A rendition such as the one given in figure 9.11 would very seldom occur in a performance for the reason

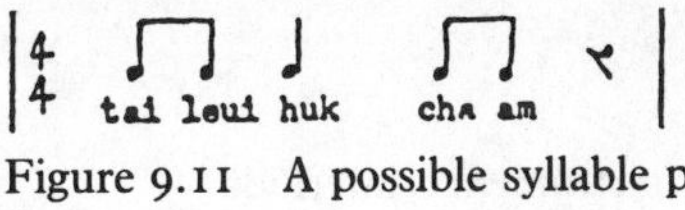

Figure 9.11 A possible syllable placement of the same phrase from figure 9.10

100 Cantonese opera

that the last syllable of P1 in either line of *Bongji Maanbaan* needs to end on a strong beat. This example demonstrates that the singer sometimes gives musical consideration a higher priority than the grammatical sense of the text. While literary criteria will identify certain groupings of multiplets, musical criteria may override them to produce a different grouping.

Three kinds of padding syllables have been discussed: syllables in the added phrase, phrase leader syllables, and multiplets. Because their presence alters the melodic structure of the aria type to varying degrees, it seems probable that the singer's treatment of these padding syllables will depend upon musical criteria as well as considerations of the grammatical structure and the meaning of the text. The next three kinds, which are less significant in so far as they generally do not alter the melodic features of the aria type, are nevertheless prominent in all performances.

Interlude fillers, tail syllables, and nonsense syllables

The fourth kind of padding syllable may be called an "interlude filler." Some aria types have relatively fixed instrumental interludes between the phrases of the vocal line. Occasionally, such an interlude is fitted with a text rather than being left as a purely instrumental line. (Using Western terminology, one may say that the instrumental interlude has been "troped" with the text.) The rest of the melody in the aria type is not affected. Interlude fillers are not generally used in *Bongji Maanbaan*, the aria type under consideration, but they are used in some other aria types, for example, the *Faansin Yiwong*. Figure 9.12 gives one line of *Faansin*

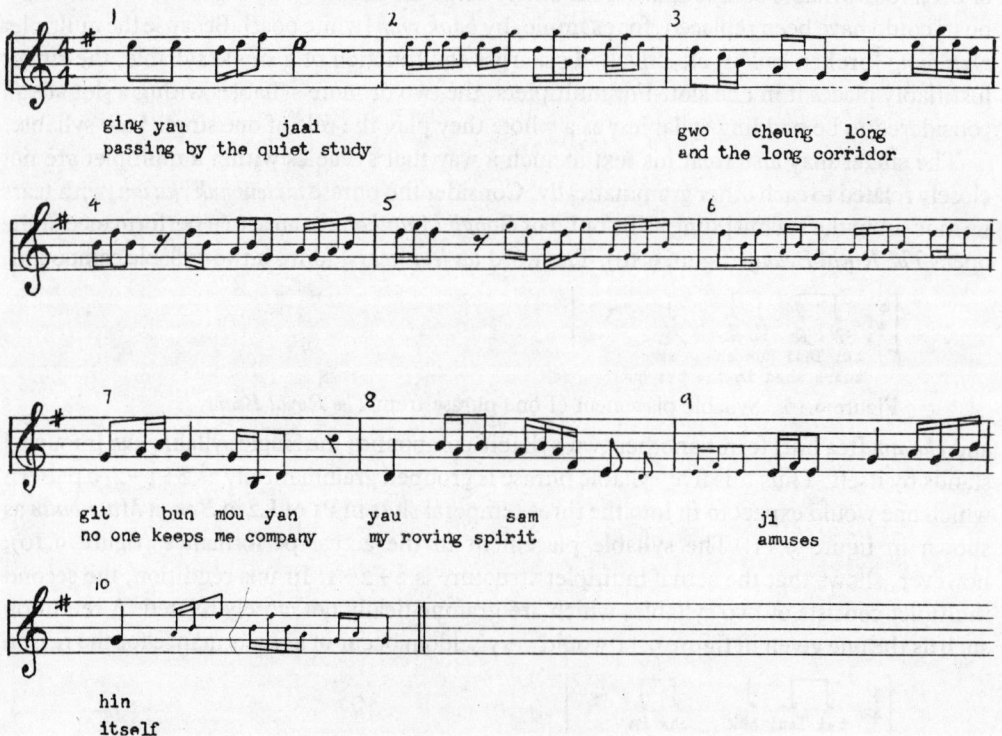

Figure 9.12 One line of *Faansin Yiwong* with instrumental interlude

Padding syllables

Yiwong without interlude fillers to be compared with one line of the same aria type *with* interlude fillers in figure 9.13. Interlude fillers differ from other padding syllables in that they are always specified as such by the scriptwriter.[7]

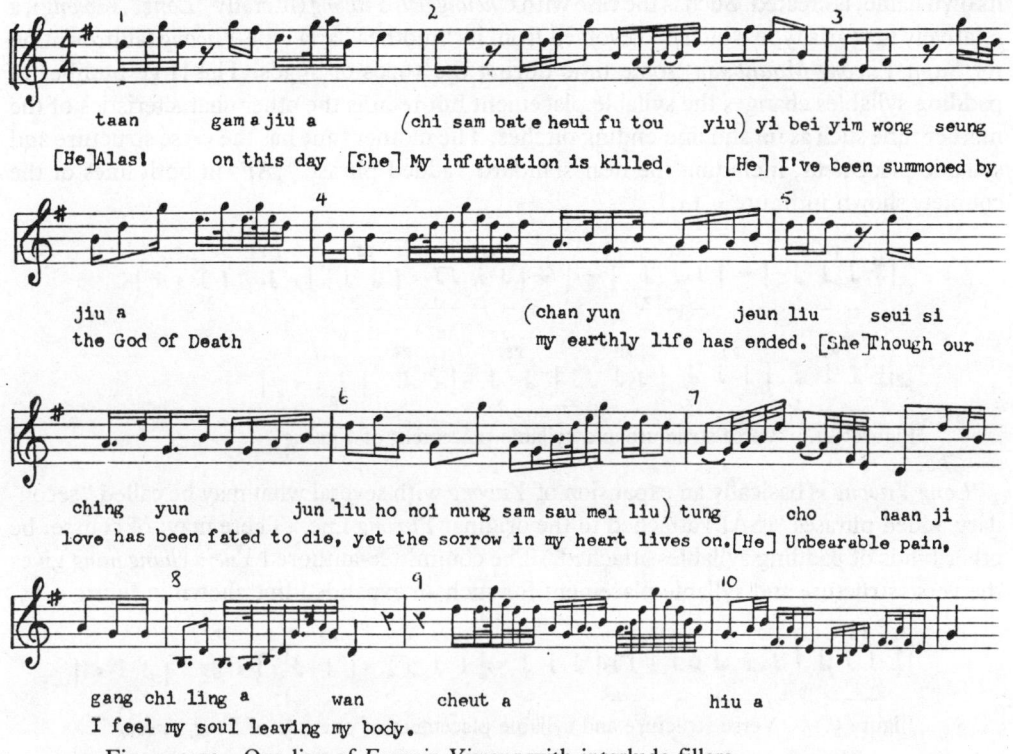

Figure 9.13 One line of *Faansin Yiwong* with interlude fillers

The fifth kind, called "tail syllables," are grammatical particles added extemporaneously by the singer to the end of a line. Meaningless by themselves, they suggest or emphasize subtle nuances in the meaning of the line as a whole.[8] When tail syllables are used, they are never sung on a strong beat of the melody. The last syllable of P2 in figure 9.8a is an illustration of a tail syllable, its function being to emphasize the exclamatory nature of the line. Tail syllables at the end of a line should not be confused with meaningless vocalizations which can occur anywhere in a line, even though they may sound alike.

The last kind of padding syllable, the nonsense syllables, occur very often but may be considered the least important. These are meaningless vocalizations such as "a," "e," and "i" which the singer uses to intone certain notes of a melisma after a regular syllable. (They might be compared to the extra syllables in Handel's "Every valley shall be exa-a-a-alted.") There appear to be some consistent patterns as to the conditions under which certain vocalizing syllables are used. For example, male singers tend to use "a" and "e," while female singers tend to use "i." The practice may depend largely on the personal styles of individual singers, but further research needs to be done before any conclusion can be drawn. The great singer Ma Shizeng was known to add the syllable "a" after almost every regular text syllable. The vocalizations "e" and "a" in figures 9.3, 9.5, 9.7, and 9.8a (except the last syllable in figure 9.8a, which is a "tail syllable") are all illustrations of this kind of padding syllable.

The case of *Long Yiwong*

Sometimes the padding syllables become permanently attached so that a new aria type, with its own name, is created. Such is the case with *Cheunggeui Yiwong* (literally *"Long" Yiwong*), a relatively new aria type which had evolved from its "mother" aria type *Yiwong* (abbreviation for *Sapji Yiwong Maanbaan*) some time during the 1920s or 1930s. The large number of padding syllables changes the syllable placement but retains the other characteristics of the mother tune such as *sin* and line-ending pitches. The mother tune has the verse structure and syllable placement, including the near-standard "added phrase" (AP) in both lines of the couplet, shown in figure 9.14.[9]

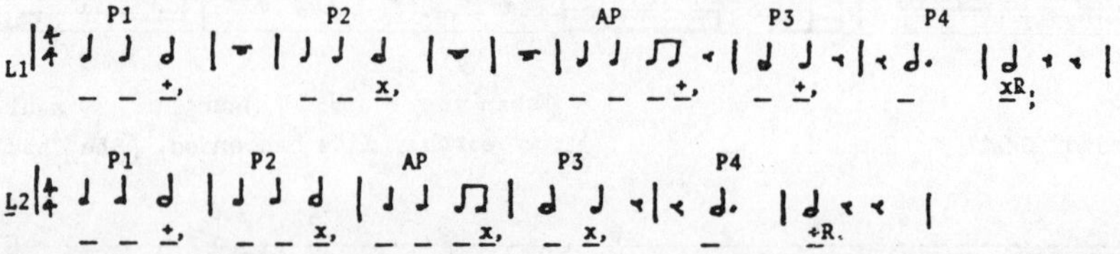

Figure 9.14 Verse structure and syllable placement of *Yiwong*

Long Yiwong is basically an expansion of *Yiwong* with several what may be called "secondary added phrases" (SAP) attached to the original *Yiwong* line. (There may, of course, be other kinds of padding syllables attached.) The committee-authored *Yueju changqiang* gives the verse structure and syllable placement for such an expanded line shown in figure 9.15.

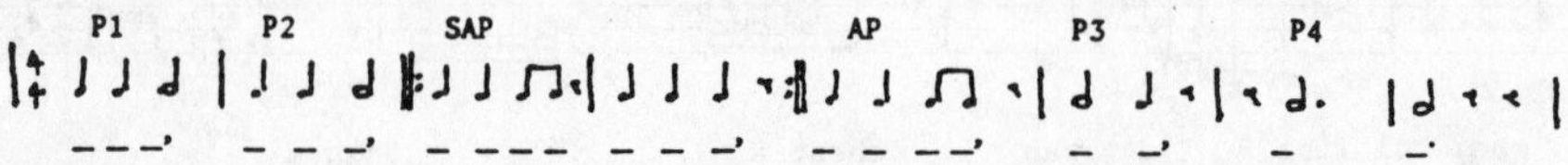

Figure 9.15 Verse structure and syllable placement of one line of *Long Yiwong*

Actual examples from performances show *Long Yiwong* is almost never sung in more than one expanded line, but rather begins with an expanded line (usually lower line), followed by a second line (upper line) that is a drastic truncation consisting of only the last four measures with eight syllables (AP, P3, P4). Such an example occurs in *The Magic Pearl* act 1 lines 337–347 and is transcribed in figure 9.16.

A survey of thirteen versions of *Long Yiwong* from different plays shows that seven followed the above pattern of upper expanded line – lower truncated line. Four versions have only one single expanded line (lower line). One version has a sequence of three lines: lower expanded line–upper truncated line–lower expanded line. One has a sequence of upper expanded line–lower truncated line–upper truncated line. Thus the formal structure of *Long Yiwong* appears to be quite flexible, so long as it contains one expanded line. The number of repetitions of the secondary added phrase vary from version to version; among the thirteen surveyed, nine have two repetitions, one has three repetitions, and three have four repetitions. The line-ending pitches of *Long Yiwong* are identical to that of *Yiwong*. Also, like *Yiwong*, it can be sung in any of the three *sins*.

A similar development occurred in *Gwanfa*, which has spawned a new aria type called *Long Gwanfa* (*Cheunggeui Gwanfa*), an example of which can be heard in *The Magic Pearl* act 1 line 319.

Padding syllables

Text

L2 P1   Ngo fan mang jou ding joi ji ling jung
          My marriage contract was determined when I was a child

    P2   Yan yau luk lai saam syu heung gong ga fung
          The six rites and the three documents of marriage have been offered to the Gong family

    SAP1 Bat gwo sap nin yan si pa ji pa leung bat tung
          But how the world has changed in ten years time

    SAP2 Luk wai gou sing ji dak yan ging jung
          [My future father-in-law] has since gained promotion, fortune, and high status

    AP   Sin fu nin chin ging hei seung
          But my own father has been demoted

    P3P4 Hung yu ha leung jau ching fung
          And lost all his wealth

L1 AP   Gam yat ngo jou fong hung kiu
          The purpose of my visit to Rainbow Bridge today

    P3P4 Mou fei yeuk haau siu long yan fung
          Is but an attempt to renew the relationship

Figure 9.16   One couplet of *Long Yiwong*

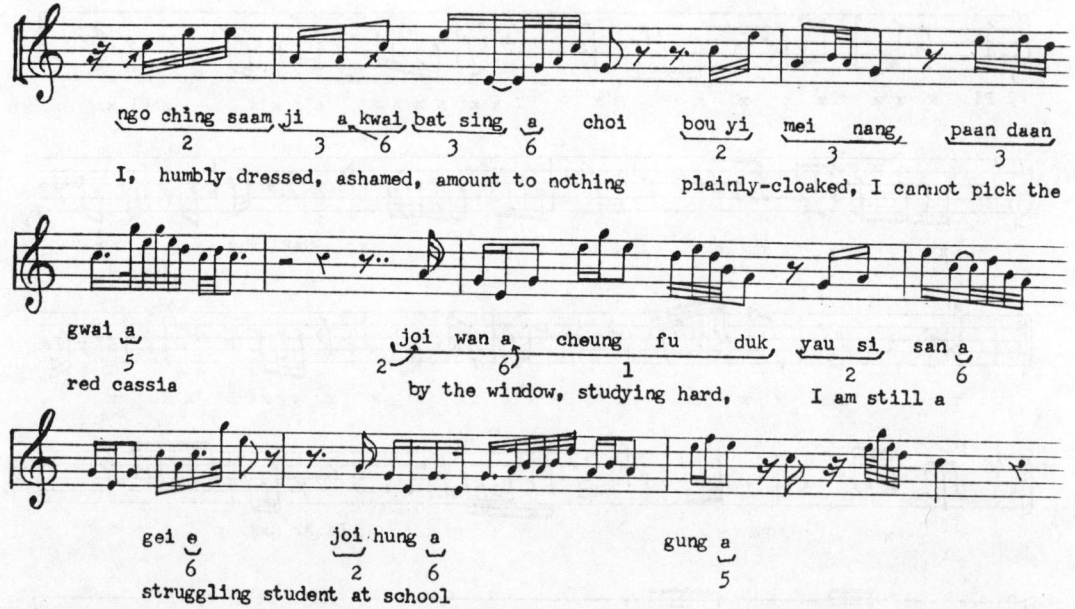

Figure 9.17 One line of *Bongji Maanbaan* showing five kinds of padding syllables

Summary

The padding syllables have been classified according to the way the singer treats the text during his performance. The study illustrates the freedom which the singer enjoys in manipulating the padding syllables and the resultant musical line. It reveals in some detail the inner creative process of the singer: the conflict he faces and the solution he chooses when he is confronted with considerations of textual meaning and musical aesthetic standards. Figure 9.17 gives a complete line of *Bongji Maanbaan* in which five kinds of padding syllables discussed in this chapter are illustrated: added phrase (1), phrase leader syllables (2), multiplets (3), tail syllables (5), and nonsense syllables (6). The source for this example is the same as that for version A of figures 9.8a and 9.8b.

The total number of syllables is twenty-nine, plus six nonsense syllables. Comparison with the standard verse structure and syllable placement as given in figures 9.1 and 9.2 illustrates the degree of difference between prescription and realization in performance. Some of the padding syllables are written into the script, others are improvised by the singer on stage. Their functions are varied; for some padding syllables, the function is to clarify the meaning of the text, for others, it is a means to create musical material. The different kinds of padding syllables affect the resultant musical line in different ways. The added phrase increases the number of metrical units of the musical line, while phrase leader syllables and multiplets alter the internal structure of the melody.

The extemporaneous addition of padding syllables depends also upon the dramatic situation and the role type. For example, singers of a comic role or of any other role during a lighter moment of the drama are more likely to improvise in this manner. The practice also

Padding syllables

depends upon the performing style of individual singers. In recent years such extemporizing has been frowned upon as improper by some performers and audience members. This may be due to the view of some literary-minded older Chinese and Western-minded younger Chinese that adhering closely to a fixed text is important in a performance.

10 *Sin*

Chapter 7 has shown that *sin* is an important structural element in the identity, categorization, and performance of aria types; but it plays an equally important role in the other oral delivery types of Cantonese opera – the fixed tunes and the narrative songs – and in Cantonese instrumental music outside of the opera. *Sin* has so far eluded a thorough understanding theoretically; the recent publications from China which attempt to investigate it on a level beyond simple description have yielded only contradictory opinions.[1]

Two facts contribute to the difficulty of the issue. First, *sin* has been going through slow but constant changes which are not consistently observed by all musicians; some embrace the changes, others are more conservative. As a result, one encounters different treatments of *sin* in practice by performers and in theory by scholars. Second, the Cantonese scale, upon which an understanding of *sin* depends, is itself a controversial issue among musicians and music scholars.

The Cantonese scale

The Cantonese heptatonic scale, already given in chapter 2, is reproduced in figure 10.1 for convenience. The reader is advised to review the discussion on the Cantonese scale in chapter 2 before proceeding.

Figure 10.1 Cantonese heptatonic scale in three octaves

The above scale, based upon two recent publications from China (see chapter 2, note 5), is an idealized model. Since there has never been a standardized tuning system, musicians disagree on some of the intervals, particularly the placement of the notes *yi* and *faan* that result in the 3/4 tones. One theory is that *yi* and *faan* can each assume two values: B^b and B, and F and F# respectively. Another theory is that *yi* and *faan* are unstable; their average values might be represented approximately by those given in figure 10.1, but their real values change from performance to performance.

The construction of musical instruments also raises questions about the scale. Some instruments, such as the two-string bowed lute (*erhu*), are unfretted; the musicians are obviously able to change finger positions to produce different values for the pitches *yi* and *faan*. Other instruments, such as the various kinds of fretted lutes (*yueqin*, *qinqin*) and particularly the struck zither (*yangqin*), produce a fixed scale.[2] It is therefore not surprising that there are different opinions on what the scale (or scales) should be. The performances, which with few exceptions involve both fretted and unfretted instruments playing in ensemble, indicate the possibility of a mixture of different scales.

The disagreement is also due at least in part to changing aesthetic standards among some musicians. During the 1920s and 1930s, Cantonese operatic music was under heavy Western influence, including the popularity of Western instruments such as the violin and the saxophone, the adoption of Western popular tunes, and the harmonization of melodies. Even though these Western elements have gradually disappeared from the scene since the 1940s, they left a deep and enduring mark on the musicians, particularly with respect to the Cantonese scale and *sin*. For example, Li Yan wrote in 1984 that "The adoption of the twelve-pitch scale will increase the expressive power of Cantonese opera."[3] This sentiment is not uncommon among Chinese musicians and even music scholars today. They are quick to point out that the twelve-pitch scale had existed in China before it did in the West, and that they are simply advocating a return to the roots of Chinese music.[4] Nevertheless, the influence of Western music from the early part of this century in shaping these opinions cannot be denied.

My own observation of performances of Cantonese opera in Hong Kong in the 1970s convinced me that musicians at one time in history, and some of the more conservative musicians and those who play the struck zither and the fretted lutes today, performed according to the scale represented by figure 10.1. The problematic intervals might not be exactly a 3/4 tone, but I believe that they were close to it and that musicians consciously and consistently chose to make them so regardless of the *sin*. This view is supported by the following published statement: "In the traditional music of Cantonese opera, the scale degrees 7 and 4 (*yi* and *faan*) *do not change pitch heights* [emphasis added] among *Jingsin*, *Faansin* or *Yifaansin*. After Liberation [1949], because of continual change and development, the pitch heights for those two scale degrees began to change: for *Jingsin* and *Faansin*, they grew closer to the equidistant chromatic scale degrees of B and F. In *Yifaansin*, 4 (*faan*) grew closer to F, but 7 (*yi*) grew closer to B^b."[5] The discussion that follows will further support this premise. For lack of a more definitive scale, the one shown in figure 10.1 will be taken as a working model for the discussion of *sin* in this chapter.

The historical interpretation of *sin*: the seven theoretical *sin*s

Sin means literally "line" or "string." It is generally acknowledged that, at one time in history, the term referred to the tuning of the strings of the two-string bowed lute, which has been the principal accompanying instrument for Cantonese opera since at least the beginning of this century (except for a lapse during the 1920s and 1930s; see chapter 3). Thus, what was called *Hochesin* meant that the two strings were tuned to the scale degrees of *ho* (Sol or G) and *che* (Re or D), *Sigungsin* of *si* (La or A) and *gung* (Mi or E), and so forth.[6]

There are two views on how the strings were tuned for different *sin*s. The first view is by Chen Zhuoying and Huang Jinpei, who say that the two strings of the lute in *Sigungsin* (La-Mi), for instance, were tuned a whole tone higher than that in *Hochesin* (Sol-Re). In other words, the absolute pitch of the scale did not change as one moved from one *sin* to another.[7] The second view is by Li Yan, who says that, when *sin* changed, the strings were not retuned; the same pitches simply served the function of different scale degrees.[8] In other words, the pitches of the two strings, which represented the notes *ho* and *che* (Sol and Re) in *Hochesin*, represented *si* and *gung* (La and Mi) instead when the *sin* was changed to *Sigungsin*. The actual pitches of the scale degrees were lowered by one whole tone as a result.

Regardless of the difference in the above views, a change of tuning would change the lowest scale degree that could be played and thus might affect the nature of the tune. Huang Jinpei points out for example that playing a tune in the wrong *sin* may result in awkward intervals in the melody. He gives the example of the following tune intended to be played on the *Chewusin* (strings tuned to *che* (D) and *wu* (A″) but at an octave lower so that, in effect, the tuning is *che'* (D) and *si* (A)). If the same tune were to be played on an instrument that was tuned to the *Hochesin* (strings tuned to G and D), the lower string of the two-string bowed lute could no longer accommodate some of the low pitches in the tune. The instrumentalist could either play the whole tune an octave higher by using a higher hand position on the fingerboard, or, more likely, he retained the tessitura of the tune at the lowest hand position, but switched the low pitches to an octave higher. The character of the resultant tune would obviously be quite different. The original tune played in *Chewusin* and the new version played in *Hochesin* are shown in figure 10.2.[9]

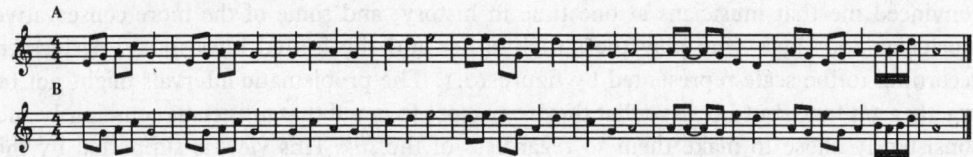

Figure 10.2 Comparison of the same tune played in (A) *Chewusin* and in (B) *Hochesin*

Theoretically there could be seven *sins*: *Hochesin* (Sol-Re), *Sigungsin* (La-Mi), *Yifaansin* (Si-Fa), *Saangliusin* (Do-Sol), *Chewusin* (Re-La), *Gungyisin* (Mi-Si), and *Faansaangsin* (Fa-Do). According to Li Yan's theory, different *sins* served to accommodate the voice-ranges of different singers. Thus for a singer with a relatively high voice-range, the two open-string pitches would represent the lower end of the scale, possibly in *Hochesin* (Sol-Re). For a singer with a relatively low voice range, the same two pitches of the open strings would represent the correspondingly higher end of the scale. When understood in this manner, the concept of *sin* appears to be similar to the Western concept of "key."

A new historical interpretation

The crucial question, however, pertains not to the absolute pitch but to the consistency of intervals that make up the scale. In order to retain the same intervals for the different tunings, the performer must have different finger positions. While musicians today generally play with different finger positions for different tunings, it is difficult to ascertain the general practice in the earlier generations, although at least some musicians apparently did not change their finger positions. Feng Yuanzhi of Hong Kong, a performer and teacher of the *erhu*, explained in 1969 that, while he played with different finger positions for different tunings, his teacher, Wang Chun, played with a fixed finger position for all tunings.[10] Qiu Hechou, in his 1916 publication on Cantonese singing, includes two diagrams of the finger positions on the *erhu*, one for *Hochesin*, and another for *Sigungsin*. In these diagrams, the finger positions are shown as identical for both *sins*.[11]

If finger positions do not change for the different tunings, then the intervals among the scale degrees naturally must differ among the *sins*. The construction of the fretted lutes and the struck zither, which have always played major roles in a Cantonese instrumental ensemble, also supports this conclusion. Assuming that these instruments are not retuned in the middle of a performance when the *sin* is changed (such retuning would be highly unlikely especially in the case of the zither, which has about forty strings), the original set of intervals is expected then to represent another set of intervals for the new *sin*. In other words, a change of *sin* unavoidably changes the intervals of the scale.

The implication of this observation is significant because it leads naturally to a new theory of what *sin* could have meant. If one designates the two kinds of intervals of the Cantonese scale as L (large, for the whole tone interval) and S (small, for the three-quarter tone interval), the lowest seven intervals for the *Hochesin* (Sol-Re) are as follows (refer to figure 10.1):

L S S L L S S

If the *sin* is to change to the *Sigungsin* so that the two open strings represent the pitches *si* and *gung* (La and Mi), the new set of intervals should be:

S S L L S S L

if the identity of the scale is to be retained. But if finger positions remain the same, then obviously some of the intervals would sound very much "out of tune." Figure 10.3 compares the discrepancies between the intervals for all seven *sins*. Some of the "transpositions" result in a greater number of "wrong" intervals (underlined) than others. For example, *Yifaansin* (Si-Fa) and *Gungyisin* (Mi-Si) have six each. On the other hand, *Saangliusin* (Do-Sol) and *Chewusin* (Re-La) result in only two "wrong" intervals each.

Hochesin (Sol-Re)	L S S L L S S
Sigungsin (La-Mi)	S̲ S̲ L L S̲ S̲ L
Yifaansin (Si-Fa)	S̲ L L S̲ S̲ L S̲
Saangliusin (Do-Sol)	L L̲ S̲ S L S S
Chewusin (Re-La)	L S S L S̲ S L̲
Gungyisin (Mi-Si)	S̲ S̲ L̲ S̲ S̲ L L̲
Faansaangsin (Fa-Do)	S̲ L S̲ S̲ L L S̲

Figure 10.3 Intervals for the seven *sins*

If finger positions do not change for the lute player and the zither player does not retune his instrument, a change of *sin* must mean more than a simple transposition of key: it results in a change in the intervals within the scale. Such an operation is somewhat similar to a change of *patet* in the gamelan music of Java. For an instrument such as the *gender*, a metal xylophone, the tuning of its individual metal "keys" stays unchanged during a performance. To play a tune in a different *patet* sometimes means simply transposing the movements of the two hands up or down the scale by one or two keys.[12] Since the tuning of the keys is not equidistant, such a change of *patet* results in a version different from the original tune. If the above interpretation of *sin* is correct, then it could have played a very similar role in Cantonese music as that of *patet* in gamelan music.

Constructing a model of *sin*

Sin today is no longer tied to the tuning of the bowed lute; the two strings are tuned to *ho* and *che* for all tunes. The names (and in one case, the meaning of a name) of *sin* have also changed; the commonly-used *sin*s today are *Jingsin*, *Faansin*, and *Yifaansin*. The word "*jing*" means regular, normal or proper, and *Jingsin* is appropriately the most often used *sin*. The word "*faan*" means "reverse" or "upside down" (while the word is identical to the scale degree *faan*, its usage as the name of a *sin* is unrelated to the scale degree), the significance of which will become clear in later discussions. *Yi* and *faan* in *Yifaansin* refer to the scale degrees, although the name *Yifaansin* does not imply tuning of the bowed lute. *Yifaansin* is also known as *Fuhau* (literally, "sad voice") because of the commonly accepted emotional content of that *sin*. The present-day meaning of *sin*, however, will be shown to still reflect on one level the significance of its new historical interpretation given above.

This study proposes a three-level model of *sin* based upon present-day practice and the analysis of actual performed examples. On the first level, the model proposes that, while all aria types use the same heptatonic scale as given in figure 10.1, an aria type in a particular *sin* emphasizes certain pitches in the scale. These pitches, which can be called principal pitches, form a principal scale within the larger heptatonic scale. Each *sin* is distinguished from the others by its distinctive principal scale, and all aria types belonging to the same *sin* share the same principal scale.

On the second level the model proposes that *sin* has a meaning similar to that of "key" in Western music; the three principal scales can be considered as a single scale transposed to different pitch levels. However, *sin* differs from the Western concept of "key" in that some of the intervals undergo small changes when the scale is transposed.

On the third level the model proposes that *sin* resembles "mode" in European medieval music. The melodic behavior of Cantonese opera is such that tunes in different *sin*s occupy different regions of the octave and have different sets of predominant notes and cadential notes.

The material for study

Since *sin* is one of the features that categorize aria types, the present study limits its material to three aria types which differ from one another only in *sin* but share the same value for the other features. The aria types chosen are:

> The *Jingsin Sapji Bongji Jungbaan* [Regular *Sin*, Ten Syllable, *Bongji*, Medium *Baan*], or *Jingsin Jungbaan*
> the *Faansin Sapji Bongji Jungbaan* [Reverse *Sin*, Ten Syllable, *Bongji*, Medium *Baan*], or *Faansin Jungbaan*, and
> the *Yifaansin Sapji Bongji Jungbaan* [*Yifaan Sin*, Ten Syllable, *Bongji*, Medium *Baan*], or *Yifaansin Jungbaan*.

Note that they possess identical verse structure, metrical pattern, and rhythmic structure for syllable placement. Their shared features allow the investigation of *sin* to be maximally free from extraneous considerations. Comparison of these aria types should reveal their differences, which are assumed to be attributable to *sin*.

In making comparative studies, consideration is given to the fact that extensive melodic variation occurs among different versions of the same aria type even though they belong to the same *sin* (see chapter 7). Therefore, more than one version of each aria type is studied so that the results are statistically convincing. Figure 10.4 shows seventeen lines in *Jingsin* from five passages (eight upper lines, nine lower lines); figure 10.5 shows seventeen lines in *Faansin* from five passages (seven upper lines, ten lower lines); figure 10.6 shows sixteen lines in *Yifaansin* from four passages (six upper lines, ten lower lines). In order to facilitate comparison, the versions of each line of the couplet in each *sin* are aligned vertically so that the metrical, rhythmic, and phrasal patterns are clear at a glance.[13]

The first level for the proposed model of *sin* states that there exists a set of principal pitches for each *sin*. The principal pitches are defined as those pitches in the heptatonic scale that play a more important role in a tune than others. From the singer's point of view, he or she places greater emphasis, or gives greater degree of preference, to the principal pitches in the scale than to others in the creation of a tune. From the listener's point of view, he or she perceives these pitches as different from others because of their heavier "weight." The determination of principal pitches thus depends upon the definition and determination of the relative degree of preference for, or "weight" of, a pitch.

One obvious factor contributing to the degree of preference, or "weight," is the relative frequency with which a pitch occurs in a tune; one assumes that the frequency of occurrence of a pitch is directly related to the degree of its preference by the singer, and to the perception of its "weight" by the listener. Other factors, such as the placement of a pitch in the metrical, rhythmic, and phrasal framework, may also reflect its degree of preference and affect its weight. For example, a pitch that occurs ten times in a tune is assumed to be "heavier" than one that occurs only once; on the other hand, a pitch that occurs as the last note of a phrase is assumed to be "heavier" than one that occurs as the penultimate note.[14]

Cantonese opera

Figure 10.4 Seventeen lines of *Jingsin Jungbaan*

Sin

Figure 10.5 Seventeen lines of *Faansin Jungbaan*

Sin

Figure 10.6 Sixteen lines of *Yifaansin Jungbaan*

Six assumptions and criteria for the determination of the "weight" of a pitch

1 All notes

The simplest and most obvious criterion is that the mere occurrence of a pitch, regardless of its position in a tune, contributes to its "weight." Consideration should, of course, be given to the duration of each occurrence. As a first approximation, each occurrence of a pitch is assumed to have equal weight, regardless of its duration.

2 Notes on strong beats

Jungbaan has a metrical pattern of "one-*baan*-one-*ding*," which is in many ways equivalent to, and therefore often transcribed into, a 2/4 meter in staff notation (see chapter 2).[15] The "weight" of a note is assumed to depend upon the strength of the metrical accent it receives. The first beat (*baan*) of each metrical unit has a relatively strong beat; the second beat (*ding*) has a relatively weak beat. The subdivisions within the *baan* and the *ding* are always binary and do not have names; one can safely assume that these subdivisions constitute even weaker beats than the *ding*. As an approximation, all notes that fall on the *baan* and the *ding* (the first and third quarter notes in the transcription) are assumed to have the same "weight," and are "heavier" than all other notes.

3 Phrase-ending notes

The standard verse structure of *Jungbaan* is such that each textual unit has two lines, each line four phrases, and each phrase either two or three syllables:

    Line 1   3 + 3 + 2 + 2
    Line 2   3 + 3 + 2 + 2

The caesura between any two phrases is reflected in the musical structure of the tune: the end of a phrase is generally sung to a note of a relatively long duration and/or followed by a break and rest of the voice. It is therefore assumed that the note that ends a phrase, in giving a sense of repose, is "heavier" than the notes preceding it.

4 Line-ending notes

The note that ends the last phrase of a line is assumed to be heavier than other phrase-ending notes for three reasons. First, the grammatical structure of the text ensures that there is a more distinct break between any two lines than between any two phrases, which gives the end of a line a greater sense of repose than the end of a phrase. Second, a passage of aria type almost always ends at the end of a line, not in the middle, before moving on to a different aria type or musical material. Therefore the line-ending note gives a sense of termination which the phrase-ending notes do not. Third, the line-ending notes (or cadential notes) employ specific pitches quite consistently from version to version. For example, *Faansin Jungbaan* always ends on *che* (or D) for its upper line, and *ho* (or G) for its lower line. To a listener familiar with the aria types, this invariance from version to version contributes a greater "weight" to the pitches involved. As an approximation, the two line-ending notes are given equal weight even though in present-day practice, a passage of aria type is more likely to end with an upper line than with a lower line (see chapter 13).

5 Standard syllable placement of the text

The syllable placement, one of the important structural features in the identity of an aria type, is determined by the *baan* of the aria type and by the number of syllables in a line. In present-day performances the verse structure of a ten-syllable line is often modified to contain additional syllables; the singer fits the so-called padding syllables into the standard syllable placement. However, the standard pattern without the padding syllables is still very much in the musical consciousness of the singers and the experienced audience. For example, when the singer performs a line that has more than ten syllables, he more likely than not places the textually more important syllables at points coinciding with the syllable placement (see chapter 9). The notes at these points are therefore assumed to be "heavier" than the others. This criterion, like the last one, demands that the audience be sufficiently sophisticated to sense the standard syllable placements of the aria type. The reader is referred to figure 7.8 for the syllable placement of *Faansin Jungbaan*.

6 Actual syllable placement
A note that is sung to the attack point of a textual syllable is assumed to be "heavier" than the other notes. This criterion is of greater significance than first appears if one understands the relationship between the linguistic tones of the text and the musical pitches that are sung to the text, a relationship that has been discussed in chapter 8. Very briefly, syllables belonging to a particular linguistic tonal category are found to be consistently sung to one (or a few) musical pitches throughout an aria type (exceptions are discussed in chapter 8). For example, in the versions of *Jingsin Jungbaan* in figure 10.4, syllables belonging to the Lower Even Tone are sung, with few exceptions, to the pitch *ho*, or G. To the experienced listener (and, of course, to the singer), some pitches within the scale stand out from the rest by virtue of their correspondences to the linguistic tones of the text. These correspondences are consistent for the tunes within a *sin*, but may differ from one *sin* to another. The sets of pitches in each *sin* that correspond to the four categories of linguistic tones are shown in figure 10.7.[16]

Figure 10.7 Tables of matching between linguistic tones and musical pitches

Sin as scale

Except for the first, each of the criterion proposes that certain notes in the tune are more important than others: they are considered as the "heavy" notes. The singer chooses some pitches in the heptatonic scale more than others for these "heavy" notes. The degree of preference is determined statistically by the frequency of occurrence of a particular pitch in a large number of versions. In other words, the singer, in his performance of the aria type, consistently uses these preferred pitches for the "heavy" notes more frequently than the others. The identity of the *sin* of an aria type is determined by the consistent use of a set of preferred pitches, and this identity is recognized by the listener through his perception of these pitches as being "heavy."

Since the degree of preference for (and the weight of) a pitch is assumed to be directly related to its frequency of occurrence, the preferred pitches can be determined through simple counting in accordance with the rules stipulated by each criterion. Thus, by the first

120   Cantonese opera

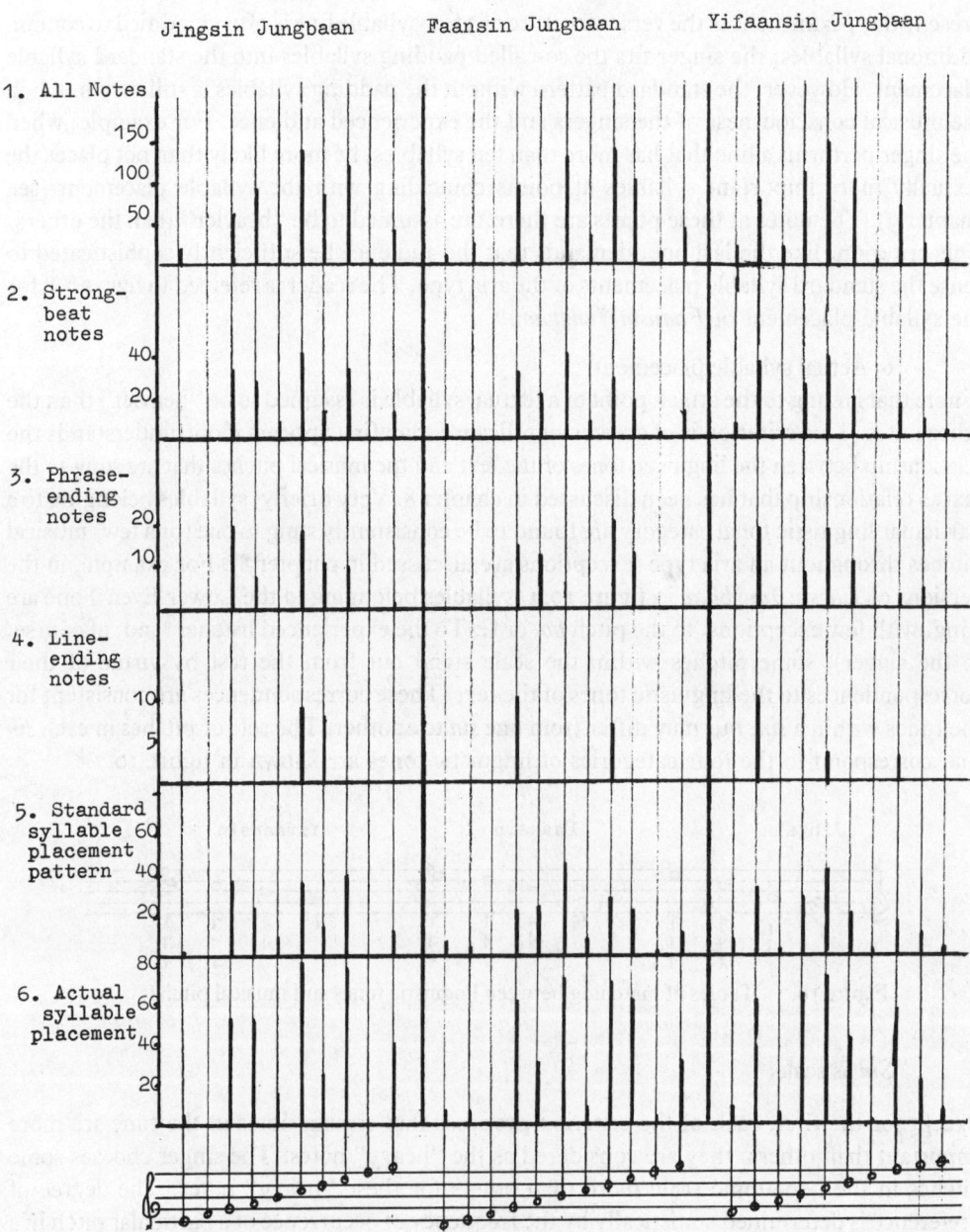

Figure 10.8 Matrix of eighteen graphs showing result of pitch counting

criterion, all the notes are counted once, and the number of occurrences for each pitch is noted. The second criterion stipulates that all notes that occur at the *baan* and the *ding* are "heavy" ones; therefore the pitches of those notes are counted. The results of the counting based upon all six criteria are given in a matrix of graphs in figure 10.8.

The way to read this matrix of eighteen graphs is as follows. The three columns correspond to the three *sin*s, while the six rows correspond to the six criteria for counting. For each

Sin

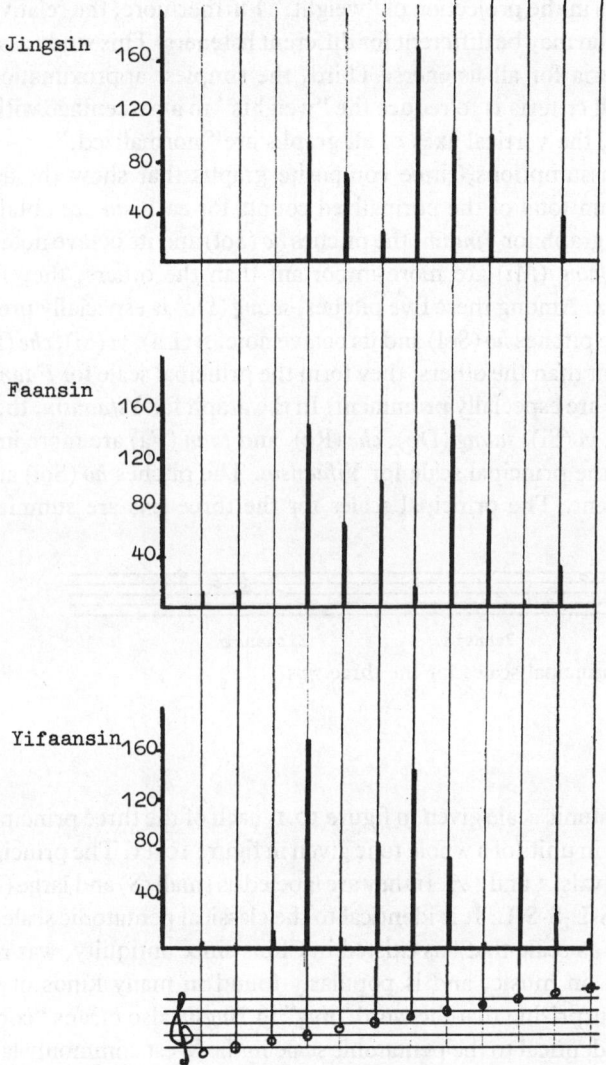

Figure 10.9 The aggregate "weight" of pitches for the three *sins*

individual graph, the horizontal axis shows the pitches of the heptatonic scale, shown at the bottom of the graphs; the vertical axis shows the number of occurrences for each pitch. Thus, the graph at the upper left-hand corner shows the result of counting the number of occurrences for all notes for the versions in *Jingsin*. It shows that the number of occurrences for the high G is forty-five, for the high F five, and so forth.

Several assumptions must be accepted to allow evaluation of the eighteen graphs in a straightforward way. First, since the "weight," or degree of preference, is indicated by the frequency of occurrences of the pitches under each criterion, the aggregate "weight" of any pitch is assumed to be some form of combined "weight" as determined by all the criteria. Second, the six criteria are very likely to exert different degrees of influence so far as the "weight" of a pitch is concerned. For example, the line-ending notes may be more important than the phrase-ending notes in the projection of "weight." Furthermore, the relative degree of importance of each criterion may be different for different listeners. This study assumes an equal "weight" for all criteria for all listeners. Third, the simplest approximation in the adding of "weights" from all criteria is to reduce the "weights" to a percentage within their own graph; in other words, the vertical axes of all graphs are "normalized."

Based upon the above assumptions, three composite graphs that show the aggregate "weight" in terms of the sum total of the normalized counts for each *sin* are obtained and shown in figure 10.9. In the graph for *Jingsin*, the pitches *ho* (Sol) and its octave note, *si* (La), *saang* (Do), *che* (Re), and *gung* (Mi) are more important than the others; they form the principal scale for the *Jingsin*. Among these five pitches, *saang* (Do) is especially prominent. In the graph for *Faansin*, the pitches *ho* (Sol) and its octave note, *si* (La), *yi* (Si), *che* (Re), and *gung* (Mi) are more important than the others; they form the principal scale for *Faansin*. The pitches *ho* (Sol) and *che* (Re) are especially prominent. In the graph for *Yifaansin*, the pitches *ho* (Sol) and its octave note, *yi* (Si), *saang* (Do), *che* (Re), and *faan* (Fa) are more important than the others; they form the principal scale for *Yifaansin*. The pitches *ho* (Sol) and *saang* (Do) are especially prominent. The principal scales for the three *sin*s are summarized as shown in figure 10.10.

Figure 10.10 The principal scales for the three *sin*s

Sin as key

In accordance with the heptatonic scale given in figure 10.1, each of the three principal scales has the sequence of intervals in units of a whole tone given in figure 10.11. The principal scale for *Jingsin* involves two intervals: 1 and 1½. If they are labeled as small (S) and large (L), then the sequence of intervals is S-L-S-S-L. It is identical to the classical pentatonic scale derived from the Pythagorean series, a scale that has existed in China since antiquity, was recorded among the earliest writings on music, and is popularly found in many kinds of Chinese music.[17] It is therefore not surprising that the word "*jing*" in *Jingsin* also means "correct" or "principal." Since it is also identical to the pentatonic scale in the West commonly labeled as Sol, La, Do, Re, Mi, the five pitches of *Jingsin* will be labeled by the Western names for ease of discussion.

Jingsin	1	1½	1	1	1½
Faansin	1	¾	1¾	1	1½
Yifaansin	1¾	¾	1	1¾	¾

Figure 10.11 Intervals of the principal scales

The sequences of intervals for *Faansin* and *Yifaansin* are more complicated, each involving more than two intervals. Nevertheless, notations of Cantonese music show that the Cantonese musicians consider these scales as transpositions of *Jingsin* (to be discussed later in this section). In other words, with some modification, the five intervals of *Faansin* and *Yifaansin* can be considered to fit the same sequence of intervals found in *Jingsin*. Given the five intervals for *Faansin* and for *Yifaansin*, the best fits are as follows:

Sin

Faansin	1	¾	1¾	1	1½
	S	S	L	S	L
Yifaansin	1¾	¾	1	1¾	¾
	L	S	S	L	S

If the five pitches of the *Jingsin* scale are Sol, La, Do, Re, Mi, then the transposed scales of *Faansin* and *Yifaansin* will have the sequence of intervals given in figure 10.12.

Jingsin:	Sol		La		Do		Re		Mi		Sol
		1		1½		1		1		1½	
Faansin:	Sol		La		Do		Re		Mi		Sol
		1		1½		1		¾		1¾	
Yifaansin:	Sol		La		Do		Re		Mi		Sol
		¾		1¾		¾		1		1¾	

Figure 10.12 Intervals of the transposed scales

The figure shows that, as a result of the transposition, some of the pitches are slightly "off" from the original *Jingsin* scale. For example, the scale degree Mi in *Faansin* is one quarter of a tone flattened, and the scale degrees Do and Sol in *Yifaansin* are both one quarter of a tone sharpened.

In summary, the second level of the model proposes that, when one *sin* changes to another, a transposition occurs. The identity of the scale is retained, but some of the intervals within the scale are changed. The transposition and the microtonal differences in intervals contribute to the identity of *sin*.

That such a transposition does actually occur in the performer's and the listener's perception is seen in the alternate name for *Faansin*: the *Saangliusin*. This name implies that the two-stringed bowed lute is tuned to the pitches of *saang* (Do) and *liu* (Sol). In fact, the tuning is not different from that of *Jingsin*, but the name implies that the open-string pitches have changed from *ho* (Sol) to *saang* (Do) and from *che* (Re) to *liu* (Sol). In other words, a transposition process has resulted in which the whole scale has been moved down by an interval of a fourth.

The meaning of the word "*faan*" (literally, reverse, upside-down) in *Faansin* also becomes clear. In *Jingsin*, the lower of the two strings is tuned to the note *ho* (Sol); in *Faansin*, the higher of the two strings *appears* to be tuned to the note *liu* (the octave equivalent of Sol). In other words, the scale degree *ho* has moved from the lower string to the upper string: the result of an "upside-down" change.

The perception of such a transposition process is further evidenced by the ways in which tunes in *Faansin* and *Yifaansin* are sometimes notated. Cantonese music has traditionally used the notation called the *gongche* system (*gungche* in Cantonese, *gung* and *che* refer to two of the pitches in the Cantonese heptatonic scale), in which the names *ho, si, yi*, and so forth are used to indicate pitches in the tune (see chapter 2). Around the turn of the century, the cipher notation, in which numerals 1 through 7 represent the pitches of the heptatonic scale, was introduced into China through Japan. As Chinese musicians and listeners became familiar with the cipher notation (and with the Western music which it represented), they realized its obvious similarity to the *gungche* system, and began to apply it to many kinds of Chinese music, including Cantonese music. The Cantonese system of *ho, si, yi, saang, che, gung, faan* was considered to be equivalent to, and often replaced by, the series 5, 6, 7, 1, 2, 3, 4 (or Sol, La, Si, Do, Re, Mi, Fa, as these numbers are pronounced by the Chinese).

Tunes in *Faansin* and *Yifaansin* are sometimes notated with numerals in this simple substitution process, but at other times are notated as if the tunes were transposed. That is, for *Faansin* the basic scale *ho, si, yi, saang, che, gung, faan* is notated as 1, 2, 3, 4, 5, 6, 7, implying a transposition of key. For *Yifaansin*, the basic scale is notated as 6, 7, 1, 2, 3, 4, 5. The notation sometimes makes this transposition explicit by providing a "key" signature: for tunes in *Jingsin* the notation will begin with the instruction of 1 = C, for tunes in the *Faansin* the instruction of 1 = G, and for *Yifaansin* the instruction of 6 = G. During the last several decades, tunes in *Faansin* and *Yifaansin* have been notated in both ways: using either the transposed or the untransposed scale.

The struck zither as evidence

The earliest published evidence indicating the Cantonese musician's perception of transposition is found in a collection of notation called *Qinxian xinbian* [A new collection of songs for the struck zither] by Qiu Hechou, who discusses in the preface how tunes of different *sin*s are to be performed on the struck zither (*yangqin*). His discussion supports the contention that a transposition process occurs with a change of *sin*, and that such a transposition involves small changes of interval, at least in so far as performances on the zither are concerned. In order to illustrate this point, some words on the construction and tuning of the zither are in order.

The Chinese struck zither is a direct descendent of the *santur* of the Near East and shares a great deal of similarity with the latter. As it existed in the early twentieth century, it consisted of fourteen sets of triple-course strings stretched horizontally over high bridges across the trapezoidal-shaped surface of the soundbox (see figures 10.13 through 10.15). The bridges, each slightly wider than the width of the triple-course strings, were attached to two strips of wood which formed two rows, one along the left side and the other along the right side of the surface of the soundbox. Every second set of strings was stretched over the left row of bridges, the other over the right row. The position of the left row of bridges was critical: they had to be placed two-fifths of the distance from the left edge so that each set of strings was divided into two portions at a ratio of two to three. Both portions of the strings were struck at a short distance from either side of the bridges; the intervallic relationship of the two notes was, of course, a fifth. The position of the right row of bridges was not critical since only the portions of the strings on the left side of the bridges were struck.

Because of this construction, the fourteen sets of strings could be considered as comprising three manuals. The seven sets of strings that stretched over the right row of bridges, struck at points immediately to the left side of the bridges, comprised the right manual. In the case of the other seven sets of strings that were stretched over the left row of bridges, that portion of the strings to the right side of the bridges comprised the middle manual, that to the left side of the bridges the left manual.

The tuning was such that the first string (counting from the longest string at the bottom of the instrument) in the right manual was tuned to the pitch *ho'* (the prime indicates that it was at an octave lower than the *ho* of the core octave, see chapter 2), the lowest pitch of the instrument. Each successive set of strings along the right manual was tuned one or two scale degrees higher, to *si'*, *saang'*, *che'*, *gung'*, *faan'*, and *ho*. The middle manual, starting from the

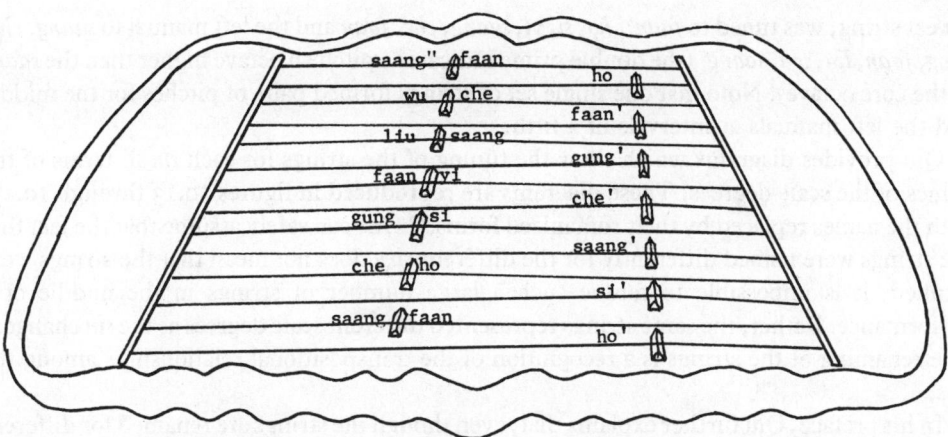

Figure 10.13 *Jingsin* tuning of *yangqin*

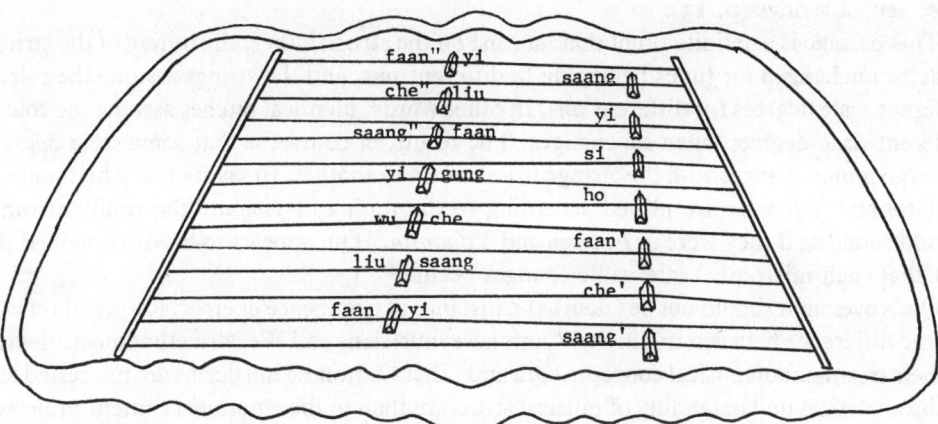

Figure 10.14 *Faansin* tuning of *yangqin*

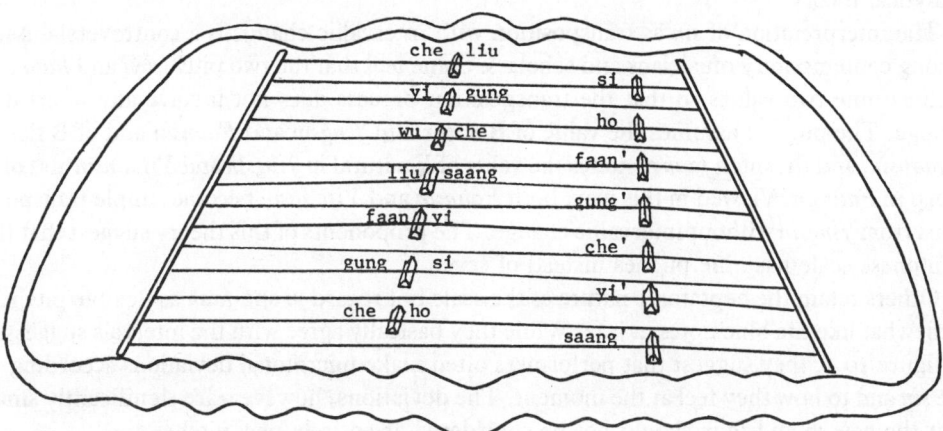

Figure 10.15 *Yifaansin* tuning of *yangqin*

lowest string, was tuned to *faan'*, *ho*, *si*, *yi*, *saang*, *che*, *faan* and the left manual to *saang*, *che*, *gung*, *faan*, *liu*, *wu*, *saang"* (the double prime indicates a pitch an octave higher than the *saang* of the core octave). Note that one single set of strings formed pairs of pitches for the middle and the left manuals at intervals of a fifth.

Qiu provides diagrams which show the tuning of the strings for each *sin* in terms of the names of the scale degrees. These diagrams are reproduced in figures 10.13 through 10.15, with the names replaced by their romanized forms.[18] One can safely assume that the fact that the strings were named differently for the different *sin*s does not mean that the strings were retuned, it is impossible to retune such a large number of strings in the middle of a performance. Rather, the same strings represented different scale degrees as the *sin* changed. The renaming of the strings is a recognition of the transpositional relationships among the *sin*s.

In his preface, Qiu further explains that, even though the strings are renamed for different *sin*s, one can easily play tunes of all *sin*s based upon the tuning of *Jingsin* so long as they are notated accordingly. The advantage, as he explains, is that one does not need to memorize three sets of strings (p. 13).

This passage is a definite proof that, at least on the struck zither, the tuning of the strings remains unchanged for tunes belonging to different *sin*s, and the strings assume the role of different scale degrees for different *sin*s. In other words, identical pitches assume the role of different scale degrees when *sin* changes. The result, of course, is that some scale degrees undergo minor changes with the change from one *sin* to another. In saying that when tunes in *Faansin* and *Yifaansin* are played according to the tuning of *Jingsin* "the resultant tunes should sound as if they were in *Faansin* and *Yifaansin*," Qiu appears to have overlooked the fact that such microtonal intervallic changes occur.[19]

Qiu's oversight should not be taken as an instance of negligence or error. Rather, it reflects a basic difference between traditional Cantonese musicians and Western ethnomusicologists in their treatment of musical concepts. Qiu and other Cantonese musicians are interested less in the analytical understanding of musical structure than in the emotional content projected by the different *sin*s. The microtonal intervallic changes, which they must certainly perceive, are simply not considered to be significant enough to be mentioned and made the subject of analytical theory.

The interpretation of *sin* as transposition with intervallic change is a controversial issue among contemporary musicians and scholars. Some feel that the two pitches *yi* and *faan* can each assume two values so that the transposition process does not involve any intervallic change. The pitch *yi* assumes the value of B natural in *Jingsin* and *Faansin* and of B flat in *Yifaansin*, and the pitch *faan* assumes the value of F natural in *Jingsin* and *Yifaansin* and of F sharp in *Faansin*. Viewed in this way, both *Faansin* and *Yifaansin* become simple transpositions from *Jingsin* without intervallic change. The proponents of this theory suggest that the Cantonese scale has nine pitches instead of seven.[20]

Others retain the heptatonic nature of the scale but regard *yi* and *faan* as flexible pitches, somewhat like the blue notes in jazz. While they basically agree with the intervals suggested in figure 10.1, they suggest that performers often make microtonal deviations according to the *sin* and to how they feel at the moment. The deviations, however, are significantly small that the new *yi* and *faan* should not be considered as entirely new pitches.[21]

Both views differ from the model suggested in this chapter and from the performance

Sin

practice on the struck zither. The most likely solution to this controversy is that all three models are valid because musicians differ in their performance practices, a result of rapid and drastic changes in Cantonese opera in this century.

Sin as mode

The matrix of eighteen graphs in figure 10.8 and the three composite graphs in figure 10.9 offer additional information. Each *sin* places different weights on the pitches of the scale; for example, *Jingsin* stresses the pitch C (or Do), *Faansin* stresses the pitches G and D (or Do and Sol, after transposition), *Yifaansin* stresses the pitches G and C (or La and Re, after transposition).

Each *sin* also has its own set of cadential pitches (line-ending pitches): for example, tunes in *Jingsin* cadence on D and C (or Re and Do) for upper and lower lines respectively, tunes in *Faansin* cadence on D and G (or Sol and Do, after transposition), and tunes in *Yifaansin* cadence on C and G (or Re and La, after transposition).[22]

Each *sin* has its own range in respect to the core octave; for example, Sol to Sol for *Jingsin*, Do to Do for *Faansin*, and La to La for *Yifaansin*. Figure 10.16 summarizes the information. Note that *Jingsin* and *Faansin* are closely related modally because of the overall predominance of the scale degree Do and its function as a cadential pitch in both *sins*. The differences are that *Faansin* stresses the scale degree Sol more than *Jingsin* does, and that the range of *Jingsin* tunes is from Sol to Sol, while that of *Faansin* is from Do to Do. Thus *Jingsin* somewhat resembles the "authentic" mode and *Faansin* the "plagal" mode of medieval Church Music in the West.

Yifaansin differs from the other two in its emphasis on the scale degrees Re and La, giving it a "minor-sounding" flavor. It is not surprising that some published notations of Cantonese operatic music in Hong Kong label the *Yifaansin* as a "minor" *sin* (*siudiu*) as opposed to *Jingsin* and *Faansin*, which are labeled as "major" *sins* (*daaidiu*).

	Jingsin	Faansin	Yifaansin
Predominant Pitches	Do	Sol, Do	Re, La
Cadential Pitches	Re, Do	Sol, Do	Re, La
Range	Sol to Sol	Do to Do	La to La

Figure 10.16 Predominant and cadential pitches and range for the three *sins*

It is noteworthy that, if the model suggested in this chapter is valid, the interval between *ho* and *yi*, that of 1¾ whole tones, should remain the same for both *Faansin* and *Yifaansin*. To the Cantonese listeners who hear both *Faansin* and *Yifaansin* as transpositions of *Jingsin*, the same interval is closer to a major third for *Faansin* but to a minor third for *Yifaansin*. Most Cantonese listeners admit that there is something especially "Cantonese" about *Faansin* and *Yifaansin* which is lost if a tune is played on the piano. Without doubt the mysterious "Cantonese" flavor in this case is a result of microtonal changes in intervals. On one level of perception, the differences are ignored; on another level, they are clearly perceived.

11 Fixed tunes

The category of oral delivery types called fixed tunes in this book comprises what the musicians themselves called *siukuk* (*xiaoqu* in Peking dialect) and *paaiji* (*paizi*).[1] *Siukik* means literally "small songs" and *paaiji* means "title." The two subcategories together are often referred to by the musicians as *kukpaai* (*qupai*). The translation "fixed tunes" is chosen to reflect the fact that, in comparison with other tunes used in the opera, the ones in these two repertories show less variation from version to version in performance. This characteristic of relative fixity is related to the process called *tinchi* (*tianci*), meaning literally "to fill in with text," by which new texts are composed for preexistent tunes with little alteration to their melodic characteristics.

The creative process of *tinchi* has great significance in the history of Chinese poetry and opera. It is generally accepted that during the early stages in the development of Chinese poetic genres such as *chi* (*ci*) and *kuk* (*qu*), poems were composed to be sung rather than simply read.[2] As certain tunes became popular among poets, new poems were composed to fit them. The procedure was feasible even for poets who were not musically oriented as long as the new texts followed the verse structure of the model with regard to patterns of beat, phrase structure, and, with some flexibility, the sequence of linguistic tones. Since the verse structure was derived from the musical characteristics of the tune in the first place, conforming to it ensured that the new poems would automatically be suitable for musical performance. Known by the title of the tune that it fits, the verse structure came to be used as a model by poets who composed poems in ignorance of the original tune. As time went on, poems were performed orally less and less often, and the tunes were gradually forgotten; they were not, with very few exceptions, preserved in notation. However, new poems were (and still are today) composed to fit particular verse structures even in the absence of the original tunes. Thus among poets, the term *tinchi* has come to denote the composing of a poem to fit a preexistent verse structure.

While the practice of composing a new poem to fit an actual tune has been long lost among poets, it is still very actively carried out in some Chinese popular musical and operatic genres today. In Cantonese opera this practice forms an integral part of the creative process for fixed tunes. Thus a study of this process is not only significant for the understanding of the performance practice of Cantonese opera but will also shed some light on how poets at one time may have composed poems according to actual tunes rather than to an abstract verse structure.

In a typical play lasting four hours, generally ten to twenty fixed tunes are used, each one lasting several minutes. (*The Magic Pearl* has four fixed tunes in the first act, seventeen in the entire play.) Each tune is identified in the script by a title, and generally without musical notation; it is assumed that the performer knows these tunes just from the titles given.

Fixed tunes

Sometimes only part of a tune may be used in a passage, in which case the script will add to the title terms such as "front section," "middle section," and so on.

An average singer or instrumentalist knows as many as two or three hundred fixed tunes. So far no survey has been made of the total number of these tunes used in Cantonese opera. Indeed such a survey would be difficult to make and, if made, difficult to keep up-to-date, because whenever a new play is written a new tune may be borrowed from outside the original repertory and premiered on stage. The new tune will then join the rank of fixed tunes. During the 1930s and 1940s, many Western popular tunes, for example, were borrowed. In the last few decades performers have been more conservative than their predecessors; to a large extent only tunes already in the repertory have been used in new plays. Furthermore, the Western popular tunes introduced into the repertory earlier are no longer in vogue today and indeed have disappeared completely from the stage.

Sources of the tunes

The fixed tunes come from many sources: any tune that has become popular in a community may be adopted again and again in different plays, thus joining the large repertory. The total repertory, as a result, exhibits a variety of melodic forms and styles. Many of the tunes are also played regularly as instrumental ensemble music without singing in the Guangdong area.[3]

Most of the *paaiji* tunes are believed to have originated from the Kunqu opera, a fact reflected in the many *paaiji* tune titles that are identical with Kunqu tune titles.[4] How they are in fact historically and musically related awaits further study.

The origin of the *siukuk* repertory is much more varied: the majority are traditional folk or urban tunes of obscure origin popular in the Guangdong area, some of which are regularly played as instrumental ensemble music. Many of their titles are identical with titles of tunes used in traditional literary genres of *chi* (*ci*) and *kuk* (*qu*); however, it is not known whether these opera tunes are related historically or musically to those from the literary genres, which, of course, are no longer in existence. Some of the tunes have titles that are not found in other regional music of China and are assumed to be indigenous to the Guangdong Province, for example, *Yuda Bajiao* [*Rain Beating on the Banana Tree Leaves*] (all song titles are given in Peking dialect) and *Ema Yaoling* [*Hungry Horse Shaking the Bell*].

Some *siukuk* are borrowed from a known source but without a known composer. A small number of tunes, for example, derive from other genres of traditional Chinese music, including a recently popularized folk tune, *Machefu Zhige* [*Song of the Horse-drawn Wagon Driver*], from the Xinjiang Province, and a tune called *Nanbangzi* [*Southern Bangzi*] from Peking opera. Another small group of *siukuk* tunes can be traced to known composers from this century, and are published in printed scores together with the names of the composers. Some examples are *Pinghu Qiuyue* [*Autumn Moon on the Calm Lake*] by Lü Wencheng, *Sailong Duojin* [*Winning the Prize in a Dragon Boat Race*] by He Liutang, and *Kaixuan* [*Triumphant Song*] by Chen Junying.

Finally, some tunes are newly composed for a new play, often by the *erhu* player in the orchestra or by someone else in the troupe who is musically gifted. If such a new play becomes popular and is performed frequently, the new tune may also become well-known and be borrowed for other plays. In the last two decades, very few new plays have been written; those that have been have seldom involved the composition of new tunes.

Choice of tune

The first step in the *tinchi* process is the scriptwriter's choice of a tune from the vast repertory to suit a particular dramatic situation in a play. His choice may be based upon certain musical characteristics which relate a tune directly to a certain dramatic situation. For example, a tune with a brisk tempo may be chosen for a scene with an excited mood. On the other hand, the exceptional popularity of a tune can be reason enough for its being used. But the most important criterion for choice is the tune title, which in most cases is of a descriptive nature: if the description fits the dramatic situation, the tune is likely to be used. For example, in act 1 of *The Magic Pearl*, the two beautiful young ladies taking a walk and admiring the scenery in a garden sing a tune called *Bubujiao* [*Dainty Steps*]; the God of Law sings the tune *Dangzhou* [*Rowing a Boat*] as he makes his appearance as a boatman.[5]

After the tune is chosen, a new poem is composed to fit it through the process of *tinchi*, the subject of investigation in this chapter. The methodology involves a comparative study of several versions of a single tune which are sung to different poems in different plays. The music and texts are transcribed from recordings, and the relationship between the verse structure of the text and the musical characteristics is investigated. An examination of this relationship will clarify the process whereby a scriptwriter composes his poem to fit the tune, and how a performer sings it.[6] To put it in another way, the study asks what the scriptwriters and performers mean by "fit" when it comes to composing a poem and singing it to a preexistent tune.

Several versions of the tune called *Pinghu Qiuyue* [*Autumn Moon on the Calm Lake*] are used; figure 11.1 shows the transcription, including the text in linguistic tonal symbols for each syllable, of three performed versions A, B, and C, and a printed version D.[7] Each phrase of the text is marked off by a comma; the numerals offer markers which allow the reader to follow the text as romanized and translated in appendix 3.

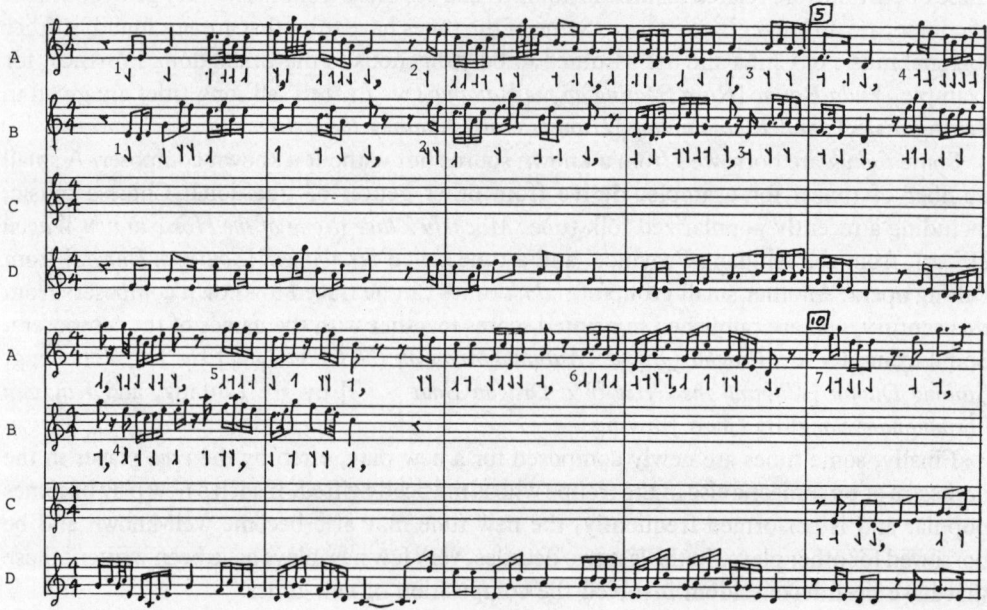

Fixed tunes

Figure 11.1 Four versions of *Autumn Moon on the Calm Lake*

The analysis which follows is in three parts. First, the verse structure of the three sets of text for A, B, and C is compared. Second, the similarities and differences in the melody of the three versions are observed. Finally, the relationship between verse structure and melody is analysed.

Verse structure of the text

The three major features of verse structure that concern traditional Chinese poets are as follows: first, the pattern of line-lengths (the number of syllables in a line); second, the pattern of rhyming among the final syllables of each line; and third, the pattern of linguistic tones of the syllables.[8] The first question is whether or not the different texts that are composed to the same tune follow the same pattern of line-lengths and, if they do, what exactly is the pattern. An examination of the three versions shows that their patterns are clearly not the same. The opening few lines of version A exhibit the pattern 7+5+10+5+5 (each numeral refers to the number of syllables in a phrase, nonsense syllables represented by "|" are not counted), while those of version B have 9+7+7+6. Version C has omitted the opening lines of the tune.

The ways in which the textual phrases are matched with the musical phrases make it obvious that the scriptwriter is not concerned with producing a fixed pattern of line-lengths for the same tune. The following combinations are found:

  7+5 (syllables) match with 9 (sung to the first musical phrase)
  10 match with 7 (sung to the second musical phrase)
  5 match with 7 (sung to the third musical phrase)
  5 match with 6 (sung to the fourth musical phrase)

132   Cantonese opera

As regards the pattern of rhyming, with few exceptions, every line of the song ends with an identical rhyme. Each version has its own rhyme: version A has -an, -am, or -aam, considered the same rhyme by scriptwriters. Version B has -ing, or -in. Version C has -ong or -eung.

As regards the pattern of linguistic tones, the last syllables of each phrase (the rhyming syllables) alternate between Oblique Tones and Even Tones in most cases. A more general rule appears to be the avoidance of several consecutive phrases with all Oblique Tone or all Even Tone. The linguistic tones of syllables which do not end phrases do not appear to adhere to any clearly defined or rigidly followed pattern.

Versions of the melody

A comparison of the melodies of the three versions can be carried out on two levels, what one might call "macro" and "micro." On the macro level, one notes that the complete tune, as represented by the printed version, has a total of twenty metrical units (or measures); each unit consists of one *baan* followed by three *ding* (one strong beat followed by three weak beats). In the first play, the complete tune was sung; in the other two, only parts of the tune were sung. Figure 11.2 summarizes the discrepancies among the versions.

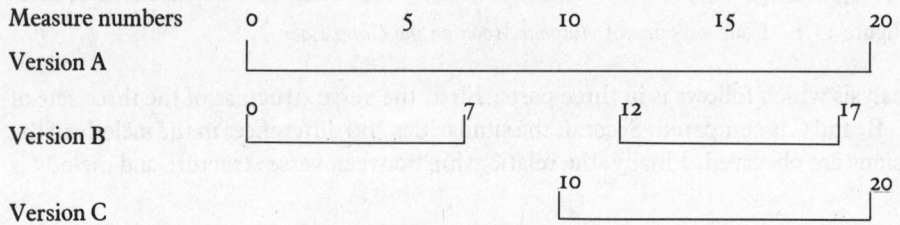

Figure 11.2   Sections of the tune *Autumn Moon* used in the three performed versions

On the micro level, the three versions are quite similar in phrase structure, melodic contour, and rhythmic characteristics; in short, they share a large percentage of individual pitches in the same metrical positions, especially the cadential pitches. Minor variations are of three kinds:

1. Minor rhythmic variations such as that found in measure 4, fourth quarter note, where version B has a dotted rhythm while version A has even sixteenth notes.
2. Addition, deletion, or alteration of passing notes, ornamental notes, anacrusis, or in general, notes on weak beats. Examples can be found in almost every measure.
3. The singing of the same melodic fragment at different octaves between two versions. See measures 10–12.

On the "macro" level, the scriptwriter obviously has the freedom to manipulate large musical units, as is evidenced by versions B and C which use only part of the tune, as long as the tune retains a relatively stable melodic structure on the local level. The identity of the tune, therefore, does not depend on its larger structure; the listener is expected to accept a portion of a tune as representing the whole. The identity is sufficiently established simply by certain melodic characteristics of individual musical phrases and their aggregates on the "micro" level.

Fixed tunes

Drawing the distinction between "macro" and "micro" levels is crucial in understanding the difference between a fixed tune and an aria type. Chapter 7 has shown that the identity of an aria type depends very little on melodic contour, which can vary greatly among versions of the same aria type. A fixed tune, on the other hand, retains the melodic contour to a large extent. Different versions of an aria type must retain the overall structure of its basic couplet form. A fixed tune, on the other hand, appears to retain its identity even when its large-scale, overall structure is altered.

Chapter 8 has shown that the variation in melodic contour among versions of an aria type is, to a large extent, due to a direct relationship between that contour and the linguistic tones of the text, which must match one another closely. Different sets of text, therefore, naturally result in different melodic contours. Since different versions of a fixed tune also have different texts, why does the melodic contour of the different versions not vary to the same degree as those of an aria type? Does the rigid rule governing the relationship between the linguistic tones of the text and the melodic contour of the tune not apply to fixed tunes? Is there a basic difference in the creative process between aria types and fixed tunes?

Relationship between verse structure and melody

In order to answer the above questions, the relationship between the verse structure of the text and the musical characteristics of the tune must be investigated. The focus will be on the relationships between textual and musical phrasing and between the linguistic tones of the text and the melodic contour of the tune.

In the three performed versions, the scriptwriters all seem to treat the phrase structure of the tune identically. For example, both versions A and B have a pause in the melody at measures 2, 5, 7, etc. Furthermore, the textual phrasing mirrors the musical phrasing: the textual phrases exhibit small syntactic breaks also at measures 2, 5, 7, etc. This phenomenon implies that the scriptwriters compose their text by molding the textual phrase patterns of the tune; pauses in the text are made to coincide with the cadential or semi-cadential points in the music. There are a few exceptions, most notably in measure 17 where the textual phrase of each of the versions breaks at different points.

It has already been shown that, when two texts are sung to the same melodic phrase, the number of syllables in the two texts is not necessarily the same. A melodic phrase, without change to its overall length, can accommodate a larger number of syllables through the addition of passing notes and anacruses added to it, and a smaller number of syllables through a reduction of the number of notes in the melody or an increase in melismaticness. By these means, the scriptwriter is enabled to fit more or fewer syllables into the same musical phrase. In other words, the concept of syllable placement, so important in aria types, does not play a role in fixed tunes.

As regards the relationship between the linguistic tonal patterns of the text and the melodic contour of the tune, the first phrase of version A shows that, as the tune moves up and down the pitch register, the linguistic tones of the text match the movement with a similar contour (figure 11.3). All three versions exemplify this rule of pitch matching, which may be formulated as follows: words are so chosen that the relative pitch levels of their linguistic tones match the relative pitch levels of the tune. The rule is most strictly observed for the beginning and ending syllables of a textual phrase (and the corresponding musical phrase).

Figure 11.3 Version A measure 1

Figure 11.4 Version B measure 1

For example, the first two syllables of both versions A and B belong to the Lower Even Tone. They are chosen so that the low pitch of the linguistic tone will match the musical pitch, which is relatively low at that point. In measure 2, the end of the melodic phrase on a low pitch is sung in both versions to syllables with the same Lower Even Tone, so that the matching is again achieved. This rule is reflected in the verse structure of the text even without reference to the music: a comparison of the ending syllables of the textual phrases in the different versions shows that they generally have the same linguistic tones, or different linguistic tones with the same pitch level. For example, Lower Even Tone is found in both versions in the fourth quarter note of measure 3; Upper Rising Tone and Upper Even Tone (both with relatively high pitch level) in the third quarter note of measure 4; Lower Even Tone for both versions in the fourth quarter note of the same measure; Lower Rising Tone and Upper Going Tone (both with medium high pitch level) in the first quarter note of measure 6, and so forth.

As was discussed in chapter 8, the matching between linguistic tones and pitch levels of the tune can be either "consistent" or "localized." In the former case, the syllables of one linguistic tonal category are consistently set to one particular pitch throughout a tune. In the latter case, the syllables of one linguistic tonal category may be set to different pitches at different points of the tune, as long as the tonal contour of a cluster of syllables still resembles the melodic contour, regardless of pitch level. In the versions of the fixed tune under study, the matching appears to be essentially of the localized kind. For example, for version A, the Lower Even Tone in measure 1 is sung to the pitch E above Middle C, but in measure 10, the Lower Even Tone is sung to D above High C; but the overall linguistic tonal contour and the melodic contour match each other locally in both cases. One should recall that, in aria types, the rule of matching between linguistic tones and pitch levels of the tune is of the "consistent" kind.

The rule of matching stated above would appear to restrict greatly the scriptwriter's freedom of choice among syllables; as the tune is relatively invariable, only a limited number of syllables are eligible to fit the melodic contour of the tune. In reality, the application of the rule can be quite flexible, especially in the middle of a musical phrase, because the singer generally makes adjustments during a performance to avoid breaking it when the linguistic tones of the text do not match exactly the melodic contour of the tune. Two kinds of adjustments are commonly used.

The singer may adjust the placement of the syllables so that they are sung to the right pitches. An example can be found in version B, measure 1 (figure 11.4). To the rendition given in this transcription two alternative renditions can be imagined, shown in figure 11.5. In both these alternatives, the syllable placement is quite plausible, although rendition 1 is

Fixed tunes

Figure 11.5 Alternate renditions of figure 11.4

unlikely due to the syntactic structure of the text, the discussion of which is beyond the scope of this book. Rendition 2, however, makes sense rhythmically because the elimination of the two sixteenth notes makes the musical phrase identical to that of version A and the printed version D. But the rule of matching will then no longer be observed: the syllable *chau* (third syllable), with an Upper Even Tone, should be sung to a relatively high pitch. If it is sung to the pitch C as in rendition 2, the syllable would sound like another syllable with an Upper Going Tone meaning "stinking" rather than the intended syllable, which means "autumn." If it is sung to the pitch E, then the nature of the tune would have to be changed at that point. Thus one sees how the singer adjusts his text to a particular syllable placement so that the rule of matching can be observed and the identity of the tune on the "micro" level is preserved. In aria types, on the other hand, the identity of the tune is defined largely by a relatively fixed syllable placement, so the singer does not have as much freedom as he does in the fixed tune to manipulate the placement of the syllable.

The singer may add or alter passing notes in order to accommodate syllables that have the "wrong" linguistic tones. This is tolerated as long as the general contour of the melody is not affected. An example can be found in measure 4, second quarter note (figure 11.6). In version B, in order to accommodate the syllable with the Upper Even Tone, the melodic contour jumps up a 4th to the pitch C and then down a 6th, while in version A the melodic progression is much more gentle. A comparison with the printed version D does not indicate which version is the "mother tune" and which is a variant form.[9] The point here is that such alterations are felt to be possible (and occur quite frequently – as the transcription shows) as a way to satisfy the rule of matching between linguistic tone and melodic contour.

Figure 11.6 Measure 4

136   Cantonese opera

Thus to understand the creative process of *tinchi* in the fixed tunes, one should not limit one's attention to the scriptwriter alone. While his duty is to choose the tune and compose a poem to fit it, the actual fitting process depends to a certain extent on the singer, who is ultimately responsible for the adjustment of the poem to the tune.

How a singer, within the restrictions of a preexistent tune, renders a text during performance is a complicated issue and may involve many factors other than the rule of matching. The first quarter note of measure 16 offers an example in which the melodic contour varies from one version to another even though the linguistic tone of the text is identical (figure 11.7). The

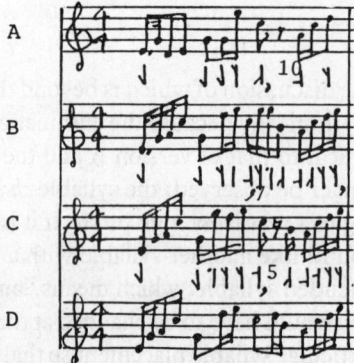

Figure 11.7   Measure 16

variations are obviously the result of factors other than the verse structure of the text, whether these be the style of a "school" of singing, the dramatic situation, or individual musical-aesthetic inclinations. These factors, however, are beyond the scope of this study.

Tinchi as creative process

To summarize, the scriptwriter first chooses a tune that he considers to match the dramatic requirements of the play. He then composes the poem to match the tune, taking into account two major factors in the verse structure. First, the phrase structure of the text is designed to match the phrase structure of the tune. Since a melodic phrase can accommodate a larger or smaller number of syllables through the addition or deletion of passing notes and anacruses, the exact number of syllables within a textual phrase is not critical. What is critical is that a textual phrase should begin and end with a melodic phrase.

Second, the choice of words for the poem is based upon a rule of pitch matching: syllables with linguistic tones of low (or high) pitch level are chosen for the portion of the tune that has low (or high) pitch levels. In general, the tonal contour of the linguistic tone of the text matches the tonal contour of the tune according to this rule. The matching, however, is "localized": so long as linguistic tonal contours match the melodic contour on a local level, the rule is satisfied. The rule may also be satisfied by the singer who either adjusts the rhythmic placement of the syllables or modifies slightly the melodic contour of the tune.

Two overriding rules affect, indeed control, the compositional process in both fixed tunes and aria types. First, the identity of a tune must be preserved in order for it to serve its dramatic function; and second, the linguistic tones of the text must match the melodic contour of the tune. How these rules are dealt with, however, is different in the two cases.

Fixed tunes

In aria types, the identity of the tune depends to a large extent upon the so-called syllable placement of the text: the number of syllables in a textual line is fixed, and they must be sung to a prescribed rhythmic pattern in the tune. This pattern does not change from version to version, and constitutes one of the important marks of identity for a particular tune. The scriptwriter, therefore, must adhere to the prescribed number of syllables in each line.[10] The identity of the tune is less dependent, however, on the melodic contour of the tune, which varies from version to version, sometimes to a considerable degree. Thus the scriptwriter has the luxury of not needing to be too much concerned with choosing the "correct" linguistic tones for the text.[11] The singer simply adjusts the melodic contour to fit the linguistic tones during a performance. One may say that, in aria types, the text determines the melodic behavior.

In fixed tunes, the identity of the tune depends to a large extent upon its melodic contour, with allowances for minor variations among the versions. The scriptwriter must compose his text carefully so that the linguistic tones match the predetermined melodic contour of the tune. The identity of the tune, however, is not affected by the syllable placement of the text. Thus the scriptwriter is given a certain degree of flexibility in his choice of pattern of phrase lengths and linguistic tones. Still, one can say that, in fixed tunes, the tune determines the linguistic tonal behavior of the text.

In the total repertory of Cantonese opera tunes, there are about thirty aria types, and several hundred fixed tunes. The two lines of an aria type are often repeated during a single musical passage, sometimes several times. The same aria type may also appear several times at different points within the same play. On the other hand, a fixed tune never appears in a play more than once and is never repeated within a single passage. Although there may be complex historical reasons for these contrasting behaviors, the examination of fixity and variability in the melodic contour of these two categories of tunes suggests possible musical-aesthetic explanations.

12 Narrative songs

The early decades of the twentieth century saw the introduction of a set of new tunes into the repertory of oral delivery types in Cantonese opera: tunes that were originally used in the so-called narrative songs of the Canton region.[1] Known as *kuk'ngai* (*quyi* in Peking dialect) [song-art] or *syutcheung* (*shuochang*) [speaking-singing], narrative songs can be described simply as the telling of a story through speech and song with minimal stage movement, bodily gesture, make-up, costume, and staging. They have been an important form of popular entertainment throughout China from at least as early as the tenth century AD, and, in the twentieth century, over 260 different regional kinds have been identified nationwide, exhibiting a rich variety of musical forms and styles.[2]

The Chinese names *kuk'ngai* and *syutcheung* reflect two important characteristics of narrative songs: they use mainly words to tell a story, and the performance involves a combination of speaking and singing. The latter characteristic takes two distinct forms: in some regional kinds, such as the *Naamyam (Nanyin)* [*Southern Tone*] of the Canton area, a performance consists of alternations of speaking and singing; in others, such as the *Saiho Daaigu (Xihe Dagu)* [*Drumsong of West River*] of northeastern China, the words are often recited in a half speech-like and half song-like manner.

Some regional kinds of narrative songs are performed by a single person, accompanying himself or herself on a string or percussion instrument. Other kinds involve one or two additional musicians, acting either solely as accompanists or as singers as well. Still other kinds are performed without accompaniment. Like operas, narrative songs use preexistent tunes; most regional kinds use a small number of tunes – in the case of some, only one tune – with a small number of variants which have evolved from them.

The most important kinds of narrative songs in the Canton area include the *Naamyam (Nanyin)* already mentioned, the *Muk'yu (Muyu)* [*Wooden Fish*], the *Lungjau (Longzhou)* [*Dragon Boat*], the *Baan'ngaan (Banyan)* [*Beats and Rests*], and the *Haamseuigo (Xianxuege)* [*Salt-water Song*]. They were widely performed in urban and rural areas around the Pearl River Delta region until the 1950s, when they began to lose their popularity; today they are scarcely performed at all.

Naamyam was widely performed in many different situations, such as private banquets in restaurants and homes, private and semi-private professional clubs or guilds formed by, and catering to, members of a particular trade or craft, and public places such as restaurants and teahouses for the entertainment of regular customers. *Muk'yu* was performed mainly in private homes for the enjoyment of housewives and maid-servants, some of whom learned to sing these songs themselves. *Baan'ngaan* was performed in brothels and opium dens, while *Lungjau* was performed by beggars on street corners. *Haamseuigo* were songs associated with the so-called "boat-people," fishermen who dwelt permanently on boats that were moored on rivers and seashores throughout the Pearl River Delta.

Narrative songs

While the Cantonese narrative songs were diverse in their social context, they shared certain general features. Singers were of either sex; many were blind and of such low social status that they were sometimes treated little better than beggars and prostitutes. Occasionally a singer's artistry might attract the attention of an educated person who would compose highly refined poems especially for the singer to perform. But in general the audience consisted of people without literary sophistication, and the songs were considered vulgar by the literary class. Changing social conditions and value systems made these songs obsolete, their social functions being replaced by movies, modern popular songs, and other forms of entertainment. In the early part of this century, their popularity allowed them to be absorbed into the operatic repertory. Today the stage is the only place one can hear these tunes, among which the *Naamyam* and the *Muk'yu* are the most often performed.[3]

1. *Naamyam*

A passage of *Naamyam* is generally composed of an opening couplet, a main body of one or two quatrains, and a closing quatrain. The verse structure of a quatrain in the main body is shown in figure 12.1 and the verse structure of the opening couplet in figure 12.2. The closing quatrain (figure 12.3) has a verse structure identical to that of the main body with the exception of an extra three- or four-syllable line added between the third and the fourth lines. Some of the rules that define the verse structure are more rigid than others. For example, the rhyming and linguistic tone patterns for the ending syllables of the second and the fourth lines must be rigidly observed, but those governing the first and the third lines are more flexible. Rules on linguistic tones are more flexible for syllables that do not end a line. The quatrain structure and the phrase structure within a line must also be rigidly observed, but padding syllables can be liberally added. For example, in the opening couplet, instead of three syllables in each phrase of the first line, there may be four or five syllables.

Naamyam uses a single "tune" which is also basically in quatrain form. As a "tune," it

$$
\begin{array}{ll}
L1 & \_\_\_\underline{+}, \_\_\underline{x}R; \\
L2 & \_\_\_\underline{x}, \_\_\underline{+}'R; \\
L3 & \_\_\_\underline{+}, \_\_\underline{x}R; \\
L4 & \_\_\_\underline{x}, \_\_\underline{+}\backslash R.
\end{array}
$$

Figure 12.1 Verse structure of main quatrain of *Naamyam*

$$
\begin{array}{ll}
L1 & \_\_\underline{x}, \_\_\underline{+}'R; \\
L2 & \_\_\_\underline{x}, \_\_\underline{+}\backslash R.
\end{array}
$$

Figure 12.2 Verse structure of opening couplet of *Naamyam*

$$
\begin{array}{ll}
L1 & \_\_\_\underline{+}, \_\_\underline{x}R; \\
L2 & \_\_\_\underline{x}, \_\_\underline{+}'R; \\
L3 & \_\_\_\underline{+}, \_\_\underline{x}R; \\
 & \_\_\underline{x}; \\
L4 & \_\_\_\underline{x}, \_\_\underline{+}\backslash R.
\end{array}
$$

Figure 12.3 Verse structure of closing quatrain of *Naamyam*

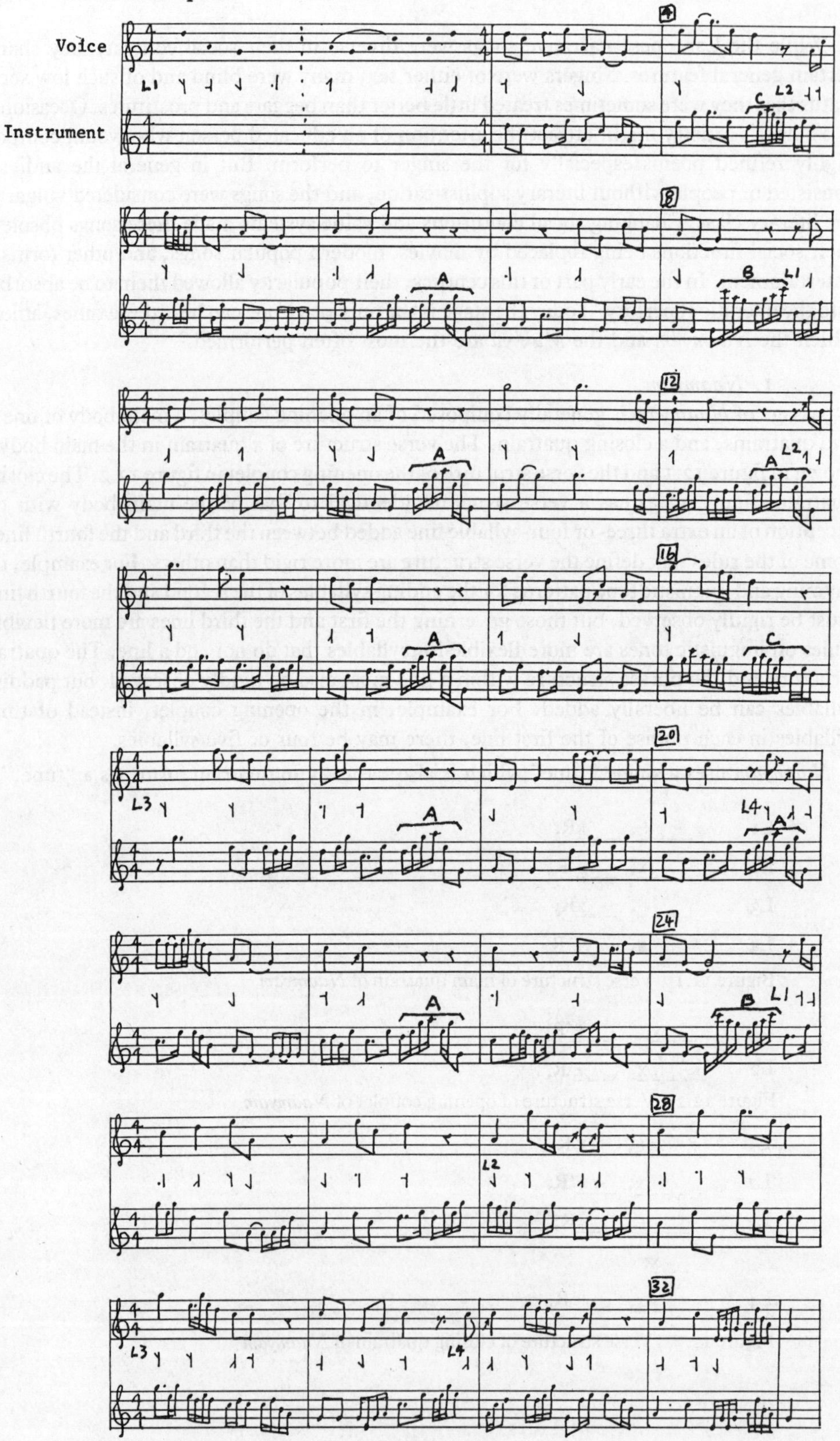

Figure 12.4 An opening couplet and two quatrains of *Naamyam*

Narrative songs

resembles the aria types in being appropriately characterized as a set of tonal and rhythmic patterns, or, from the singer's point of view, a set of rules for composing the melody. The melodic contour is flexible and depends to a large extent upon the linguistic tones of the syllables to which the tune is sung. The tune is also identified by a distinct instrumental prelude and several interludes. Figure 12.4 shows an example of *Naamyam* comprising an opening couplet and a main body of two quatrains (without a closing quatrain). The transcription also shows the instrumental accompaniment and interludes.

The syllable placement is an important identifying mark in the *Naamyam* tune. Three different kinds of syllable placement are commonly used, each of them resulting in a variant form of the tune. Known as *maanbaan* [slow *baan*], *jungbaan* [medium *baan*], and *faaibaan* [fast *baan*], they are shown in figure 12.5.

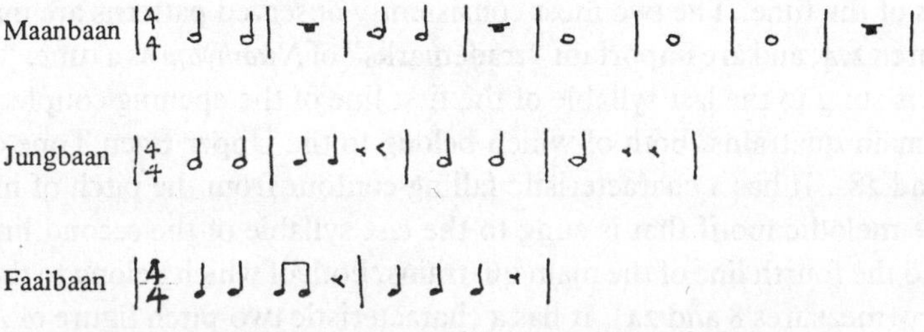

Figure 12.5 Syllable placement of three variants of *Naamyam*

The example shown in figure 12.4 is representative of a *Naamyam* passage used in many plays. It has an opening couplet which begins in free rhythm without a regular and steady beat (indicated by noteheads without stems in the transcription) and without instrumental accompaniment. By the second phrase of the first line, the tune assumes a beat and becomes metrical, and the instrumental ensemble joins in. It is followed by two quatrains (without a closing quatrain); the first is sung according to *jungbaan*, and the second according to *faaibaan*. The many padding syllables in the text are fitted into the prescribed pattern of syllable placement mostly as phrase leader syllables.

The meter for both the *maanbaan* and the *jungbaan* belongs to a pattern called one-*baan*-three-*ding* (one strong beat followed by three weak beats, see chapter 2), transcribed here as a 4/4 meter. The *faaibaan* belongs to a pattern called one-*baan*-one-*ding*, transcribed here as a 2/4 meter. In metronomical terms, the tempo in all three cases is usually about ♩ = 60. Most passages of *Naamyam* comprise one or two quatrains of *jungbaan*. When a passage includes more than one *baan*, it usually begins with one quatrain of a slower *baan* (either slow or medium), followed by a second quatrain of a faster *baan*, as is the case in figure 12.4. The singer in the above example, in lieu of a closing quatrain, adds a melisma to the last syllable which extends the length of the tune for an additional measure.

Naamyam is sung in two *sin*s, the *jingsin* and the *yifaansin*, the latter also known as *muifahong* [plum-blossom style]. The meaning of *sin* here is identical to that which it bears in connection with the aria types: tunes of each *sin* emphasize five of the seven pitches in the Cantonese heptatonic scale. All the quatrains in figure 12.4 are in *jingsin*.

Line-ending pitches are prescribed rigidly for lines with even tones as the last syllable (including both lines in the opening couplet and the second and fourth lines in all the quatrains) and less rigidly for lines which end on an oblique tone (the first and third lines of

Cantonese opera

		jingsin	yifaansin
Opening couplet	L1	D	D
	L2	G	G
Quatrains	L1	D (C, E)	C (F)
	L2	D	D
	L3	C (A)	C
	L4	G	G

Figure 12.6 Line-ending pitches for *Naamyam*

the quatrains). Figure 12.6 shows these line-ending pitches for both *jingsin* and *yifaansin* versions of *Naamyam*. The pitches in parenthesis are occasional variants.

Although the melodic contour is flexible, it contains formulaic patterns that occur at certain fixed points of the tune. The two most consistently observed patterns are marked as "a" and "b" in figure 12.4, and are important "trademarks" of *Naamyam* as a tune: "a" is the melodic motif that is sung to the last syllable of the first line of the opening couplet and the second line of the main quatrains, both of which belong to the Upper Even Tone category (measures 4, 16, and 28). It has a characteristic falling contour from the pitch of high G to pitch D; "b" is the melodic motif that is sung to the last syllable of the second line of the opening couplet and the fourth line of the main quatrains, both of which belong to the Lower Even Tone category (measures 8 and 24). It has a characteristic two-pitch figure of A-G (the melismatic figure added to measure 32 obscures the figure).

Formulaic patterns are even more prominent in the instrumental prelude and interludes. The prelude to *Naamyam* is one of the most popular tunes in the repertory, often performed independently as a song with a poem written to fit it. An example is found in act 1 of *The Magic Pearl* (lines 173–181), where the scholar Si sings the prelude as a way of introducing himself (transcribed in figure 12.7 with the text omitted).

Figure 12.7 Prelude to *Naamyam* sung to a poem

Short instrumental interludes which follow each vocal phrase of the opening couplet and main quatrain (for the *maanbaan* and *jungbaan* versions) are relatively fixed and formulaically placed. Three recurring interludes are marked "A," "B," and "C" in figure 12.4, and are reproduced in figure 12.8. They are placed formulaically according to the pattern shown in figure 12.9. In other words, pattern A is played after phrase 1 of all the lines, and after phrase 1 of lines 1 and 3 of the main quatrain; pattern B is played after phrase 2 of line 2 of the opening couplet and after phrase 2 of line 4 of the main quatrain; pattern C is played after

Narrative songs

Figure 12.8 Three interludes of *Naamyam*

phrase 2 of line 1 of the opening couplet and after phrase 2 of line 2 of the main quatrain. Notice that the placement of some of the interludes is directly related to the linguistic tones of the final syllable of the preceding phrase; in particular, pattern C follows phrases which have an Upper Even Tone as an ending syllable, and pattern B follows phrases which have a Lower Even Tone as an ending syllable.

		P1	P2
Opening Couplet	L1	–	C
	L2	A	B
Main Quatrain	L1	A	A
	L2	A	C
	L3	A	A
	L4	A	B

Figure 12.9 Placement of interludes

The instrumental accompaniment is also characterized by the omission of those instruments with a bright tone color, namely the *erhu* (the two-string bowed lute commonly used as a leading accompanying instrument for most oral delivery types) and the *dizi* (horizontal flute). In their place are the much mellower sounding two-string bowed lute called the *yehu* (two-string bowed lute with half a coconut shell as the soundbox) and the *xiao* (vertical flute). The general effect is a darker and mellower tone quality.

2 *Muk'yu*

The verse structure of *Muk'yu* is identical to that of *Naamyam* as given in figures 12.1, 12.2, and 12.3. Its most distinctive musical characteristic is that it is performed in free rhythm and does not have any instrumental accompaniment. Naturally it does not have different variants according to *baan*. It can, however, be sung in either the *jingsin* or the *yifaansin*. The melodic contour is highly flexible; line-ending pitches are rigidly prescribed for lines 2 and 4, shown in figure 12.10.

	jingsin	yifaansin
L2	E	D
L4	G	G

Figure 12.10 Line-ending pitches for *Muk'yu*

Even though *Muk'yu* does not have a regular beat, its tune nevertheless displays certain discernible rhythmic patterns. For example, the first four syllables are always sung in close temporal succession, while the last three syllables are spaced further apart by being sung with longer note values. The general impression is a tighter first half and a freer second half for each line. The voice always breaks between the two halves. Figure 12.11 shows two quatrains of *Muk'yu* (without the opening couplet or the closing quatrain) taken from lines 55–83 of act 1 of *The Magic Pearl*.

144   Cantonese opera

Naamyam is the most often used narrative song in Cantonese opera. It is chiefly used in tender dialogue scenes between a husband and wife or a pair of lovers, scenes in which the gentle melody and the mellow instrumental accompaniment help to express the emotions of love. The mood can be playful, as in the case of the example in figure 12.4, melancholic, or even tragic. As a rule, the version in *jingsin* is sung to convey a happy mood, while the version in *yifaansin* is sung during tragic moments. At the end of the act 3 of *The Magic Pearl*, Lady Pearl and her lover sing a long passage of *Naamyam* in *yifaansin* before they are forced to bid farewell. *Muk'yu* is used either in dialogue or in a monologue expressing a character's inner emotion. The unaccompanied voice projects a feeling of loneliness and desolation.

Figure 12.11 Two quatrains of *Muk'yu*

13 *Three levels of creative process*

The foregoing chapters have discussed the rules according to which the scriptwriter and, more importantly, the singer create oral delivery types on stage; in most instances they do so without the benefit of musical notation or rehearsal. The focus has been on the identity of individual oral delivery types and on specific factors that affect the creative process, such as the linguistic tones of the text, padding syllables, and *sin*. In this chapter, three broader issues concerning the creative process of music in Cantonese opera will be discussed. First, the script translated in chapter 5 will be used to illustrate how oral delivery types are assembled in relation to one another in an actual dramatic situation. Second, the entire gamut of oral delivery types available for the musical design of an opera will be examined in the context of a speech-song spectrum. Such a spectrum illustrates the diversity of musical expression and suggests the larger historical process through which music evolved to fulfill an aesthetic need. Third, a specific micro-level process in the creation of new versions of a melody will be discussed.

Design and organization of oral delivery types in an act

Act 1 of *The Magic Pearl*, translated in chapter 5, is divided into six scenes, a division based upon this researcher's analysis of the dramatic content of the script. Each scene marks a turn in the dramatic events, often accompanied by the entrance of a main character.

Scene 1. Village people discussing the demons in the lake.
2. Enter God of Law; self-introduction; dialogue with God of Earth.
3. Enter Golden Scale; self-introduction and search for Lady Pearl.
4. Enter Lady Pearl and Little Bou; stroll by the lake.
5. Enter Si; self-introduction; joined by God of Law as boatman and the two women; negotiation on sharing the boat-ride.
6. Boat-ride.

The oral delivery types used in each scene (except *Plain Speech*) are listed in the table shown in figure 13.1. The first column indicates the scene number; the second column gives the location of the oral delivery type in terms of the line numbers used in the translation in chapter 5; the third column lists the names of the oral delivery types; the fourth column specifies the length of the passage in terms of the number of couplets (or quatrains, where applicable) and the internal structure of the aria types ("a" indicates upper line and "b" indicates lower line); the fifth to eighth columns identify whether an oral delivery type belongs to the category of speech type, aria type, fixed tune, or narrative song. Other symbols will be explained in the discussion that follows.

146 Cantonese opera

Scene	Line	Oral delivery type	Number of couplets	Speech Type	Aria Type	Fixed Tune	Narrative Song
1	1	*Patter Speech.*	5 couplets [abab . . .]	×			
2	28	*Poetic Speech–*	1 quatrain	×			
		Percussion Speech–	11 lines	×			
		Gwanfa.	1 couplet [ba]		×'		
		Muk'yu–	2 quatrains				×
		Gwanfa.	1 couplet [ba]		×'		
		Rhymed Speech–	1 quatrain	×			
		Faaidim–	1/2 couplet [b]		×		
		Gwanfa.	1/2 couplet [a]		×'		
3	116	*Faaidim–*	1 and 1/2 couplet [bab]		×		
		Gwanfa.	1/2 couplet [a]		×'		
		Gwanfa.	1 couplet [ba]		×'		
4	136	*Dainty Steps.*				×	
		Gwanfa–	1 couplet [ba]		×'		
		Supported Speech–		×			
		Gwanfa.	1 couplet [ba]		×'		
5	173	*Naamyam* (prelude)–					×
		Gwanfa.	1 couplet [ba]		×'		
		Rowing a Boat.				×	
		Gwanfa.	2 couplets [baba]		×'		
6	243	*Bongji Maanbaan* (interspersed with *Supported Speech*).	2 couplets [baba]	×	×		
		Chatjiching.	3 couplets [bababa]		×		
		Monk Dreams of a Wife.				×	
		Long Gwanfa–	1 couplet [ba]		×		
		Gwanfa.	1 couplet [ba]		×'		
		Long Yiwong.	1 couplet [ba]		×		
		When the Petals Fall.				×	
		Gwanfa.	1 couplet [ba]		×'		
		Gwanfa.	2 couplets [baba]		×'		

Figure 13.1 Summary of oral delivery types in act 1 of *The Magic Pearl*

The core of a scene comprises several song passages, which are usually separated by *Plain Speech*. Each song passage consists either of several oral delivery types sung in sequence, such as the *Poetic Speech – Percussion Speech – Gwanfa* sequence in scene 2, or of two oral delivery types in alternation as in the *Bongji Maanbaan – Supported Speech* pattern in scene 6. Occasionally a song passage consists of a single oral delivery type, such as the fixed tune *Dainty Steps* in scene 4 and the *Patter Speech* in scene 1. Figure 13.1 identifies the end of a song passage by a period "."; oral delivery types belonging to the same song passage are connected by dashes "–".

The grouping of several tunes to form a "suite" is a practice found in many kinds of Chinese opera, including the *zaju* of the Yuan dynasty and the Peking opera of today. Various patterns of such groupings have been developed for some particular kinds of regional opera.

Three levels of creative process

In Peking opera, for example, a particularly elaborate pattern consists of grouping several aria types in a sequence that progresses from slow to fast tempo, "eventually the aria reaches such a high pitch that the only way to bring it to a close is to break down the rhythm in the last line, using more rubato and long, held notes."[1] A similar pattern is known to be used in Cantonese opera before the major reforms in the early part of this century; a typical grouping began with a free-rhythmed aria type called *Saubaan* [Introductory *Baan*] followed by *Maanbaan* [Slow *Baan*] and *Jungbaan* [Medium *Baan*], ending with the free-rhythmed *Gwanfa*.[2]

The above table suggests that, for Cantonese opera today, elaborate groupings such as the slow-to-fast sequence involving three or more aria types are not employed. Instead, there appears to be a simple rule involving the use of the aria type *Gwanfa* as a terminal marker for a song passage and for a scene. *Gwanfa*, indicated by ×' in the table, is obviously the most often used among all the oral delivery types (except *Plain Speech*). Figure 13.1 indicates that all the scenes (except scene 1) end with *Gwanfa*. Furthermore, many of the song passages (except for the ones in scene 6, which will be discussed later) also end with *Gwanfa*. Using scene 2 as an example, such passages include the *Poetic Speech – Percussion Speech – Gwanfa* sequence, the *Muk'yu– Gwanfa* sequence, and the *Rhymed Speech – Faaidim – Gwanfa* sequence. Thus *Gwanfa* serves an important structural function. It is interesting to note that the *Gwanfa* of Cantonese opera is known to be historically related to the *yaoban* of Peking opera, and that the two share the distinct feature of being free-rhythmed; that they also share a similar function in their relation to other aria types underscores the common origin of the two kinds of operas.[3]

Scene 6, which is the longest and the core of the entire act, is quite different from the others in the design of oral delivery types. The scriptwriter clearly intended it to be one long lyrical scene in which the lovers express their feelings for each other and discover that their love is futile. The entire scene consists of one song passage after another without any apparent grouping. The *Long Gwanfa – Gwanfa* sequence used in the middle of the scene is intended not as a terminal marker but to draw attention to a dramatically significant moment: Lady Pearl is going to give up her Magic Pearl. This use of *Gwanfa* to heighten a dramatic moment further parallels the use of similarly free-rhythmed aria types in Peking opera.[4]

Often *Plain Speech* is wedged in between two oral delivery types within a song passage, and sometimes even in between two lines of a single oral delivery type. In scene 6 between lines 326 and 331, the two lines of *Gwanfa* sung by Lady Pearl are interrupted in the middle by Little Bou with a line of *Plain Speech* that comments on Lady Pearl's first line.

Plain Speech sometimes alternates with another oral delivery type to form a repetitive pattern; an example is in scene 2, lines 55–83, where the God of Law interrogates the God of Earth using *Muk'yu* and *Plain Speech*. Another example of such alternation is in scene 6, lines 245–276, where the four main characters carry on a dialogue by singing *Bongji Maanbaan* and alternating each line with *Supported Speech*.

Oral delivery types are often used in passages of dialogue in which characters each sing a line in turn. An example is the *Muk'yu* in scene 2 shared by the Gods of Law and Earth as they converse. In scene 6, the scriptwriter carefully designed the two couplets of the *Bongji Maanbaan* so that each of the four characters sings one line in turn. The instrumental interludes for this aria type are conveniently used as the accompaniment for lines of *Supported Speech* that are wedged in between the four sung lines.

Plain Speech may also be inserted in the middle of a line, as in scene 5, lines 219–227, where a line of *Gwanfa* is interrupted by an exchange in *Plain Speech*, and again in scene 6, lines 336–345, where a line of *Long Yiwong* is broken into two segments. Although many of these insertions are extemporaneously added by the performers, the examples given above are all written into the script. It should be noted that insertions of *Plain Speech* in the middle of a line occur only in aria types and narrative songs but never in fixed tunes, which are always sung as an uninterrupted whole. Speech types with rigid verse structure, such as *Poetic Speech* and *Percussion Speech*, are also never interrupted.

Aria types and fixed tunes occupy a much greater proportion of performing time (about 90 per cent) than speech types and narrative songs (not counting *Plain Speech*). Even though figure 13.1 shows that many more aria types than fixed tunes are used in an act, each category occupies about the same amount of time because aria types are much shorter, sometimes extending no further than a single line. Speech types and narrative songs each occupy about 5 per cent of the time. This observation on the distribution of the oral delivery types is based on a quick survey of about a dozen opera scripts. As a general rule, the scriptwriter designs the music so that the fixed tunes and aria types are evenly distributed relative to one other. Act 1 of *The Magic Pearl* illustrates this rule clearly, although the fact that the four fixed tunes in the act are separated by exactly three aria types in each instance is probably coincidental.

The speech types and the narrative songs, whether they are in couplet form (*Patter Speech*) or in quatrain form (*Poetic Speech, Rhymed Speech, Muk'yu*), always appear in one complete unit or multiple of units; in other words, such an oral delivery type always begins with the first line of a unit and end with the last line. The situation is different for aria types: always in couplet form, they appear most often singly, sometimes in a string of two or more couplets, and occasionally in half-couplet segments. With few exceptions, aria types begin with the lower line and end with the upper line; this is indicated in the table above by the letters "a" and "b" in square brackets. This phenomenon reflects two important rules pertaining to the verse structure (and therefore to the tune) that govern the relationship between the aria types throughout an entire opera. First, all the lines of aria types in the entire opera consistently alternate between upper line and lower line, regardless of whether or not two consecutive lines are interrupted by other kinds of oral delivery types. As an example, extracting all the aria types in scene 6 in their sequence of occurrence, one gets: *Bongji Maanbaan* [b-a-b-a]–*Chatjiching* [b-a-b-a-b-a] – *Long Gwanfa* [b-a] – *Gwanfa* [b-a] – *Gwanfa* [b-a] – *Gwanfa* [b-a]. Note that two fixed tunes are fitted in between some of these aria types, while others are interrupted by *Plain Speech* and other dramatic happenings on stage. Nevertheless the alternation of upper line and lower line is rigidly observed.

Second, again taking scene 6 as an example, one notes that all song passages (with one or more aria types) begin with the lower line and end with the upper line, a pattern which can be seen not only in the rest of the play, but in all plays of Cantonese opera. This rule was emphasized by the noted performer Mai Bingrong (in an interview dated August 9, 1975), who explained that "ending a passage after an upper line adds a sense of suspense and anticipation and thus helps the forward momentum of the play; if passages end with a lower line, there is too much of a sense of finality." Mai added that an exception to the rule is the final song passage which ends a play: the aria type then ends with a lower line. Mai also pointed out that the *paizi* tune which accompanies the raising of the curtain at the start of a play serves the function of an upper line; consequently the first aria type of the play always begins with the lower line, as exemplified by act 1 of *The Magic Pearl* in which *Gwanfa* in scene 2 (the first aria type of the play) begins with the lower line.

When there are more than one aria types in a song passage, it is often the *Gwanfa* that ends such a passage with half a couplet. For example, in scene 2, half a couplet of *Faaidim* (lower) ends with half a couplet of *Gwanfa* (upper); in scene 3, one and a half couplets of *Faaidim* end with half a couplet (upper) of *Gwanfa*. In both cases, a single upper line of *Gwanfa* replaces the upper line of *Faaidim* to serve as a terminal marker. Such usage of *Gwanfa* is quite common, resulting in an odd number of lines of the original aria type it replaces in the passage (such as the b-a-b sequence of *Faaidim* in scene 3).[5]

The scriptwriter of *The Magic Pearl*, Su Weng, discussed the writing of a script at an interview conducted on July 19, 1975. On the general structure of a Cantonese opera, Mr. Su says that there is no rigid rule on the number of acts or scenes, but that the whole play should last somewhere between three and four hours. After having decided on a rough outline of the story, he designs the acts and scenes which must revolve around major and minor dramatic high-points. At the end of an act, there should be suspense so that the audience is led to look forward to the next act. According to him, some scriptwriters write various parts of the script out of order of the progression of the play; but he writes from the very beginning through to the end. When he comes to those parts that need to be sung, he "knows" which oral delivery type should be used; he then writes the song text accordingly.

As regards the dramatic meaning of the various oral delivery types, he says that some have obviously strong and specific associations, while others do not. The choice of an oral delivery type often depends on other factors, such as a consideration of the overall balance and distribution of the various oral delivery types by reason of their musical properties. He says that sometimes he chooses one type solely because it has not been used in the rest of the play.

The aria type called *Faansin Jungbaan* (short for *Jingsin Sapji Faansin Jungbaan*) is the most popular today among audiences. For this reason, a scriptwriter always tries to include several passages in a play. In fact the aria type has gained such status that the privilege of singing it tends to be reserved for, and demanded by, the principal male and female roles, almost to the exclusion of supporting performers. Its dramatic associations are somewhat sad and romantic, but not tragic. Because of its romantic nuance, it is never sung by comic roles. In its place, *Muk'yu*, which is also for sad moments, but not romantic, is likely to be used (see scene 2 of act 1 of *The Magic Pearl*). For tragic moments, various aria types in the *yifaansin* are used. But for truly heart-wrenching scenes, the only effective oral delivery types are certain fixed tunes.

Some oral delivery types have quite specific functions, such as *Patter Speech*, which is used as a vehicle to narrate a large quantity of information, as in the beginning of *The Magic Pearl* (scene 1). *Poetic Speech* is used as a means for self-introduction (scene 2), and *Rhymed Speech* for dialogues (scene 2).

Speech–song spectrum

One of Mr. Su's most intriguing observations is that the choice of oral delivery type often does not depend on dramatic demands but rather on considerations of overall balance and distribution among all the oral delivery types in a particular act or scene. This point is also reflected in the published statements in *Yueju changqiang*. "In linking together aria types and fixed tunes, one should first consider their [musical] properties so that the dramatic situation and characterization are appropriately expressed. In addition, one should also consider whether the melodic transition is smooth, and whether rhythmic change and modal design are rich and varied" (p. 244). "There is no rigid rule on how the aria types and fixed tunes follow each other. In most cases, the fixed tunes are wedged among aria types so that modal and melodic diversity is enhanced" (p. 326).

It is beyond the scope of this study to determine the specific aesthetic standards of "balance and distribution" of oral delivery types. However, it is worthwhile to note the great variety of musical material available for use in Cantonese opera, which is one of its outstanding characteristics. For example, both aria types and fixed tunes, as well as several different speech types, are used. Comparatively, most regional operas use only aria types or only fixed tunes, and few employ a diversity of speech types.

Until the early part of this century, Cantonese opera did not use fixed tunes or narrative songs. The number of aria types was smaller than it is today, and there did not exist a variety of speech types. During the first few decades of the century, particularly in the 1920s and 1930s, fixed tunes and narrative songs were introduced and became a regular part of the musical vocabulary. New aria types were developed from existent ones, and new speech types emerged. Different *sin*s came to be regularly employed for many kinds of oral delivery types. Although it is not known exactly how, when, and by whom these new musical materials were introduced and promoted, one can assume that their appearance and wide usage met an aesthetic demand for variety. Such variety also generated the overall "balance and distribution" of oral delivery types that are evident in today's performances. From the larger historical perspective, the marked increase of musical diversity reflects a collective creative process within the Cantonese operatic community.

In order to assess the diversity analytically, this section will examine the whole gamut of speech types, aria types, fixed tunes and narrative songs in the context of a speech–song spectrum. Speech and song are two modes of auditory communication, both of which comprise words expressed in terms of rhythmic and tonal patterns; the dividing line between them is at times difficult to draw. In this book, instead of regarding them as two mutually exclusive entities, a single term "oral delivery" has been used to embrace both modes of communication. A spectrum can be constructed along which various modes of communication can be located, at one end of the spectrum is what is generally accepted as "speech," at the other end "song."

Cantonese opera, in which a performer delivers his words in a great number of oral delivery types, offers the opportunity to study this spectrum; the spectrum in turn clarifies the precise nature of the diversity of musical material. At one end is *Baak* [*Plain Speech*], which has no particular verse structure and does not involve any prescribed rhythmic or tonal patterns in its delivery. At the other end are various fixed tunes, each of which involves a well-defined melody and a text that must fit that melody's tonal and rhythmic structure; a fixed tune is unambiguously a "song" in the conventional sense of the word because it has a well-defined musical identity. In between these two extremes are other oral delivery types, each of which is characterized by various kinds of rhythmic and tonal patterns.

The presence of certain rhythmic and tonal patterns makes an oral delivery type more like a "song," while their absence makes it more like "speech." One can therefore propose several "musical parameters," the presence or absence of which determines the "degree of musicality" and thus the position of an oral delivery type along the spectrum. These proposed musical parameters can be summarized as follows:

Three levels of creative process

1. A verse structure in the text that involves prescribed patterns on rhyming and linguistic tones.
2. The verse structure of the text that defines the number of syllables in a phrase, the number of phrases in a line, and the number of lines in a cyclical unit of text.
3. A definite and steady beat in the oral delivery.
4. Musical tones, understood here as tones with stable pitches and with consistent intervallic relationships among them such that a scale can be abstracted.
5. Prescribed rhythmic patterns.
6. Prescribed melodic patterns.
7. Instrumental accompaniment.

Figure 13.2 shows eight representative oral delivery types listed in columns, and the musical parameters that each one comprises listed in rows. The boxes indicate the value of the parameters, which depends on the presence and absence of a pattern. For the purpose of a preliminary study, only three values will be assigned: black signifies the presence of a pattern used with consistency, white signifies the absence of any pattern, and grey signifies either a pattern used flexibly or a pattern that is relatively simple in terms of its structure. The number of black and grey boxes in a column therefore suggests the degree of musicality of an oral delivery type.

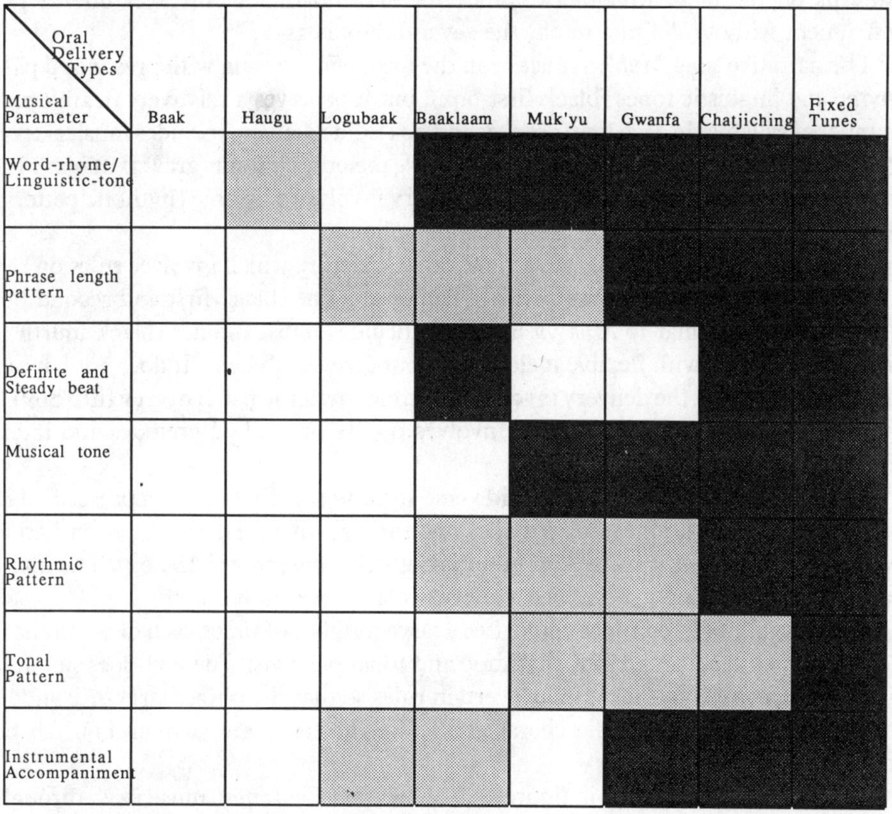

Figure 13.2 Oral delivery types in a speech–song spectrum

The eight oral delivery types, all of which have been discussed in earlier chapters, are ordered in a sequence according to their degree of musicality, and are briefly discussed as follows. *Baak*, or *Plain Speech*, has no black boxes because its text and delivery do not conform to any pattern. It is the least "musical" of all the oral delivery types.

The speech type *Haugu*, or *Rhymed Speech*, has a couplet structure that does not involve restrictions on the number of syllables in each line but does entail somewhat flexible rules on the rhyme and linguistic tonal patterns for the last syllables of each phrase (grey first box). There is no prescribed manner for the delivery of the text.

The speech type *Logubaak*, or *Percussion Speech*, has no rigid verse structure, nor is it required to observe rules on rhyme and linguistic tones. It observes a somewhat flexible pattern of four syllables in each phrase (grey second box). There is no prescribed manner for the delivery, but instrumental accompaniment is obligatory and must follow certain patterns. Since the accompaniment involves only percussion instruments which do not have definite pitch, the seventh box is grey rather than black to indicate relative simplicity.

The speech type *Baaklaam*, or *Patter Speech*, exhibits a verse structure that defines rhyme and linguistic tonal patterns (black first box) and somewhat flexible patterns as regards the number of phrases in each line and the number of syllables in each phrase (grey second box). The singer and the percussion ensemble must follow a definite beat (black third box) and a flexible set of rhythmic patterns (grey fifth box). The delivery is accomplished by prescribed patterns on the large woodblock. Since the accompaniment involves only a percussion instrument without definite pitch, the seventh box is grey.

The narrative song *Muk'yu* must be in the form of a quatrain with prescribed patterns for rhyme and linguistic tones (black first box), but it observes a relatively flexible rule on the number of syllables in each line (grey second box). The delivery includes musical tones (black fourth box) and cadential formulas with flexible melodic contour (grey sixth box). It does not have a definite and steady beat, but the delivery involves a flexible rhythmic pattern (greyed fifth box). There is no instrumental accompaniment.

The aria type *Gwanfa* observes a rigid verse structure which involves rules on rhyme and linguistic tones and on the number of syllables in a line (black first and second boxes). Its delivery is very similar to *Muk'yu* in that it includes musical tones (black fourth box) and cadential formulas with flexible melodic contour (grey sixth box). It does not have a definite and steady beat, but the delivery involves a flexible rhythmic pattern (grey fifth box). There is instrumental accompaniment which involves rigidly prescribed preludes and interludes to the voice (black seventh box).

The aria type *Chatjiching* has a rigid verse structure, definite beat, a prescribed rhythmic pattern, and musical tones (black boxes one through five). There are prescribed cadential patterns but the specific melodic contour is quite flexible (grey sixth box). The instrumental accompaniment follows prescribed patterns (black seventh box).

The category of fixed tunes comprises a large number of tunes each of which has definite beat and pitch, and prescribed rhythmic and tonal patterns. The text does not adhere to a rigid text structure, but must follow certain rules so that the phrase structure and linguistic tonal patterns fit the melodic characteristics of the tune (see chapter 11). All boxes are therefore black.

The analysis summarized in figure 13.2 shows that Cantonese musicians, through change and innovation since the turn of the century, have exploited the permutations of various

Three levels of creative process

musical parameters to produce a wide variety in the manner of text-delivery along the speech–song spectrum. It is a relatively more "finely-tuned" spectrum than those that could be constructed for other Chinese operas. On a more general level, the analysis illustrates the problem of defining speech and song as two mutually exclusive modes of communication. At least in Cantonese opera, a single concept of oral delivery, within which are recognized many modes of communication, seems to be a more accurate reflection of reality.

Tempo change and melodic expansion and contraction

A singer uses a variety of means to vary an oral delivery type, among which an important process is one based upon tempo change coupled with melodic expansion or contraction. Most oral delivery types are performed at different tempos, although within particular passages the tempo is usually quite constant. A quick check shows that the nine versions of *Chatjiching* shown in figure 7.2, which are drawn from four passages, vary in metronomic markings from ♩ = 102 to ♩ = 126, with an average of about 120. However, the version of *Chatjiching* in act 1 of *The Magic Pearl* (line 279), transcribed in figure 13.3, has a metronomic marking of only about ♩ = 32, almost four times as slow as the other versions, even though it is still labeled as *Chatjiching*.

The various features that identify this aria type, such as verse structure, syllable placement, cadential pitches, and so forth, remain unchanged. What is significantly different is that the melody is very melismatic: the versions in figure 7.2 are almost all in quarter notes and eighth notes, while the version in figure 13.3 uses many sixteenth and even thirty-second notes. Despite such differences, the density of notes in real time remains about the same. However, the density of text-syllables sung in real time is quite different: in one case, the syllables are spaced far apart temporally while in the other they are closely bunched together.

The two kinds of *Chatjiching* exemplify how some aria types can be performed in two or three somewhat standardized and distinct ways based upon what may be best described as "tempo" differences. In the case of *Chatjiching*, the melismatic version is sometimes desig-

Figure 13.3 A "slow" version of *Chatjiching*

nated by means of the prefix *maan*, meaning "slow." The syllabic version is generally not so designated. A third version of *Chatjiching* designated by means of the prefix *faai*, meaning "fast," is actually the aria type *Faaidim*. Sometimes these "tempo" differences are indicated in the opera script; at other times they are not. It should also be noted that the nomenclature applied to the various versions is not consistent. For example, in *The Magic Pearl*, the slow version is labeled *Chatjiching* without a prefix, the medium version is *Chatjiching* prefixed with the word *song*, meaning "crisp," and the fast version is called *Faaidim*.

The difference between the "fast" and the "slow" versions of an aria type is obviously not the same as a simple "tempo" difference in Western music. The Western concept of tempo has more to do with subjective evaluation than the objective measurement of a structural feature. There is still no generally accepted method by which to measure the degree of "fastness" or "slowness" of a piece of music, or to compare quantitatively the tempo of two pieces.[6] However, the same piece of music is often performed at different tempos, which can be distinguished quantitatively by metronomic markings. In such cases, tempo difference is defined as a change in the real-time density of the same set of musical events. In other words, tempo change involves a proportional change in the duration of tones and of pauses between all adjacent pairs of tones that form the tune. The tune itself, in so far as the number and sequence of tones and their rhythmic relationships are concerned, remains unchanged.

In Cantonese opera (and many other kinds of Chinese music), when a tune slows down to beyond a certain point (or is simply performed at a slower "tempo" throughout), new tones may be inserted so that the real-time density of musical events is either the same or actually increases. Nevertheless, the tune *does* create the effect of having been slowed down because its original tones are further apart in real time; and more importantly, the pulse defined by the original tune, often marked by a woodblock in Cantonese opera, moves more slowly than before.

In order to study what new tones are inserted among the old ones and according to what rhythmic configurations are they inserted, it is necessary to examine versions of an aria type that are sung to the same text so that adjustments to linguistic tones do not become a factor. Figure 13.4 shows two versions of the aria type *Jingsin Sapji Yiwong Maanbaan*: one is prefixed with *maan*, "slow," the other with *faai*, "fast"; the two versions are sung to the same text. Instrumental interludes are included in the transcription with stems up.[7]

A comparison of the two versions shows that the "fast" version comprises mainly quarter and eighth notes while the "slow" version comprises a large number of sixteenth and thirty-second notes. Yet the melodies are in fact quite similar because of the pitches that are shared at what may be called "nodal" points: many of the attack points of the syllables and some of the strong beats of each measure. Eight out of ten attack points (for the ten syllables) and twenty out of thirty-two strong beats are sung to the same pitches for the two versions.

In some places, such as the first two beats of measure 2, the "nodes" are close to one another; the "slow" version simply inserts two, three, or four notes in between the notes of the "fast" version. In others, the nodes are spaced further apart; for example, in measures 4 and 5, the two versions of melody cross paths only at the first strong beat of measure 4, the first of measure 5, and the last of measure 5. Between these "nodes," the "slow" version develops the melody in the high tessitura; the "fast" version in the low tessitura. That the two interludes at measures 4 and 5 develop at different tessituras is related to the vocal phrase immediately preceding them. It is a general rule that the instrumental ensemble imitates the

Three levels of creative process

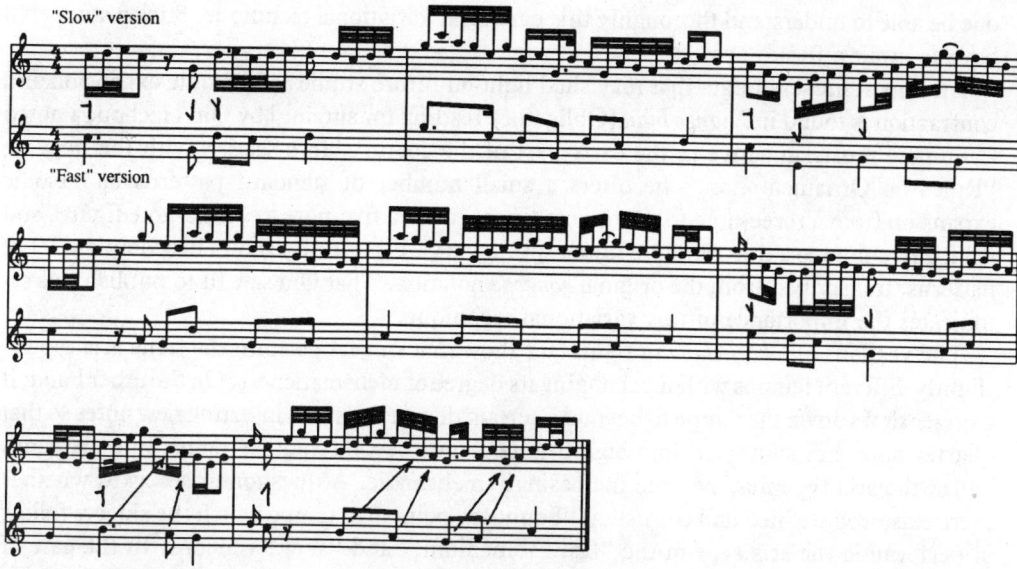

Figure 13.4 "Slow" and "fast" versions of *Jingsin Sapji Yiwong Maanbaan*

vocal line to create interludes. In this case, the sixth syllable (third beat of measure 3) is sung to a melodic phrase that swirls up to the high G in the "slow" version, while in the "fast" version, it stays at the vicinity of the low G. The interludes in the respective versions simply imitate and elaborate these vocal phrases.

A comparison of the two versions should of course go beyond an examination of the static "nodes." Measure 8 offers an example of a different kind of melodic variation, which may be termed "rhythmic displacement." The arrows in figure 13.4 show that the melodic figures at the second and third beats in the "fast" version are "displaced" into a later point in the "slow" version.

The above discussion illustrates one way in which Cantonese operatic singers and instrumentalists create new versions of an old tune by what may be appropriately called melodic expansion (or contraction) of a tune coupled with "tempo" change. Each process involves two steps carried out simultaneously. In melodic expansion, the tune "slows down" and new notes are inserted into the melody; in melodic contraction, the tune "speeds up" and some of the notes in the original melody are deleted. The aggregate result is that, in expansion, the new tune is longer in duration than the old tune, and, in contraction, it is shorter. The note-density (number of notes in every unit of real time) generally does not change significantly in either case. From the historical-evolutionary perspective, it is not known which of the versions in figure 13.4, both of which are performed today, is the original tune and which the derivative.[8]

It is also clear from the brief and preliminary analysis above that melodic expansion and contraction involve more than a process of simply adding or deleting notes. For example, the distances between "nodes" are different at different points of the tune; the melodic expansion may be affected by the preceding phrase; and other variational techniques such as "rhythmic displacement" may occur. Only by analysing a large quantity of such versions will one be able to understand thoroughly this particular variational technique. Such a study will have to await a future project.

An important set of data that may shed light on future studies of melodic expansion and contraction is found in *Xiange bidu* [Obligatory reading for singing] by Qiu Hechou, a noted Cantonese musician active in the early part of the century. In a section with the heading "Rules on Ornamentation," he offers a small number of standard patterns of melodic expansion from a three-note to a five-note figure, from a five-note to a nine-note figure, and from a five-note to a thirteen-note figure (pp. 43–45). Figure 13.5 shows his complete set of patterns, transcribed from the original *gongche* notation. That Qiu saw fit to publish this set indicates the importance of this variational technique.

The versions of *Chatjiching* in figure 7.2 show that singers perform the same aria type at slightly different tempos without changing its degree of melismaticness. On the other hand, if a singer slows down the tempo to beyond a certain degree, he starts inserting new notes so that quarter notes are converted into eighth notes, and, beyond another point, into sixteenth notes; the aria type may become increasingly melismatic. A question arises as to whether there exist well-defined and consistent "boundary points" in tempo which the singers follow in performing the aria type in the "fast," "medium," and "slow" versions. In the case of *Chatjiching*, a survey of a large number of versions indicates that no such rigid and precise "boundaries" are discerned. On the other hand, neither do there exist versions slower than about ♩ = 100 with mostly quarter notes. Indeed, the singer is given a certain degree of choice in varying the tempo of a tune without ascending or descending to a new level of "melismaticness."

Figure 13.5 Rules on melodic expansion by Qiu

Three levels of creative process

The technique of variation through tempo change coupled with melodic expansion or contraction is a standard one in many other kinds of Chinese music, notably the instrumental ensemble music called *Jiangnan Sizhu*.[9] Such changes are sometimes referred to as a change of *baan* (*ban* in Peking dialect). In Cantonese opera (and other kinds of regional opera such as Peking opera), however, a change of *baan* is similar but not identical to the process described here. As is discussed in some detail in chapter 7, a change of *baan* involves mainly a change in syllable placement, but sometimes also in metrical pattern (of strong and weak beats) and in the melismaticness of the tune-text relationship. Thus changes in *baan* and in "tempo" are independent: examples in figure 13.4 illustrate that there can be "tempo" changes within one and the same *baan*. Both the *maanbaan* and *jungbaan* categories of aria types within the *bongji* family can be sung in two or three different "tempos."

However, changes of *baan* and of "tempo" may also be historically related. The theory proposed here is that a change of "tempo" might lead to the evolution of a new version based upon a different *baan*. This theory is supported by the three "tempo" versions of *Chatjiching*. It has already been mentioned that its "fast-tempo" version, referred to as *Faai-Chatjiching* (or fast-*Chatjiching*), is identical to *Faaidim*. Chapter 7 has shown that *Faaidim* has a different syllable placement from that found in the slower versions of *Chatjiching*. To many musicians today, and in many opera scripts, *Faaidim* is considered an aria type different from *Chatjiching*. To others, it is simply another version of *Chatjiching* with a faster "tempo." Thus we have an example of an intermediary stage in the evolution of aria types based upon different *baan*.

Appendix 1 Linguistic tones, romanization system, and pronunciation guide

Linguistic tones

Chinese is a so-called tonal language, one in which pitch is used not only as intonation for speech, but also as a syllable-differentiating agent, serving the same distinctive function as vowels or consonants. The relative pitch levels, the contour of pitch movement, and the duration of pitch, may all be phonemically significant in the spoken language. A linguistic tone refers to these pitch properties of a spoken syllable. Each Chinese dialect has a small number of tonal categories, into which all syllables spoken in that dialect fall.

Cantonese dialect refers to the dialect of Canton (Guangzhou), the capital of the southern province of Guangdong. As one of the nine main groups of dialects in China, it and its variants are spoken in the western half of the province (including Hong Kong), in the southern half of Guangxi province, and in many overseas settlements. Compared to other dialects, Cantonese has a relatively complex system of nine tonal categories, involving different pitch levels, rising and falling inflections, and long and short durations. Their characteristics can be transcribed with simple symbols: a simplified time-pitch graph is drawn to the left of a vertical reference line that represents pitch height. The pitch height is divided into five points, 1, 2, 3, 4, 5, representing relatively low to high pitch levels respectively. Thus, "⌐", or 55, stands for a tone that begins high, remains high, and ends high. "⌐", or 12, stands for a tone that begins very low and rises to a medium low point. "⌐", or 5, stands for a tone that begins high but is short and ends abruptly. Using these linguistic tonal symbols, the nine tones, with their names, can be represented in figure A1.1.[1]

Nonsense syllables, which do not have specific linguistic tones, are given the symbol "|" when they are transcribed in the musical examples in this book.

Linguists do not completely agree on the behavior of the nine tones and have published different models of the tones. The major disagreement is in the two Even Tones. Beijing suggests that both Even Tones should have level contours (55 and 11).[2] Hashimoto and Wong suggest that both Even Tones could have either level contours (55 and 11) or falling

Upper Even	Upper Rising	Upper Going	Upper Entering
53 or 55	35	33	5

			Middle Entering
			3

Lower Even	Lower Rising	Lower Going	Lower Entering
21	23	22	2

Figure A1.1 Table of linguistic tonal symbols

contours (53 and 21 ↘).³ Chao's model, different from the above, has been presented in figure A1.1. In this book, since the discrepancies among the models will not cause any major problem in the discussion, the two Even Tones are assigned falling contours throughout. The result of this study may shed some light on the discrepancies (see chapter 8). The actual pitch of the levels and the size of intervals depend upon sex, individual style, and the speaker's mood.

Among the syllables with abrupt endings (Entering Tones), linguists distinguish some which have relatively longer duration than the others. Similarly, among syllables without abrupt endings (all other tone categories), linguists distinguish some that have relatively longer durations than others. In this book, all Entering Tone syllables are considered to have a relatively shorter duration than the other tonal categories. This has been experimentally verified.⁴

There is another prosodic rule of long standing which separates all Chinese tones into two large categories. One is the so-called even tones, which include the upper even and the lower even tones of the present-day Cantonese, and the other is the oblique tones, which include the other seven tones of Cantonese. This classical dichotomy of tones has been used by poets for many centuries, and is still honored by scriptwriters and performers of Cantonese opera.

Romanization system

The romanization system in the Peking dialect is according to the *pinyin* system. In the Cantonese dialect, it is an adaptation of the so-called Yale system.⁵ The following are guides for pronunciation for the Cantonese dialect.

A pronunciation guide to initials for the Yale system

Initial	As in
B	s<u>p</u>ill
CH	between i<u>ts h</u>igh and rea<u>ch h</u>igh
D	s<u>t</u>ill
F	<u>f</u>ar
G	s<u>k</u>ill
GW	s<u>qu</u>ill
H	<u>h</u>oe
J	between <u>j</u>udge and a<u>dds</u>
K	ro<u>ck h</u>ill
KW	as<u>k wh</u>y
L	<u>l</u>ay
M	<u>m</u>a
N	<u>n</u>o
NG	si<u>ng</u>
P	u<u>ph</u>ill
S	between <u>s</u>he and <u>s</u>ee
T	an<u>th</u>ill
W	<u>w</u>et
Y	<u>y</u>

Appendix 1

A pronunciation guide to finals for the Yale System

Final	As in
A	pa (father)
AAI	eye
AAU	cow
AAM	palm
AAN	barn
AANG	gong (in standard American English pronounced with vowel of "father")
AAP	harp
AAT	art
AAK	ark
AI	tight
AU	no English equivalent; German bau
AM	sum
AN	sun
ANG	hung
AP	cup (the "p" is not exploded)
AT	but (the "t" is not exploded)
AK	duck (the "k" is not exploded)
E	yes or air
ENG	length
EK	echo
EI	sleigh
EU	her without the "r" sound
EUNG	urn changing the "n" sound to "ng" without the "r"
EUK	jerk without the "r"
EUI	no English equivalent; hurry without the "rr"
EUN	no English equivalent; sun with lips rounded
EUT	no English equivalent; jut with lips rounded
I	see
IU	view
IM	teem
IN	seen
IP	deep
ING	half way between -eng and -ing
IK	sick
O	saw
OI	hoist
ON	lawn
ONG	long
OT	ought
OK	hawk
OU	so
U	too

UI	ph<u>ooey</u>
UN	m<u>oo</u>n
UT	b<u>oo</u>t
UNG	no English equivalent; German j<u>ung</u>
UK	b<u>ook</u>
YU	no English equivalent; German <u>ü</u>
YUN	no English equivalent; French <u>une</u>
YUT	no English equivalent; French <u>ut</u>

"A word" and "a syllable"

One problem in romanizing Chinese is the confusion between "a word" and "a syllable." The written Chinese consists of individual and well-defined ideograms (or characters) each of which is pronounced as a single syllable. This led to the view that Chinese is "monosyllabic." However, even though many of these single characters are "words" in the sense that "a word" means in English, some Chinese "words" are composed of more than one character, and hence more than one syllable. Thus Chinese should not be considered monosyllabic.

In romanizing names, titles, and technical terms, the general practice today is to take the polysyllabic nature of Chinese into consideration and group the syllable-compounds that are considered as "a word" in Chinese into "a word" in English. For example, the instrument *erhu*, though written in two separate characters in Chinese, will be romanized as one single English word rather than two separate words such as *er hu*. Such groupings also serve to avoid the appearance of a string of short "words." In cases where the division between syllables is not clear, so as to create difficulty in pronunciation, such as the word *baanngaan* (a kind of narrative song), a prime will be used to separate the two syllables as follows: *baan'ngaan*.

In romanizing song texts, each written Chinese character will be romanized separately in English. Thus if *erhu* appears in the song text, it *will* be romanized as *er hu*.

Appendix 2   Notes on transcription symbols

The following are the symbols and their meanings used in this book to represent verse structure of text:

"_" = a syllable
"," = end of a phrase
";" = end of a line
"." = end of a couplet or a quatrain
x = oblique tone
+ = even tone, unspecified
+' = upper even tone
+\ = lower even tone
R = rhyme
L1 or "a" = first line of couplet (or quatrain)
L2 or "b" = second line of couplet (or quatrain)
L3 or "c" = third line of quatrain

162 *Appendix 3*

　　　　L4 or "d" = fourth line of quatrain
　　　　P1 = first phrase
　　　　P2 = second phrase
　　　　P3 = third phrase
　　　　P4 = fourth phrase

The following are the symbols and their meanings used in the transcription of music in staff notation:

　　　♩̇ = a staccato note
　　　↗♩ = an upward or downward glide to or from a note. The interval is indefinite but is usually small. The duration is indefinite but is usually short.
　　　♩̃ = slightly higher or lower than the given pitch. The departure from the given pitch is indefinite but does not exceed a quarter note.
　　　♩̽ = a spoken syllable with uncertain pitch
　　　, = a short break in the continuity of the voice.

Other symbols used in specific examples are explained in the text.

Appendix 3　Text of musical examples in translation, romanization, and linguistic tones

Figure 7.2　Nine versions of Chatjiching

Version A
L1　
　　Nei wan do hung mun jou bat hang;
　　You have fallen into this gate of emptiness (nunnery), an unfortunate fate;

L2　
　　Chai leung san sai sat e naan ham e.
　　A dreary and desolate life, one that is difficult to bear.

Version B
L1　
　　Ngo sat e yi fo cheung tin ngaai chai yan e;
　　I, having failed my Examination, wander the land;

L2　
　　Yat bun dou tung si leun lok e yan e.
　　Both of us are lost souls.

Version C
L1　
　　Hung fu choi wa yu sau gam e;
　　In vain are your talents, bright as embroidered brocades;

L2　
　　Lin hing wai jat yu laan e sam e.
　　I pity your wisdom, and your heart like an orchid (purity of heart).

Text of musical examples in translation 163

Version D
L1
Yuk dai mou ching si seui yun yeung gaan;
The heartless Jade Emperor, he tore up the marriage contract;

L2
Fan fu yau han leui sa fung wong tan.
This human folk shed tears at the Phoenix Altar.

Version E
L1
Ji siu do ching seui gin e man;
I laugh at my own love-sickness, who would understand me?

L2
Keuk mou yat yu daap lou yan.
But I have no word to answer the old man.

Version F
L1
Mung leui wan hing chyun sam e ham;
Tenderness and dream still lingers in my heart;

L2
Sau chaan mou haan yu naan chan a.
Embarrassed and shamed I cannot speak out.

Version G
L1
Gwai jung ye duk jing man hon;
Studying late into the night, you know your books well;

L2
Hap gaau choi neui pui choi long.
A cultivated lady will match a cultivated man.

Version H
L1
Zat pa yuk yu king lau naan paan seung;
Alas! the jade palace I cannot enter;

L2
Hou mun bat naap bou yi long.
A wealthy family will not take this lowly man.

Version I
L1
Ga fu bat kau gam maan leung;
My father does not seek ten thousand catties of gold;

L2
Mou choi syun sai jeui dung chong.
He wants a talented son-in-law to be drafted into his service.

Appendix 3

Figure 7.11 Three lines of Faaidim

L2
Fung wan chui fu long chui lung
The wind obeys the tiger; the waves obey the dragon

L1
Maan lei gong ho chin bo yung
Ten thousand miles of river; one thousand surging waves

L2
Bin seui hung jaak yat ho tung
Bin River and Lake Hung Jaak are but one body of water

Figure 7.14 Four couplets of Gaamji Fuyung

Version A
L1
Nei jing yat joi syu fong, ho loi do nga hing
You all day stay in the study, what makes you so engrossed?

L2
Hoi gyun nang yik ji, ngo fu duk wai kau jing
Reading increases knowledge, I study hard to improve myself.

Version B
L1
Nei pou fu kok fei faan, ling nung sang oi ging
You have extraordinary ideals, I truly love and respect you;

L2
Ngo wai long yi fai cham, nei mong sik wai ho ching?
I lost sleep for your sake, you neglected your meals for whom?

Version C
L1
Ho bin yat deui baak tin ngo, cheung yau bik bo seung
On the river a pair of white swans, having a swim on the blue water;

L2
Ho yi yat jeik joi chin bin heui a, yat jeik joi hau min taan gu hon?
Why does one swan stay in front, the other left behind sad and lonely?

Version D
L1
Ho siu hung niu ji gu chin hang, bat gaai fu cheui fu cheung;
How absurd the male swan stays in front, knowing not the joy of togetherness.

L2
Leung hing mei dung kei jung yi, kam lin chi niu giu tyun cheung.
Dear Leung does not understand what I mean, pity this female swan crying with a broken heart.

Text of musical examples in translation   165

Figure 7.19 Three couplets of Gwanfa

Version A
L2
   Ngo daap po hung kiu cham lai ying, ji mong hung kiu jeun chyu yin sin jung.
   I look everywhere in search of the beautiful girl; I hope to catch a glimpse of her on the other side of Rainbow Bridge.

L1
   Hon chi cheun mun yan gaan fa tou heung, gang naan aat ching yin hing heung dung;
   Such earthly Spring, such fragrant flowers, how can I stop the love-chords in me from singing?

Version B
L2
   Daai dei seung yin hung ji jaat, seui dai ha hak am fui mung.
   How colorful it is here on land; how black and murky under the water.

L1
   Gwaai bat dak wa ji sin yun yeung bat sin sin, keui yau cheun dou ji wai faan sam dung;
   No wonder people say: better to be a pair of mandarin ducks than a lone god; she is taking this stroll because she yearns for love;

Version C
L2
   Ngo jyun wai yan gaan siu mo jeung, na heui yiu mat ching long hung.
   I am here to save men from demons, they shall do no more harm.

L1
   Mou bin faat lik ngo jin kei nang, hap sap lin mong ba jan yin jung;
   With my magic power, I clap my hands and summon;

Figure 11.1 Three versions of Autumn Moon on the Calm Lake

Versions A
1
   Yin loi keuk si wa yau yan / a ye hei ngo sau pan /
   His words are meaningful / they stirred up my sorrowful thoughts /

2
   Ta na leui ji yun gu daan taan jik sam / ngo yik a a yau tung gam /
   He is lamenting on his loneliness / I feel the same way /

3
   Chai ching taan jik sam/
   Alone and lonely /

4
   Pa si nin wa yung yi lou / heui dou hung ngaan luk ban /
   Grieving the passing of time / witnessing the transience of beauty and youth /

Appendix 3

5. Ngaan hon yau yeuk lau seui cheun gwai heui / ta sam ngo yi tung pou sau wo han /
As the river water and the Spring of yesteryear that never shall return / he and I share the same woe /

6. Jam a ho yi jeun sou jung kuk / ngo bun cheut ga yan /
But how shall I express myself / for I have taken my vows /

7. Ngo yiu ching a waai ji gam / seung gung a nei sau si ying keui ban /
I must restrain myself / dear sir: away with your sorrowful thoughts /

8. Gun gwan / gun gwan / yau chi hou hok man / jung fei gau kwan /
Look / look at yourself / a gentleman with great learning / you will not be detained long /

9. Yau jiu dak a ji bou ching wan / ho sau mou gaai leui /
One day when your aspiration is realized, you will walk the clouds / then you shall easily find a good companion /

10. Wai gwan nei bun duk joi laan fong / siu nim dang /
Accompanying you while you study / smilingly adjusting the flame of your lamp /

11. Yu fu man jeun mou chyu / sam hung yau yun ya jung heui /
I'm like a fisherman searching for water, but not knowing whom to enquire / afraid that my opportunity might be lost /

12. Mou mat chyu / ji sam gaai leui miu naam cham /
Where shall I look / for such a truly understanding mate? /

Version B

1. Ying ying chau bo chi seui heung long ying /
Glistening like an autumn lake, my eyes are upon you /

2. Seung si yi sam mung yik sing / bun long deui dang sai heung tin /
My longing is deep, my dream is coming true / by your side, in front of the lamp, facing heaven I swear /

3. Mong tin sam gaam yu sing / yun chi hau cheui long sing /
Hoping heaven will see my earnestness / I declare from now on I shall take your name /

4. Ngo wai long fu bat bin sam / ching oi dong gin wing /
I shall be your woman, never be regretful / my love will be for ever /

Text of musical examples in translation

5 Sat ging / sat ging / gin kei ching / yam e wa kwai dak e sing /
   Shocking / shocking / witnessing such a scandal / this wanton woman of no virtue /

6 Long keui seung oi yik gin jung sing / yat jan wong mui fung e ging /
   My man refuses her love, showing his fidelity / a sudden gust of "yellow plum breeze" of jealousy /

7 Syun dak ngo leui mun heung soi / chit chi tung han /
   So sour it causes tears to cover my face / with teeth-biting bitterness /

8 Mou yin ngo am tan sing /
   I kept silent, swallowing my words /

Version C

1 Lou mong mong / na fong wong /
   The road is long / where does it lead to? /

2 Fong heung sai dung seung mei ming lou ging / yin dak gwai ga wong /
   East? west? I don't know which is the right way / how will I ever reach home /

3 Saan sai jo gaak chin lei ngoi / yau yeuk wan gaak ching a tin a long /
   One thousand miles separate me from the province of Saansai / like clouds separating me from the clear sky /

4 Seui a yun a fuk a saan a cheung / gwai gok ngo mei bat ji fong heung /
   The water is far, the mountain is long / this humble and helpless woman is lost, knowing not where to turn /

5 Ngo gwai kau yan gung nei / paan mong seui lin jok jyu jeung /
   I kneel in front of you, my benefactor / pray be my master and guide me along /

6 Waan heung waan ga chin wong / ngo yin ho joi doi nei jok jyu jeung /
   Go home, go home / but I can no longer serve as your guide /

7 Yin ng ngo chung chung gon lou ma tai mong /
   The urgent pace of my horse shall not be slackened /

Appendix 3

Figure 12.4 One couplet and two quatrains of Naamyam

a. Hing dai tung yap miu, ha lai kau ling gwong.
   You and I enter the temple together, we bow and pray to the Goddess.

b. Yau gin gam tung yuk neui lit leung pong.
   We notice on either side stand Gold Boy and Jade Girl

a. Keui leung wai fan ming fu chai yeung.
   They obviously look like husband and wife.

b. Jam noi sam jung yau yi hau naan jeung.
   But voiceless, they cannot express their feelings.

c. Gun yam yat fu chi bei seung.
   The goddess Gun Yam has kindness and compassion all over her face.

d. Dong wui wai chi naam yun neui jyut fung wong.
   She surely would play the matchmaker for a lovesick couple.

a. Gei si yuk neui gam tung yun yat deui.
   Since Jade Girl and Gold Boy are meant to be together.

b. Leung hing yu ngo yik yat seung.
   You, brother Leung, and I also form a pair.

c. Gun yam yau yi wai mui jing.
   Gun Yam shall be our witness.

d. Ngo yu hing kwai sau gung baai tong.
   You and I, holding hands, take our vows.

Figure 12.11 Two quatrains of Muk'yu

a. Tou dei saan san gei heung fo dou bun yau yan gung fung.
   The God of Earth should be rich with offerings from human beings.

b. Jan hai laang lok miu tong ngo sik gan sai bak fung.
   My temple is empty, I only have the Northwest wind to fill my stomach.

Text of musical examples in translation

c. Mok bat si nei jyut mou sing ling ji bat wui bei yan hon jung.
You mean you've lost your supernatural power, and no one respects you any more?

d. Bat guo ming chin si gwaai ngo wui naau kung.
My poverty simply comes from bad fortune.

a. Mok fei ling san ya yau sat si tung.
Could it be even a God can sometimes fall into hard times?

b. Jau hai yau seui mou sing ying jyu wu jung.
Because there is a water demon living in the lake.

c. Wu jung mou dyun yau hung seui yung.
For no apparent reason, the water overflows from the lake.

d. Gam jau bei keui hoi dak ngo ni go tou dei gung gung bin jo yat gau bei tai chung.
That's what reduced this poor God of Earth into a helpless worm.

Figure 13.3 Four lines of Chatjiching

L2 Yau yun ping seui yik seung fung.
It is destined that our paths should cross.

L1 Yan sang dou dai yu cheun mung.
Life is like a Spring dream.

L2 Ping jung jeui saan taai chung chung.
Meetings and partings happen all too swiftly.

L1 Siu je yun ngoi ji yam gung ji a nei ho chang dung.
Has the young gentleman understood the meaning of her words?

Figure 13.4 One line of Sapji Jingsin Yiwong Maanbaan

L1 Hon san jau, jin kei hung, cheun leui heung dong.
Looking at San Jau, red battle-flags, Spring thunder roaring.

Appendix 4　Text of musical examples in Chinese characters

Figure 6.1

張千真消息啊抑或假消息啊
聞道帝女回生我就心戚戚
未到庵堂就更非寒食
借尸還魂事未當庵堂那有鬼堆積
我對富貴不忘對公主長相憶
張千啊張千你有冇認錯人抑或睇錯色

Figure 6.2

吾乃
紫竹林中護法天尊韋陀是也
只因洪澤湖水氾濫
泗州江太守
上祭天庭
驚動了大慈大悲觀世音菩薩
為請救百姓蒼生
就此命俺韋陀前來
查探一番
若然真有妖物為害
嘿嘿　俺韋陀定就把他除去

Figure 6.4

普渡眾生顯神通　積下功德萬萬重
手上金剛降魔杵　妖魔鬼怪一掃啊空

Musical examples in Chinese characters

Figure 6.6

啊　原來那水妖練就一顆分水的玄珠啊　分水玄珠乃是妖物吸取日月精華　更加以玄珠修練　佢原來有此寶物傍身　難怪佢有恃無恐啊
還有啊　因為汴水小龍垂涎水母美色　時常到來探訪　每來一次　就興起波浪滔滔啊
哈哈　汴水老龍為何不把他兒子管教呢　好　待本護法回天上奏之時　一定懲罰那老龍將兒子放縱定啦
其實洪澤湖水氾濫　由于水母練珠所致　亦因汴水小龍而起　一邪一正，才害苦了我呢個土地公公啊

Figure 6.8

桃花紅　杏花紅　　萬花錦繡舞春風
泗州城外花如海　　虹橋一座跨西東
虹橋之下係洪澤湖　騷人墨客皆詩誦
可惜今時無盛況　　憶昔撫今嘆不同
以前虹橋邊　　　　是青陽市集用
一到墟期日　　　　水泄都也不通
可惜近年來　　　　洪水氾濫湧
傷人和害命　　　　禍物又傷農
江太守祭天　　　　仍然係無作用
洪水依然有　　　　一定有怪物在其中

Figure 7.2

你淪墮空門遭不幸　　淒涼身世實難堪
我失意科場天涯棲隱　一般都同是淪落人
空負才華如繡錦　　　憐卿慧質與蘭心
玉帝無情撕碎鴛鴦束　凡夫有恨淚洒鳳凰壇
自笑多情誰見憫　　　卻無一語答老人
夢裡溫馨存心坎　　　羞慚無限語難陳
閨中夜讀精文翰　　　合教才女配才郎
則怕玉宇瓊樓難攀上　豪門不納布衣郎
家父不求金萬兩　　　慕才選婿贅東床

Figure 7.11

風雲隨虎浪隨龍
萬里江河千波涌
汴水洪澤一河通

Figure 7.14

你整日在書房　　　何來多雅興
開卷能益智　　　　我苦讀為求精
你抱負確非凡　　　令儂生愛敬
我為郎而廢寢　　　你忘食為何情
河邊一對白天鵝　　暢遊碧波上
何以一隻在前邊去啊　一隻在後面嘆孤寒
可笑雄鳥只顧前行　不解婦隨夫唱
梁兄未懂其中意　　堪憐雌鳥叫斷腸

Musical examples in Chinese characters

Figure 7.19

我踏遍虹橋尋儷影　　只望虹橋盡處現仙蹤
看此春滿人間花吐香　更難壓情絃輕響動
大地上嫣紅紫妊　　　水底下黑暗灰朦
怪不得話只羨鴛鴦不羨仙　佢遊春都只為凡心動
我專為人間消魔障　　那許妖物逞狼兇
無邊法力我展奇能　　合什連忙把真言誦

Figure 9.3

嚴世藩　統三軍　一品大員　豈容冒犯

Figure 9.5

海剛峰　小御史　區區五品官銜

Figure 9.7

飄零猶似斷蓬船　慘淡更如無家犬　我青衫自愧不成材　嘆一句布衣未能攀丹桂啊

Figure 9.12

經幽齋　過長廊　結伴無人　遊心自遣

Figure 9.13

嘆今朝　痴心不許賦桃夭　已被閻王相召　塵緣盡了　雖是情緣盡了　可奈儂心愁未了　痛楚難支　更似靈魂出竅

Figure 9.16

我婚盟早訂在稚齡中　　因有六禮三書向江家奉
不過十年人事怕兩不同　　祿位高升只得人敬重
先父年前經棄上　　空餘下兩袖清風
今日我造訪虹橋　　無非欲效蕭郎引鳳

Figure 9.17

我青衫自愧不成材　布衣未能攀丹桂啊　在芸窗苦讀　猶是身寄在鶯宮啊

Figure 11.1

言來卻是話有因　惹起我愁鞏　他那裡自怨孤單嘆寂岑　我亦有同感淒清嘆寂岑　怕是年華容易老　虛渡紅顏綠鬢　眼看有若流水春歸去　他心我意同抱愁和恨　怎可以盡訴衷曲　我本出家人　我要情懷自禁　相公啊你愁思應驅擯　觀君　觀君　有此好學問　終非久困　有朝得志步青雲　何愁無佳侶　為君你伴讀在蘭房　笑拈燈　漁夫問津無處深恐有緣也總虛　無覓處　知心佳侶渺難尋

盈盈秋波似水向郎凝　相思已深夢亦成　伴郎對燈誓向天　望天心鑒愚誠　願此後隨郎姓　我為郎婦不變心　情愛當堅永　失驚　失驚　見奇情淫娃虧德性　郎拒相愛亦見忠誠　一陣黃梅風勁　酸得我淚滿香腮　切齒痛恨　無言我暗吞聲

路茫茫那方往　方向西東尚未明路徑　焉得歸家往　山西阻隔千里外　有若雲隔情天朗　水遠復山長　閨閣娥媚不知方向　我跪叩恩公你盼望垂憐作主張　還鄉還家前往　我焉可再代你作主脹　延誤我匆匆趕路馬蹄忙

Musical examples in Chinese characters

Figure 12.4

兄弟同入廟下禮叩靈光　又見金堂玉女列兩旁
佢兩位分明夫妻樣　　　怎奈心中有意口難張
觀音一副慈悲相　　　　當會為痴男怨女撮鳳凰
既是玉女金童原一對　　梁兄與我亦一雙
觀音有意為媒証　　　　我與兄攜手共拜堂

Figure 12.11

土地山神慨香火本有人供奉
真係冷落廟堂我食緊西北風
莫不是你絕冇聖靈至不會被人看重
不過命蹇時乖我會鬧窮
莫非靈神也有失時痛
就係有水母成形住湖中
湖中無端有洪水涌
咁就被佢害得我呢個土地公公變佐一舊鼻涕蟲

Figure 13.3

有緣萍水亦相逢　　　人生到底如春夢
萍蹤聚散太匆匆　　　小姐絃外之音公子啊你可曾懂

Figure 13.4

看神州　戰旗紅　春雷響動

Appendix 5 Sources of musical examples

Figure 6.1   Sung by Xin Haiquan, in *Dinühua* [*The Royal Beauty*] act 4; recorded from a live performance on January 2, 1975.
Figure 6.2   Sung by Liang Xingbo, in *The Magic Pearl* recorded July 14, 1975.
Figure 6.4   Sung by Liang Xingbo, in *The Magic Pearl* recorded July 14, 1975.
Figure 6.6   Sung by Liang Xingbo and unknown actor, in *The Magic Pearl* recorded July 14, 1975.
Figure 6.8   Sung by four unknown actors, in *The Magic Pearl* recorded July 14, 1975.
Figure 7.2   Nine versions of *Chatjiching*. Versions A, B, C sung by Lü Yulang in *Yuzanji* [*The Jade Hairpin*], China Records M-377; Version D sung by Lin Jiasheng in *Tianji Songzi* [*Heavenly Maiden Delivers a Son*], Tienshing Records SSLP-2053; Versions E, F sung by Jiang Ping in *Mudanting* [*Peony Pavillion*], Hesheng Records (no number); Versions G, H, I sung by Lin Jiasheng and Li Baoying in *Liang Shanbo yu Zhu Yingtai* [*The Butterfly Lovers*], Tienshing Records TSLP-2046.
Figure 7.10 From Guangdongsheng, *Yueju changqiang*, p. 90.
Figure 7.11 Sung by Ruan Zhaohui, in *The Magic Pearl* recorded July 14, 1975.
Figure 7.13 From Guangdongsheng, *Yueju changqiang*, p. 91.
Figure 7.14 Versions A and B sung by Lin Jiasheng and Li Baoying, in *Sanxi Enqing Ershizai Chou* [*Three Nights of Love, Twenty Years of Hate*], Tienshing Records TSLP-2035; versions C and D sung by the same two singers in *Liang Shanbo yu Zhu Yingtai* [*The Butterfly Lovers*], Tienshing Records TSLP-2046.
Figure 7.18 From Guangdongsheng, *Yueju changqiang*, p. 76.
Figure 7.19 Sung by Li Long, Nan Hong, and Liang Xingbo in *The Magic Pearl* recorded July 14, 1975.
Figure 7.20 From Guangdongsheng, *Yueju changqiang*, p. 69.
Figure 7.21 From Guangdongsheng, *Yueju changqiang*, p. 70.
Figure 7.22 From Guangdongsheng, *Yueju changqiang*, pp. 69, 115.
Figure 9.3   Sung by Jing Cibo in *Dahongpao* [*The Red Robe*], Funghang Records FHLP-139.
Figure 9.5   Sung by Ren Jianhui in *Dahongpao* [*The Red Robe*], Funghang Records FHLP-139.
Figure 9.7   Sung by Long Jiansheng in *Dinühua* [*The Royal Beauty*], recorded from a live performance on January 2, 1975.
Figure 9.8   Sung by Ruan Zhaohui in *The Magic Pearl*, recorded from live performances on July 8, 1975 (version A) and on July 14, 1975 (version B).
Figure 9.10 Sung by Long Jiansheng in *Dinühua* [*The Royal Beauty*], recorded from a live performance on January 2, 1975.
Figure 9.12 From Chen Zhuoying, *Yuequ xiechang changshi*, p. 99.
Figure 9.13 Sung by Wen Qiansui and Chen Haoqiu in *Nüerxiang* [*Fragrant Beauty*], Funghang Records FHLP-449.
Figure 9.14 From Chen Zhuoying, *Yuequ xiechang changshi*, pp. 49–52.
Figure 9.15 From Chen Zhuoying, *Yuequ xiechang changshi*, p. 68.

Sources of musical examples

Figure 9.16   Sung by Ruan Zhaohui in *The Magic Pearl* recorded July 14, 1975.
Figure 9.17   Sung by Ruan Zhaohui in *The Magic Pearl* recorded July 8, 1975.
Figure 10.2   Huang Jinpei, "Lun 'Yueyue'", p. 13.
Figure 10.4   Passage 1 (lines 1–3) sung by Ren Jianhui in *Taohuameng [Peach Blossom Dream]*, Funghang Record Co. (Hong Kong) FHLP-132; passage 2 (lines 4–6) sung by Liang Tianyan in *Shenyuan Chunmeng [Spring Dream in Shen Garden]*, New Wave Record Co. (Hong Kong) MWLP-4; passage 3 (lines 7–11) sung by Mai Bingrong in *Yesong Jingniang [Escorting Lady Jing in the Night]*, Tienshing Record Co. (Hong Kong) TSLP-2040; passage 4 (12–13) sung by Hong Xiannü *Yulong Xifeng [Dragon Flirts with Phoenix]*, Meeshing Record Co. (San Francisco) M-3311; passage 5 (14–17) sung by Ren Jianghui in *Tang Bohu Xi Qiuxiang [Tang Bohu Flirts with Qiuxiang]*, Meeshing Record Co. (San Francisco) M-3356.
Figure 10.5   Passage 1 (lines 1–5) sung by Mai Bingrong in *Bieyao [Farewell at the Cave]*, Roxy Record Co. (Hong Kong) CSLP-1013; passage 2 (lines 6–8) sung by Wen Qiansui in *Nüerxiang [Fragrance Beauty]*, Funghang Record Co. (Hong Kong) FHLP-449; passage 3 (lines 9–11) sung by Wu Junli in *Yuewangyuan [Sorrow of King Yue]*, Funghang Record Co. (Hong Kong) FHLP-424; passage 4 (lines 12–14) sung by Chen Haoqiu in *Nüerxiang [Fragrance Beauty]*, Funghang Record Co. (Hong Kong) FHLP-449; passage 5 (lines 15–17) sung by Lü Yulang in *Yuzanji [The Jade Hairpin]*, China Records (Beijing) M-377.
Figure 10.6   Passage 1 (lines 1–3) sung by Wu Junli and Ren Jianhui in *Taohuameng [Peach Blossom Dream]*, Funghang Record Co. (Hong Kong) FHLP-132; passage 2 (lines 4–6) sung by Yu Jia in *Xue Dingshan yu Fan Lihua [Xue Dingshan and Fan Lihua]*, Funghang Record Co. (Hong Kong) FHLP-456; passage 3 (lines 7–16) sung by He Feifan in a live performance of *Xinlingjun Yeji Weiwangfei [Duke Xinling Offers Sacrifices to Lady Wei]* in Hong Kong on February 23, 1973.
Figure 11.1   Text for three versions of *Autumn Moon on the Calm Lake*. Version A sung by Lin Xiaoqun and Lü Yulang in *Yuzanji [The Jade Hairpin]*, China Records (Beijing) M-377; Version B sung by Bai Xuexian and Ren Bing'er in *Pipa Xiangkou Gurenlai [An Old Friend Comes to Loquat Lane]*, Tienshing Record Co. (Hong Kong) TSLP-2018; Version C sung by Mai Bingrong and Li Fenfang in *Yesong Jingniang [Escorting Lady Jing in the Night]*, Tienshing Record Co. (Hong Kong) TSLP-2040.
Figure 12.4   Sung by Lin Jiasheng and Li Baoying in *Liang Shanbo yu Zhu Yingtai [The Butterfly Lovers]*, Tienshing Record Co. (Hong Kong) TSLP-2046.
Figure 12.7   Sung by Ruan Zhaohui in *The Magic Pearl*, recorded July 14, 1975.
Figure 12.11   Sung by Liang Xingbo and an unnamed actor in *The Magic Pearl*, recorded July 14, 1975.
Figure 13.3   Sung by Nan Hong and Ren Bing'er in *The Magic Pearl* recorded July 14, 1975.
Figure 13.4   From Guangdongsheng, *Yueju changqiang*, pp. 126–128.
Figure 13.5   From Qiu, *Xiange bidu*, pp. 43–45.

Items on the cassette

Side 1

Number 1. Nine versions of *Chatjiching*, corresponding to figure 7.2 [1′ 58″]
Number 2. Four versions of *Gaamji Fuyung*, corresponding to figure 7.14 [1′ 43″]
Number 3. Three lines of *Jingsin Sapji Bongji Jungbaan*, corresponding to lines 1, 2, and 3 of figure 10.4; five lines of *Faansin Sapji Bongji Jungbaan*, corresponding to lines 1 through 5 of figure 10.5; three lines of *Yifaansin Sapji Bongji Jungbaan*, corresponding to lines 1, 2, and 3 of figure 10.6 [3′ 53″]
Number 4. Three versions of *Autumn Moon on the Calm Lake*, corresponding to figure 11.1 [5′ 22″]
Number 5. Ten lines of *Naamyam*, corresponding to figure 12.4 [2′ 10″]
Number 6. First act of *The Magic Pearl*, corresponding to lines 1 to 122 in chapter 5 [12′ 13″]

Side 2

Continuation of Number 6 from Side 1: first act of *The Magic Pearl*, corresponding to lines 122 to 325 in chapter 5 [28′ 27″]

Notes

1 Introduction to Chinese opera

1. A readable introduction in English on the origins and antecedents of Chinese opera is William Dolby, *A History of Chinese Drama* (London: Paul Elek, 1976), pp. 1–13. See also Zhou Yibai, "Zhongguo xijude xingcheng he fazhan" [The origin and development of Chinese theater] in Zhou Yibai, *Zhongguo xiqu lunji* [Essays on Chinese opera] (Beijing: Zhonghua Xiju Chubanshe, 1960), pp. 1–30; Zhou Yibai, *Zhongguo xijushi* [History of Chinese theater] (Shanghai: Zhonghua Shuju, 1953), pp. 9–73. For discussion on the origin of Chinese puppet theater, see Sun Kaidi, *Kuileixi kaoyuan* [The origin of puppet theater] (Shanghai: Shangza Chubanshe, 1952). For the influence of Sanskrit drama on Chinese theater, see Xu Dishan, "Fanju tili jiqizai hanjushangde diandian didi" [The form of Sanskrit drama and its traces in Chinese drama] in *Zhongguo wenxue yanjiu* [Studies of Chinese literature], ed. Zheng Zhenduo (Shanghai: Shangwu Yinshuguan, 1927).
2. Dolby, *A History of Chinese Drama*, p. 14. On discussions of *zaju*, see Zhou Yibai, *Zhongguo xijushi*, pp. 99–124.
3. Wenzhou *zaju* is also known as Yongjia *zaju*. See Qian Nanyang, *Xiwen gailun* [General study of *xiwen*] (Shanghai: Guji Chubanshe, 1981). Also see Sauyan Chan, "The arrangements of tunes in Nanxi (Southern drama) of the Song dynasty (960–1279 AD)" (M.A. thesis, University of Pittsburgh, 1984).
4. Writings on Yuan *zaju* are numerous, most of which are concerned with its literary content; among those dealing with aspects of its music are Yang Yinliu, *Zhongguo gudai yinyue shigao* [Draft history of ancient Chinese music] (Beijing: Renmin Yinyue Chubanshe, 1982), pp. 552–630; Aoki Masao, *Zhongguo jinshi xiqushi* [History of Chinese drama of the recent centuries] in Japanese, translated into Chinese by Wang Gulu (Shanghai: Shangwu Yinshuguan, 1936), pp. 34–74; and Dale Johnson, *Yuarn Music Dramas: Studies in Prosody and Structure and a Complete Catalogue of Northern Arias in the Dramatic Style* (Ann Arbor: Center for Chinese Studies of the University of Michigan, 1980).
5. Its full name is *Jiugong dacheng nanbeici gongpu* [A compendium of northern and southern arias in nine *gong*] in eighty-two volumes, published in 1746 under the imperial edict of the Qing dynasty and containing material drawn from the preceding 1,000 years. Much basic bibliographical research still needs to be carried out on this vast amount of material, which constitutes one of the most valuable musical sources in the history of Chinese vocal music.
6. For a discussion on this aspect of Yuan *zaju*, see Yang Yinlui, *Zhongguo gudai yinyue shigao*, pp. 599–628.
7. Yang Yinliu, *Zhongguo gudai yinyue shigao*, p. 629; Zhou Yibai, *Zhongguo xijushi*, p. 294.
8. For *nanxi* of the Yuan dynasty and *chuanqi* of the Ming dynasty, see, for example, Dolby, *A History of Chinese Drama*, pp. 71–101; Yang Yinliu, *Zhongguo gudai yinyue shigao*, pp. 640–724, 856–979.
9. Zhou Yibai, "Zhongguo xiqu shengqiangde sanda yuanliu" [The three main vocal styles in Chinese opera] in Zhou Yibai, *Zhongguo xiqu lunji*, pp. 204–229. For a brief English summary, see Colin P. Mackerras, *The Rise of the Peking Opera 1770–1870* (Oxford: Clarendon Press, 1972), pp. 4–11.
10. For Kun opera, see Lu Eting, *Kunju yanchu shigao* [Draft history of the performance practice of Kun opera] (Shanghai: Wenyi Chubanshe, 1980); Yang Yinliu, *Zhongguo gudai yinyue shigao*, pp. 862–979.
11. Yang Yinliu, *Zhongguo gudai yinyue shigao*, p. 863.
12. *Ibid.*, p. 864.

13. Structural elements such as melody and rhythm are relatively easily notated, but at the same time more restrictive. When notation restricts the freedom of a performer, it allows the identification of a "composer." On the other hand, features pertaining to the manner of performance, for example the adding of ornamentation, are not easily notated, and consequently a performer is allowed to exercise individual creativity. The greater flexibility of the music as rendered by different performers makes the identification of a single composer more difficult.
14. Yang Yinliu, *Zhongguo gudai yinyue shigao*, p. 342.
15. The term *pihuang* is a composite of *xipi* and *erhuang*.
16. Among the copious writings on Peking opera, see Mackerras, *The Rise of Peking Opera*; on its music, see the many works of Rulan Chao Pian listed in the bibliography.
17. Su Yi, "Quanguo juzhong chubu tongji" [A preliminary listing of operatic genres in China], *Xiju luncong* [Collected Papers on Theater], 1 (1957), 215–223.
18. Qi Rushan, *Guoju yishu huikao* [A study of the art of Peking opera] (Taipei: Chongguang Wenyi Chubanshe, 1962), p. 3.
19. *Ibid.*, p. 4.
20. The bare stage could, of course, be attributed to economic factors, as well as to the fact that many performances are by itinerant troupes that require a simple stage for ease of travel. The importation of Western spoken plays and motion pictures from the early twentieth century led to the introduction of realistic stage sets and props into a few regional operas such as Cantonese opera. Since the 1960s many other operas have adopted these innovations.
21. Bertolt Brecht, "Alienation effects in Chinese acting" in *Brecht on Theater: The Development of an Aesthetic*, ed. and transl. John Willett (New York: Hill and Wang, 1964), pp. 91–99.
22. Xia Ye, *Xiqu yinyue yanjiu* [Research on operatic music] (Shanghai: Wenyi Chubanshe, 1959), pp. 4–5.
23. Bruce E. Brooks, "Chinese aria studies" (Ph.D. dissertation, University of Washington, 1964).
24. Rulan Chao Pian, "Aria structural patterns in the Peking opera" in *Chinese and Japanese Music-Drama*, ed. J. I. Crump and William P. Malm, Michigan Papers in Chinese Studies, No. 19 (Ann Arbor: University of Michigan Press, 1975), pp. 65–89.
25. Tanaka Issei, "Mindai no minetzu chihogeki ni tsuite" (An outline of Min Yüeh local drama during the Ming dynasty], *Tohogaku* [Eastern Studies], 42 (August 1971), 82–97, and "Development of Chinese local plays in the seventeenth and eighteenth centuries" *Acta Asiatica, Bulletin of the Institute of Eastern Culture*, 23 (1972), 42–62.
26. See Tanaka Issei, *Chugoku saishi engeki kenkyu* [Ritual theaters in China] (Tokyo: Institute of Oriental Cultures, University of Tokyo, 1981); Barbara E. Ward, "Regional operas and their audiences: evidence from Hong Kong" in *Popular Culture in Late Imperial China*, ed. David Johnson, Andrew J. Nathan and Evelyn S. Rawski (Berkeley: University of California Press, 1985), pp. 161–187.
27. It should, however, be noted that operas were exploited as the major medium for the dissemination of ideological messages under strict government control during the decade between the mid-1960s and mid-1970s. See Bell Yung, "Model opera as model" in *Popular Chinese Literature and Performing Arts in the People's Republic of China, 1949–1979*, ed. Bonnie McDougall (University of California Press, 1984), pp. 144–164.
28. In some cases the dialect spoken on stage differs from that spoken on the street because a regional opera developed out of one imported from another province. At one time Cantonese opera used a dialect different from street Cantonese.
29. For example, the two *qiang* used in Peking opera (*xipi* and *erhuang*) are known to correspond historically to the two *qiang* used in Cantonese opera (*bongji* and *yiwong*) respectively. Yet any opera-goer will testify that *xipi* sounds quite different from *bongji*, and *erhuang* from *yiwong*.
30. For a discussion of the history of Cantonese opera in English, see Bell Yung, "The music of Cantonese opera" (unpublished Ph.D. dissertation Harvard University, 1976), chapter 3; Colin P. Mackerras, *The Chinese Theater in Modern Times* (Amherst: University of Massachusetts Press, 1975), pp. 145–152; in Chinese, see Mai Xiaoxia, "Guangdong xiqu shilüe" [A brief history of the Cantonese opera] in *Guangdong wenwu* [The cultural things of Guangdong] ed. Guangdong Wenwu Zhanlanhui [Committee on the Exhibition of Cultural Things of Guangdong] (Hong Kong:

Zhongguo Wenhua Xiejinhui 1940), vol. VIII, pp. 141–185, and Ouyang Yuqian, "Shitan yueju" [A preliminary study of Cantonese opera] in *Zhongguo xiqu yanjiu ziliao chuji* [The first collection of research material for the study of Chinese opera], ed. Ouyang Yuqian (Beijing: Yishu Chubanshe, 1956), pp. 109–157.
31. Leung Puikam, *Yueju yanjiu tonglun* [Study of Cantonese opera] (Hong Kong: Longmen Shudian, 1982), pp. 282–304.
32. Ronald Riddle, *Flying Dragons, Flowing Streams – Music in the Life of San Francisco's Chinese* (Westport, CT: Greenwood Press, 1983).
33. See Yung, "Model opera as model."

2 Essential elements of Cantonese opera as performing art

1. All Chinese terms in this chapter, unless otherwise noted, are romanized first according to the pronunciation of the Peking dialect, followed in parenthesis by that of the Cantonese dialect.
2. Note that the consistency is in intervallic relationships rather than the frequency value of individual tones; thus while the pitch level is generally held constant within a performance, it might vary between performances. In other words, the performance tradition as a whole does not follow a rigid standard of absolute pitch.
3. Cantonese opera, until recent times, has always been performed in temporarily erected sheds called *xipeng* (*heipaang*) or opera sheds. These were bamboo structures with the roof covered with mats. Three of the four sides were open to the elements; the fourth side, the back of the stage, was also covered with mats. Today the mats have been replaced by aluminium sheets.
4. Some Cantonese musicians also use the so-called cipher notation, or "number" notation in which numerals from 1 through 7 represent the scale degrees, and horizontal lines underneath the numerals suggest proportional durations. This system, though widely used in published notations and scholarly works, is seldom used in relation to professional operatic performances.
5. There have been disagreements among Chinese scholars on the intervals of the Cantonese scale. The one presented here is according to the following two sources: Guangdongsheng Xiju Yanjiushi [Center for Operatic Research of Guangdong Province], ed. and compiler, *Yueju changqiang yinyue gailun* [A general study of the melodic styles of Cantonese opera] (Beijing: Renmin Yinyue Chubanshe, 1984), p. 35; and Li Yan, "'Xian' lun" [Theory on *xian*], *Guangzhou Yinyue Xueyuan Xuebao* [Journal of the Canton Conservatory of Music], (1983.3), 12–22, p. 13.
6. The tune is in the "scale" of *faansin*, which means that, in the performance, it is transposed down a fifth from the notation. The issue of "scale" will be discussed in chapter 10.
7. Notable exceptions are the early part of this century and during the Cultural Revolution (1966–76), when stories set in the contemporary period were staged.
8. The early 1970s, when the popularity of Cantonese opera in Hong Kong was at a low point, saw a few attempts at innovation in programming, none of which had a lasting effect. For example, two medium-length plays were staged in the same evening, each with a different set of performers. Experiments were also made in presenting a number of scenes of relatively short duration from different plays.
9. The scriptwriter was Su Weng. It was first performed in Hong Kong from June 8 through 14, 1975 by the Jinlinian Troupe [Year of Golden Profit] with Yuan Zhaohui and Nan Hong as principal male and female singers.
10. See Tao Junqi, compiler, *Jingju jumu chutan* [A preliminary compilation of Peking opera titles], (Beijing: Zhongguo Xiju Chubanshe, 1963), p. 419.
11. Names in the opera are romanized in the Cantonese dialect.
12. A translation of act 1 can be found in chapter 5.

3 Musical instruments

1. The list of instruments is based upon field work observation in Hong Kong. Some instruments differ slightly from published sources. See Guangdongsheng ed., *Yueju changqiang*, pp. 359–361, and Guangzhoushi Wenhuaju Xiqu Gongzuoshi [Center for Operatic Study of the Ministry of

Culture of Canton], compiler, *Yueju luogu jichu zhishi* [Fundamentals of percussion music in Cantonese opera] (Guangzhou: Guangdong Renmin Chubanshe, 1979), p. 2.
2. For percussion patterns of Cantonese opera, see Guangzhoushi, compiler, *Yueju luogu*.
3. Relevant to this issue are Rulan Chao Pian's two articles which touch upon percussion music in Peking opera: "The function of rhythm in Peking opera" in *The Music of Asia*, ed. Jose Maceda (Manila: The National Council of the Philippines in Cooperation with the UNESCO National Commission of the Philippines, 1971), pp. 114–131; and "Rhythmic texture in the opera 'The Fisherman's Revenge'," *Asian Culture Quarterly*, 7: 4 (Taipei, 1979), 19–26.
4. About fifty *paizi* tunes together with their "scenes" are listed in Guangdongsheng ed., *Yueju changqiang*, pp. 452–517.
5. For a detailed organological discussion of some of the instruments mentioned in this section, see *The New Grove's Dictionary of Music and Musicians*, ed. Stanley Sadie (London: Macmillan, 1980), pp. 262–279.
6. Violins, saxophones, guitars, and others were widely used as the principal accompanying instruments in Cantonese opera during the 1920s, 1930s and 1940s. See Yung, "The music of Cantonese opera," pp. 76–78.

4 Social context

1. An informative article in English on the social context of Cantonese opera in Hong Kong is Ward, "Regional operas and their audiences," which outlines four main types of live professional opera that could be seen in Hong Kong during the 1970s, according to sponsorship and place of performance (p. 164):

    1. Community sponsored, normally in shed theaters;
    2. Privately sponsored, in restaurants and private dwellings;
    3. Officially and municipally sponsored, in public auditoria, shed theaters, and public parks;
    4. Entrepreneurial sponsorship, in opera houses, adapted cinemas, public auditoria, amusement-park theaters, and mat-shed [opera-shed] theaters.

    On the ritual context of opera in Hong Kong see also Tanaka, *Chugokku saishi engeki kenkyu*. Mackerras, *The Rise of Peking Opera*, chapter 2, has a discussion of the relation between the theater and the life of the people in other parts of China.
2. An example of the former was the Dalongfeng [The Great Dragon and Phoenix] Opera Troupe; an example of the latter was the Jiabao Opera Troupe, which was made up of one word each from the names of the two principal performers Luo Jiaying and Li Baoying.
3. Mackerras, *The Rise of Peking Opera*, p. 193.
4. Leung Puikam, *Yueju yanjiu tonglun*, p. 177.
5. Interviews in 1973 with Mr. Yuan Zhanxun, owner of the Taiping Theater.
6. According to a survey in 1975, there were approximately 1,600 ritual performances and 90 secular ones of Cantonese opera in a year. See Ward, "Regional operas and their audiences," p. 163.
7. Tanaka, "Development of Chinese local plays," pp. 42–62.
8. Mai Xiaoxia, "Guangdong"; and Ouyang Yuqian, "Shitan yueju."
9. Issei Tanaka, "The social and historical context of Ming-Ch'ing local drama" in *Popular Culture in Late Imperial China*, ed. David Johnson, Andrew J. Nathan and Evelyn S. Rawski (Berkeley: University of California Press, 1985), pp. 143–160.
10. See, for example, the chapter on "Evaluation and the future of Cantonese opera" in Leung Puikam, *Yueju yanjiu tonglun*, pp. 316–323.
11. Ward, "Regional operas and their audiences," states that "In Hong Kong the number of festival [ritual] performances was actually higher in the early 1980s than it was in the early 1950s" (p. 162). That there was a gradual increase in the number of festival performances over the years is supported by this researcher's own observation during the period from the early 1970s to the early 1980s.
12. On the religious festivals in Hong Kong, see, for example, V. R. Burkhardt, *Chinese Creeds and Customs* (Hong Kong: South China Morning Post, 1953).

13. For an account of the preparation of such a village performance, see Cornelius Osgood, *The Chinese. A Study of a Hong Kong Community* (3 vols., Tucson: University of Arizona Pess, 1975), vol. II, pp. 893–894.
14. The significance of the temple was illustrated by a performance of a Swatow opera in honor of the birthday of the Queen of Heaven which this researcher attended on May 1, 1981. It was the first afternoon performance of a three-day series, which, as usual for a Swatow opera, began with three ritual pieces: *Baxian Heshou* [*Birthday Greeting from the Eight Immortals*], *Tiaojiaguan* [*Dance of Promotion*], and *Tianji Songzi* [*Heavenly Maiden Delivers a Son*]. At the end of the last item, a short dance-like performance lasting about five minutes, the Heavenly Maiden, accompanied by her husband and four guards, carried the "baby" (represented by a doll) off the stage, walked down the aisle of the audience area, out of the opera shed, and across the courtyard separating the shed from the temple, then entering the temple, prostrated herself before the image of the Queen of Heaven and offered the baby to the deity, depositing it on the altar. I was told that the baby would be retrieved and brought back onto the stage at the end of the third night of performance (the last performance of the series). This ritual process, however, had not been observed in a Cantonese opera performance.
15. For an account of such a performance, see Bell Yung "A trip to Sok Gu Wan with a Cantonese opera troupe," *Chinoperl Papers* 7 (1977), 49–59.
16. Pan gave a series of interviews which was published serially in the Hong Kong newspaper daily *Xingdao Ribao* from May 21 to June 9, 1953. The mention of the four kinds of non-operatic performances of the music was in the May 29 issue.
17. For a brief account of the life and work of a male blind singer, see Bell Yung, "Reconstructing a lost performance context: a field work experiment," *Chinoperl Papers*, 6 (1976), 120–143; and "Popular narratives in the pleasure houses of the south," *Chinoperl Papers*, 11 (1982), 126–149. An account written in Chinese is "Guangzhou shiniang" [Blind songstresses of Canton], based upon an autobiographical narration of Wen Lirong, in *Guangdong quyishi ziliao* [Source material on the history of Cantonese popular narrative song], compiled by Guangdong Yinyue Quyituan (Guangzhou: Guangdong Yinyue Quyituan, 1980), pp. 1–120.
18. "Guangzhou nüling" [Female entertainers of Canton] narrated by Xiong Feiying, Yuan Miaosheng, Yuan Yinghe, Huang Peiying in *Guangdong quyishi ziliao*, pp. 13–37.
19. The one teahouse is Zuiqionglou Restaurant in the Wanchai district on Hong Kong island. Among the singers active in the 1970s, the best-known was Jiang Yanhong, famous for her ability to sing both the female and military male role types. As an institution, singing of operatic excerpts in teahouses also existed in north China in the early part of this century, as told in the autobiography of Zhang Cuifeng. See Zhang Cuifeng, "My life as a drum singer," transl. Rulan Chao Pian, *Chinoperl Papers*, 13 (1984); 7–106.
20. The following section is based upon field work carried out in Hong Kong during the mid-1970s.
21. The only substantial study is Alan Kagan, "Cantonese puppet theater: an operatic tradition and its role in the Chinese religious belief system," (Ph.D. thesis, Music, University of Indiana, 1978).
22. Mai Shaotang (Mak Siutong) was the leader of the Hanhuanian (Honwa'nin) [The Prosperous Years], the only Cantonese rod-puppet troupe in Hong Kong. In the late 1970s, Mr. Mai, then aged over 70, had only one disciple, Mr. Chen Hongyu, an architect by profession who had been studying with Mr. Mai since the early 1970s and had been participating in the performances regularly.

5 The opera script

1. Interviewed on August 9, 1975.
2. The following section is based upon firsthand observations during 1973 and 1975 of preparations for new operas by the following opera troupes with their respective principal male and female singers: the Feifanxiang Troupe [Unearthly Sound] with He Feifan and Wu Junli; the Jinlungfeng Troupe [Golden Dragon and Phoenix] with Mai Bingrong and Fenghuang Nü; the Jinlinian Troupe [Year of Golden Profit] with Yuan Zhaohui and Nan Hong; and the Juexinsheng Troupe [New Voice] with Lin Jiasheng and Li Baoying.

3. An opera troupe's unpublished working scripts are treasured possessions, and are rarely shared with outsiders. I am grateful to Su Weng, the scriptwriter of *The Magic Pearl*, for giving me his personal working copy.
4. The format and content of the original script are retained as much as possible, but since the performance differs from the script, the translation follows the performance whenever it departs from the script in a major way so that the reader might follow the translation as he listens to the recording. Minor improvisation, such as short dialogues, exclamations, and repetitions of some text are not incorporated into the translation. This translation also provides the couplet and quatrain structures of the oral delivery types: a superscript "a" or "b" before a line indicates that the line is either the upper or lower line of a couplet respectively, and superscripts "c" or "d" in addition to "a" and "b" indicate the four lines of a quatrain. Note that titles of percussion patterns, speech types, and fixed tunes are given in their translated form, while titles of aria types and narrative songs are given in their romanized form. All romanization is according to the Cantonese pronunciation. The translation is by Bell Yung.
5. See Sauyan Chan, "Improvisation in Cantonese operatic music" (Ph.D. dissertation, University of Pittsburgh, 1986).

6 Speech types

1. Rulan Chao Pian discusses this aspect in Peking opera in "The function of rhythm in Peking opera."
2. See James Liu, *The Art of Chinese Poetry* (Chicago: Chicago University Press, 1962), p. 29.
3. Interview on August 8, 1975.

7 Aria types

1. The exact number depends upon how one counts. The tunes are closely related to each other structurally; whether two tunes are merely variants of the same tune, or distinct from one another, each with its own identity, is subject to individual interpretation.
2. Another reason for using the term "aria type" is that the term was first introduced by Rulan Chao Pian in her study of Peking opera (for example, see "Text setting with the shipyi animated aria" in *Words and Music: the Scholar's View*, ed. Laurence Berman (Cambridge: Harvard University Press, 1972)). Since the "aria types" of Peking opera and Cantonese opera are related and share many characteristics, it seems appropriate to continue using the term.
3. Cantonese musicians today seldom apply the terms "strong" and "weak" to beats but call them *baan* and *ding*. Qiu Hechou in *Qinxian xinbian* [A new collection of songs for the struck zither] (Publication source unknown, 1921), wrote that *baan* beats should be strong and *ding* beats should be weak (p. 12). In an actual performance, *baan* is generally accompanied by a tap on the large woodblock, which has a more resonant, lower-pitched tone, while *ding* is accompanied by a tap on one of the smaller woodblocks, which has a less resonant, higher-pitched tone. The *baan* beats are consistently accompanied, while the *ding* beats may or may not be. The total impression is that *baan* beats are stronger than *ding* beats.
4. The entry "Mode" in *The New Grove's*.
5. Charles Seeger uses the terms "structure" and "function" to explain a similar idea: "By 'structure' I refer ... to such examples as the physical form of a particular artifact and of aggregates of artifacts. They are perceivable as facts, past or present phenomena in the physical, external universe of the senses. Structure, small or large, seems to 'stay still' ... Function has to do with action, movement, force, process towards an end." See Charles Seeger, "The music compositional process as a function in a nest of functions and in itself a nest of functions," in *Studies in Musicology 1935–1975* (Berkeley: University of California Press, 1977), pp. 141–2.
6. Noam Chomsky and Morris Halle, *The Sound Pattern of English* (New York: Harper and Row, 1968), pp. 5, 293–329. In phonetics, each feature is "a physical scale defined by two points, which are designated by antonymous adjectives: high-nonhigh, voiced-nonvoiced, and so forth" (p. 299). In the present discussion of music, the possible values of each feature are more complicated and cannot be defined in terms of a linear scale.

7. See Chen Zhuoying, *Yuequ xiechang changshi* [Guide to writing and singing Cantonese opera] (2 vols., Guangzhou: Nanfang Tongsu Chubanshe, 1952), vol. II, p. 6.
8. In terms of the Cantonese scale given in figure 2.5 in chapter 2, the range of male voice types is between *gung'* and *liu*, that of female voice types is the same in notation but an octave higher in absolute pitch, that of the "big" voice type is between *saang* and *gung"*.
9. The name *Faaidim* appears to be used only in Hong Kong. In Mainland China, the aria type is known as a fast version of *Jingsin Chatji Bongji Jungbaan*, even though the two aria types have distinctly different syllable placements. See Guangdongsheng ed., *Yueju changqiang*, p. 88.
10. See Chan, "Improvisation in Cantonese operatic music," pp. 203–216
11. These numbers are based upon my own survey of opera scripts and supported by the list of aria types discussed in Guangdongsheng ed., *Yueju changqiang*.

8 Linguistic tones

1. Yuenren Chao, "Tones, intonation, singsong, chanting, recitative, tonal composition, and atonal composition in Chinese" in *For Roman Jacobson*, compiled by Morris Halle (The Hague: Mouton, 1956), pp. 52–59; John Hazedel Levis, *Foundations of Chinese Musical Art*, 2nd edn (New York: Paragon, 1964); Lindy L. Mark and Fangkuei Li, "Speech tone and melody in Wu-Ming folk songs" in *Essays Offered to G. H. Luce*, ed. Ba Shin, Jean Boisselier and A. B. Briswold (2 vols., Ascona, Switzerland: Artibus Asiae, 1966), vol. I, pp. 167–186; Pian, "Text setting with the shipyi animated aria," pp. 237–270; Marius Schneider, "La relation entre la melodie et le langage dans la musique chinoise," *Anuario Musical*, 5 (1950), 62–69; Yang Yinliu, *Zhongguo gudai yinyue shigao*, pp. 886–900.
2. Diana L. Kao, *Structure of the Syllable in Cantonese* (The Hague: Mouton, 1971), p. 82.
3. *Ibid*.
4. The small number of Entering Tones in these examples makes the result statistically unconvincing. However, a random check of a number of other versions of *Chatjiching* indicates that the matching is quite consistently observed.
5. John McCoy has suggested that this may be the musical equivalent of tone sandhi in speech, which refers to a change in the actual value of the linguistic tone when certain syllables are juxtaposed. (Private communication.)
6. Except for a newly-composed play which is being performed for the first time. See chapter 5.
7. Pian, "Text setting with the shipyi animated aria," pp. 237–270; Marjory Liu, "The influence of tonal speech on K'unch'ü vocal art," *Selected Reports in Ethnomusicology* (Los Angeles: Institute of Ethnomusicology, University of California), 2:1 (1974), 62–86.

9 Padding syllables

1. Johnson, *Yuarn Music Dramas*, p. 29. It should be noted that in Yuan *zaju* and some other forms of operas and poetry, the prescribed pattern of line-lengths may be irregular, that is, the text is not in couplet structure, and the number of syllables per line may vary from line to line.
2. *Ibid*.
3. For example, Tong Fei, *Yuanqu xuanzhu* [Yuan drama with annotation] (Taipei: Shangwu Yinshuguan, 1965), specifies that the padding syllables cannot be sung on the *ban* [strong beat], but must fall on the *yan* [weak beat], within the metrical pattern of a tune. Yoshikawa Kojiro, *Genzatsugeki kenkyu* [A study of Yuan drama] (Tokyo: Iwanami Shoten, 1948), refers to performance when he discusses padding syllables. He speculates that padding syllables were sung lightly and quickly in relation to base syllables.
4. Yu Huiyong, *Shandong dagu* [Shandong drumsong] (Beijing: Yinyue Chubanshe, 1957).
5. On Peking Drumsong, see Rulan Chao Pian, "Feng Yeu Guei Jou 'Boat Return in the Rain,' a transcription with commentary," *Don Bang Hak Chi* [Journal of Far Eastern Studies] (Seoul: Institute of Korean Studies, Yonsei University), 23–24 (February 1980), 389–403; on Shandong Drumsong, see Yu Huiyong, *Shandong dagu*, p. 16.
6. The nonsense syllables "a" in the transcription will be discussed in a later section in this chapter.

7. In figure 9.12, the instrumental interludes are shown in small noteheads. In figure 9.13, the interlude fillers are marked between brackets. Note that the four syllables *chan yun jeun liu* are sung to the end of the vocal melisma of the same phrase in figure 9.12 (the second half of measure 4 in both figures 9.12 and 9.13). Strictly speaking, these four syllables should then be called melisma fillers rather than interlude fillers.
8. In the Cantonese dialect, grammatical particles are very frequently added to the end of sentences in daily speech. See Cheung Hungnin, Samuel, *Xianggang yueyu yufade yanjiu* [Cantonese as spoken in Hong Kong] (Hong Kong: The Chinese University of Hong Kong, 1972), p. 168.
9. The syllable placement of *Yiwong* is more flexible than other aria types. For example, the last syllable of P2 and P4 may have a long melisma that extends for one or more additional measure, and the instrumental interludes between P1 and P2, and between P2 and AP may also be extended for one or more additional measure.

10 Sin

1. Huang Jinpei, "Lun 'yueyue' yifanxian biaoxiande yinyue xingxiang" [On the musical image of *yifanxian* in Cantonese music], *Guangzhou Yinyue Xueyuan Xuebao* [Journal of the Guangzhou Conservatory of Music], 2 (1983), 8–24; Li Yan, "'Xian' lun," pp. 12–22; Guangdongsheng ed., *Yueju changqiang*, pp. 32–58.
2. It should be mentioned that one kind of fretted lute *pipa* is also widely performed as a solo instrument, in which case a musician may change the pitches microtonally by pushing a string sideways along the fingerboard.
3. Li Yan, "'Xian' lun," p. 13.
4. *Ibid.*, p. 15.
5. Guangdongsheng ed., *Yueju changqiang*, p. 45.
6. The Cantonese scale names generally imply only intervallic relationships rather than absolute pitch, and are therefore equivalent to the Western solfege system of the Movable-Do. In this chapter, the Western names of Sol, La, Si, Do, Re, Mi, Fa are sometimes used to represent the Cantonese names of *ho, si, yi, saang, che, gung, faan* respectively for the convenience of readers. Note that the Cantonese *si* is always italicized to distinguish it from the Western Si, which is not italicized but capitalized.
7. Chen Zhuoying, *Yuequ xiechang changshi*, vol. II, p. 10; Huang Jinpei, "Lun 'yueyue'," p. 11.
8. Li Yan, "'Xian' lun," p. 12.
9. Huang Jinpei, "Lun 'yueyue'," p. 13.
10. This information is supplied by the young *erhu* player Yu Siuwah who studied under Feng.
11. Qiu Hechou, *Xiange bidu* [Obligatory reading on singing] (publication source unknown, 1916), pp. 31–32.
12. According to my *gender* teachers John Pemberton of Ithaca and Djokowaluya of Yogyakarta, from whom I took *gender* lessons in 1977 and in the summer of 1983 respectively. Also see Susan Pratt Walton, *Mode in Javanese Music* (Athens, Ohio: Ohio University Center for International Studies, 1987), p. 27.
13. The somewhat bewildering numbering system of the upper and lower lines in figures 10.4 through 6 is because the examples are taken from passages in different operas; some passages begin with the upper line, others with the lower line; and some passages have an even number of lines, others an odd number. The number is based upon the sequence that the lines appear in on the cassette. For example, in figure 10.4, lines 1, 2, 3 (lower-upper-lower) belong to passage 1; lines 4, 5, 6 (upper-lower-upper) belong to passage 2; lines 7, 8, 9, 10, 11 (lower-upper-lower-upper-lower) belong to passage 3; lines 12, 13 (upper-lower) belong to passage 4; lines 14, 15, 16, 17 (upper-lower-upper-lower) belong to passage 5. Figures 10.5 and 10.6 are similarly numbered. The sources for the passages and the number of lines in each passage are listed in appendix 5. The reason that there are more lower lines than upper lines for each of the three *sins* is discussed in chapter 13 (see chapter 13 note 5). The text is relevant to this analysis only in so far as the verse structure and linguistic tones are concerned; therefore the Chinese characters of the text, their romanized form, and their meaning are not provided. In their place are schematic symbols representing the linguistic

tones of the syllables. The caesuras within a line are marked off by commas, the end of an upper line by a semi-colon, the end of a lower line by a period.

14. As used in this section, "note" refers to all the notes that occur in a tune; "pitch" refers to the scale degrees in the Cantonese scale that the tune uses. Therefore, a tune is made up of a large number of "notes," but uses only a small number of "pitches," or scale degrees.
15. For ease of reading, figures 10.4 to 10.6 use a 2/2 meter because of the large number of small note values.
16. As has been discussed in chapter 7, the different voice types (male voice, female voice, and "big" voice) affect the tessitura of the tune, and therefore may result in different tables of matching. Male voice and female voice are exactly one octave apart; they are treated as if the tunes are in the same octave in regard to the table of matching. The "big" voice lies at a tessitura half way between the male and female voices; the table of matching is therefore quite different. Note that lines 11, 13, and 15 in figure 10.6 are sung in the "big" voice, and have a different table of matching from the other lines. The table of matching for *Yifaansin* in figure 10.7 has not included these three lines. Note also that the aria type *Gaamji Fuyung* has a built-in tessitura change in its tune regardless of voice type, which is discussed in chapters 7 and 8.
17. Strictly speaking, the Pythagorean pentatonic scale produces two intervals whose ratios are 204 to 294 rather than 2 to 3.
18. Qiu used the name *Fuhau*, or "sad voice" for *Yifaansin*. Qiu also provided a fourth diagram for a fourth *sin* called *Faansin*. The *faan* in this case is a different word (from the one that means "reverse"), meaning "Buddhist"; tunes in this *sin* were presumably related to Buddhist chants. Since this *sin* is no longer used today, it is not included in the present discussion.
19. Unless, of course, the scale is equidistant, which has been proposed by some musicians; see Chen Tianguo, "Guangdong minjian yinyuede qi pingjunlü" [The equal-tempered heptatonic scale of Cantonese folk music], *Zhongguo Yinyue* [China Music] 4 (1981), 7–8. The equidistant scale is rejected by many; see Hu Yun, "Dui Guangdong yinyue 'qi pingjulü' de yixie yiwen" [Some questions on the 'equal-tempered heptatonic scale' of Cantonese folk music], *Minzu Minjian Yinyue* [Chinese National Folk Music] 1 (1986), 43–44. Such a scale is also obviously contrary to actual performances.
20. Wang Yuesheng of Hong Kong, through interview.
21. Dong Weisong of Beijing, through interview.
22. The graph for the line-ending notes (*Yifaansin*) shows an anomaly that needs some explanation. The cadential notes for the upper line of *Yifaansin Sapji Bongji Jungbaan* should be C. But among the six upper lines shown in figure 10.6, only three end on the expected C, while the other three end on high F. The reason is that the three latter versions are sung in the so-called "big" voice which has a different cadential pattern (see note 15 in this chapter).

11 Fixed tunes

1. Some of the *paizi* tunes are used only as instrumental accompaniment for certain scenes. See chapter 3.
2. James Robert Hightower, *Topics in Chinese Literature*, Harvard–Yenching Institute Studies, vol. VI (Cambridge: Harvard University Press, 1953), p. 90.
3. J. Lawrence Witzleben, "Cantonese instrumental ensemble music in Hong Kong: an overview with special reference to the Gou Wu (Gao Hu)" (M.A. thesis, University of Hawaii, 1983).
4. Chen Zhuoying, *Yuequ xiechang changshi*, p. 6; Guangdongsheng ed., *Yueju changqiang* also mentions Yiyang style opera as another source for *paaiji* tunes (p. 291).
5. By far the majority of tune titles in the fixed tune repertory are descriptive in nature, as illustrated by the few examples quoted above. This is consistent with the generally-accepted view that Chinese music is almost always programmatic. How a tune is chosen in Cantonese opera certainly reflects the significance of its programmatic title. However, the question still remains as to whether a programmatic title indeed reflects any programmatic content of the music. See Kuohuang Han, "Titles and program notes in Chinese musical repertories," *The World of Music*, 27: 1 (1985), 68–75

and Mingyue Liang, *Music of the Billion: An Introduction to Chinese Musical Culture* (New York: Heinrichshofen Edition, 1985), pp. 177–184.
6. The study of *tinchi* can also be approached by interviewing scriptwriters who practice the art today. The author intentionally chose to concentrate on actual musical examples; he based the decision to do so on his conviction that what is done is often more informative than, or at least offers an alternate source of information to, what is said. Interviews on this subject have also been conducted during field work in Hong Kong in 1972–73 and 1974–75. "What is done" is generally verified by "what is said."
7. The tune is attributed to Cantonese composer Lü Wencheng, a renowned performer on the *erhu* active from the 1920s to the 1970s. Four published versions are located: *Yueyue mingquji* [Collection of famous Cantonese tunes] compiled by Li Xiaotian (3 vols, Hong Kong: Xincheng Shuju, 1971), vol. 1, p. 37; *Guangdong yinyue* [Cantonese music] (Hong Kong: Taiping Shuju, 1963), p. 3; *Guangdong yinyue quji* [Collection of Cantonese music] (Beijing: Renmin Yinyue Chubanshe, 1981), p. 25; *Guangdong yuequ yibaishou* [One hundred pieces of Cantonese music] (Jilin: Renmin Yinyue Chubanshe, 1981), p. 7. The first version is used in figure 11.1.
8. Liu, *The Art of Poetry*, pp. 21–22.
9. The question whether a "mother tune" exists may not be valid in this case despite the fact that *Autumn Moon on the Calm Lake* has been attributed to a specific composer. A comparison of the four published versions of this tune reveals four slightly different versions. One probably should not assume that the identity of a fixed tune can be represented by a single, unambiguous configuration of pitches with "variants" or "versions." The identity may instead be constituted by the aggregate of all existing versions.
10. The aria types, of course, employ so-called padding syllables, which obscure the syllable placement to some degree. See chapter 9.
11. As has been pointed out in chapter 7, the identity of an aria type depends upon several other factors as well, among them cadential pitches. It is the responsibility of the scriptwriter, therefore, to ensure that the syllables that are to be sung to the cadential pitches should have the "correct" linguistic tones. Furthermore, aesthetic principles prohibit certain behavior in the tune, such as a melodic contour that stays on one pitch level for an extended period. This puts a further degree of restraint on the scriptwriter in his choice of syllables for the text. However, relatively speaking, he has a greater degree of freedom than when he composes the text for the fixed tunes.

12 Narrative songs

1. Guangdongsheng ed., *Yueju changqiang*, p. 8.
2. There is no general and comprehensive discussion of narrative songs published in English. The reader is referred to the brief article by Catherine Stevens in *The New Grove's*, pp. 258–260, under the heading of "China."
3. Yung, "Reconstructing a performance context" has a brief discussion of *Naamyam*; for a biographical sketch of a blind singer, see Wen Lirong, "Guangzhou shiniang."

13 Three levels of creative process

1. Pian, "Aria structural patterns," p. 72.
2. See Guangdongsheng ed., *Yueju changqiang*, pp. 243–244.
3. As Pian writes in "Aria structural patterns": "The singing of Dramatic Aria [*Yaoban*] can also be used merely for formal purposes, that is, serving as entrance and exit songs, markers of transition from one scene to another, and even markers of short episodes within a scene when a new subject of discussion is introduced." (p. 77)
4. Pian writes in "Aria structural patterns": "The short rhapsodic melodies of the Interjective Aria and the Declamatory Aria [two kinds of free-rhythmed aria types in Peking opera] are perfect vehicles for emotional outbursts or dialogue during dramatically tense moments" (p. 76).
5. This explains why the examples in figures 10.4, 10.5, and 10.6 have more lower lines than upper lines.

6. See, for example, Dieter Christenson, "Inner tempo and melodic tempo," *Ethnomusicology*, 4 (1960), 9–14; and Mieczyslaw Kolinski, "The evaluation of tempo," *Ethnomusicology*, 3 (1959), 45–57.
7. These examples are taken from Guangdongsheng ed., *Yueju changqiang*, pp. 126–128.
8. This kind of tempo change bears a close similarity to the concepts of *irama* in Indonesian music and of *taw* in Thai music. See Judith Becker, "A Southeast Asian musical process: Thai *thaw* and Javanese *irama*," *Ethnomusicology*, 24: 3 (1980), 453–464.
9. See J. Lawrence Witzleben, "Silk and bamboo: Jiangnan Sizhu instrumental ensemble music in Shanghai" (Ph.D. dissertation, University of Pittsburgh, 1987), chapter 6.

Appendix 1

1. This table is taken from Yuenren Chao, *The Cantonese Primer* (New York: Greenwood Press, 1947), p. 24. The abrupt endings are conventionally indicated with ending consonants of -p, -t, -k when romanized into English. The symbols for the three Entering Tones have been modified from Chao's short, horizontal strokes: ⏋ to dots in this paper: ⏋ to avoid confusion with the other tones.
2. Beijing Daxue Zhongguo Yuyan Wenxuexi (Department of Chinese Language and Literature, University of Beijing), *Hanyu fangyin zihui* [A glossary of Chinese characters according to dialect] (Beijing: Wenzi Gaige Chubanshe, 1962).
3. Oikan Yue Hashimoto, *Phonology of Cantonese* (London: Cambridge University Press, 1972) and Huang, Xiling (Wong, S. L.), *Yueyin yunhui* [A Chinese syllabary pronounced according to Cantonese dialect] (Hong Kong: Zhonghua Shuju, 1954).
4. Chan Yuenyuen Fok, *A Perceptual Study of Tones in Cantonese* (Hong Kong: University of Hong Kong, 1974).
5. Parker Pofei Huang and Gerard P. Kok, *Speak Cantonese* (New Haven: Institute of Far Eastern Studies, Yale University, 1960).

Glossary 1 Names of performers, plays, and opera companies

Bai Xuexian	白雪仙	Long Jiansheng	龍劍笙
Baxian Heshou	八仙賀壽	Lü Yulang	呂玉郎
Bieyao	別窰	Luo Jianying	羅劍英
Chen Haoqiu	陳好逑	Mai Bingrong	麥炳榮
Chen Hongyu	陳洪宇	Mai Shaotang	麥少棠
Dahongpao	大紅袍	Mudanting	牡丹亭
Dalongfeng	大龍鳳	Nan Hong	南紅
Dinühua	帝女花	Nüerxiang	女兒香
Feifanxiang	非凡響	Pipa Xiangkou Gurenlai	枇杷巷口故人來
Fenghuang Nü	鳳凰女	Ren Bing'er	任冰兒
Hanhuanian	漢華年	Ren Jianhui	任劍輝
He Feifan	何非凡	Ruan Zhaohui	阮兆輝
Hongqiao Zengzhu	虹橋贈珠	Sanxi Enqing Ershizai Chou	三夕恩情廿載仇
Jiabao	嘉寶	Shenyuan Chunmeng	沈園春夢
Jiang Ping	江平	Taiping	太平
Jiang Yanhong	蔣艷紅	Tang Bohu Xi Qiuxiang	唐伯虎戲秋香
Jing Cibo	靚次伯	Tang Disheng	唐滌生
Jinlinian	金利年	Taohuameng	桃花夢
Jinlungfeng	金龍鳳	Tianji Songzi	天姬送子
Juexinsheng	覺新聲	Tiaojiaguan	跳加官
Li Baoying	李寶瑩	Wen Qiansui	文千歲
Li Fenfang	李芬芳	Wu Junli	吳君麗
Li Long	李龍	Xianfengming	仙鳳鳴
Liang Shanbo yu Zhu Yingtai	梁山伯與祝英台	Xin Haiquan	新海泉
Liang Tianyan	梁天雁	Xinlingjun Yeji Weiwangfei	信陵君夜祭魏王妃
Liang Xingbo	梁醒波	Xue Dingshan yu Fan Lihua	薛丁山與樊梨花
Lin Jiasheng	林家聲	Yesong Jingniang	夜送京娘
Lin Xiaoqun	林小群	Yu Jia	羽佳
Liuguo Fengxiang	六國封相	Yuan Zhanxun	源詹勳

Other terms

Yuewangyuan	越王怨	Zhang Cuifeng	章翠鳳
Yulong Xifeng	遊龍戲鳳	Zuiqionglou	醉瓊樓
Yuzanji	玉簪記		

Glossary 2   Other terms

baak	白	ching	清
baaklaam	白欖	chou*	丑
baan	板	chouseng*	丑生
baan'ngaan	板眼	chuanqi*	傳奇
bai*	白	ci*	詞
ban*	板	daaidiu	大調
banghuang*	梆簧	daaihau	大喉
bangzi*	梆子	daanda	單打
banqiangti*	板腔體	daanhau	旦喉
banyan*	板眼	dadi*	大笛
banzhu*	班主	dagu*	大鼓
bayin*	八音	dagulao*	打鼓佬
Beidi*	北帝	dahu*	大胡
bendiban*	本地班	dan*	旦
bongji maanbaan*	梆子慢板	daxi*	大戲
bongji	梆子	di*	笛
bongwong	梆王	diao*	調
budiao*	布調	dihu*	低胡
chang*	唱	ding	叮
chatji	七字	dizi*	笛子
chatjiching	七字清	dok'kuk	度曲
che	尺	dongxiao*	洞簫
chenzi*	襯字	duoju*	垛句
cheung	唱	duqu*	度曲
cheunggeui yiwong	長句二王	erbanghua*	二幫花
chewusin	尺五線	erhu*	二胡
chi*	詞	erhuang*	二簧

faaibaan	快板	hudieqin*	蝴蝶琴
faaidim	快點	jiamao*	加帽
faaijungbaan	快中板	jiangxi shiye*	講戲師爺
faan	反	jiangxi*	講戲
faansaangsin	反上線	jiaose*	角色
faansin yiwong	反線二王	jie*	介
faansin	反線	jiekou*	介口
fahau	苦喉	jing*	淨
gaaihau	介口	jingbo*	京鈸
gaamji fuyung	減字芙蓉	jingju*	京劇
gaobianluo*	高邊鑼	jingli*	經理
getan*	歌壇	jingluo*	京鑼
gong*	工	jingsin	正線
gongche*	工尺	jueju*	絕句
gonghei siye	講戲師爺	jungbaan	中板
gonghei	講戲	juzhong*	劇種
guan*	管	Kai Tak	啓德
Guanyin*	觀音	kou*	口
guji*	瞽姬	kuk	曲
gung	工	kuk'ngai	曲藝
gungyisin	工乙線	kukpaai	曲牌
gwanfa	滾花	kunqu*	崑曲
haamseuigo	鹹水歌	Lai Chi Kok	荔枝角
haugu	口古	lauseuibaan	流水板
hediao*	河調	lengbanqu*	冷板曲
ho	合	lengqing*	冷清
hochesin	合尺線	lianquti*	聯曲體
Hong Sheng*	洪聖	logubaak	鑼鼓白
houguan*	喉管	longleuibaak	浪裡白
hu	胡	longzhou*	龍舟
Huaguang*	華光	lungjau	龍舟

Other terms

luo*	鑼	sauying	手影
luogudian*	鑼鼓點	shang*	上
mubang*	木梆	sheng*	生
muk'yu	木魚	shengqiang*	聲腔
mutou gungzaixi*	木頭公仔戲	shi*	士
muyü*	木魚	shouyin*	收音
naamyam	南音	shouying*	手影
nanxi*	南戲	shuimoqiang*	水磨腔
nanyin*	南音	shuochang*	說唱
ninbaak	念白	si	士
nüling*	女伶	sibaak	詩白
paaiji	牌子	sigungsin	士工線
paichang*	排場	sin	線
paizi*	牌子	siudiu	小調
pengmian*	棚面	siukuk	小曲
pipa*	琵琶	song	爽
qiang*	腔	suluo*	蘇鑼
qiangdiao*	腔調	suona*	嗩吶
Qijie*	七姐	syutcheung	說唱
qinqin*	秦琴	taicheung	提場
qu*	曲	taigong	提綱
qupai*	曲牌	taoshu*	套數
saanbaan	散班	tianci*	填詞
saang	上	Tianhou*	天后
saangliusin	上六線	tichang*	提場
saiho daaigu	西河大鼓	tigang*	提綱
san ban*	散板	tinchi	填詞
sanghau	生喉	tokbaak	托白
sanxian*	三絃	waijiangban*	外江班
sapji	十字	wanbaak	韻白
saubaan	首板	wanjia*	玩家

wenchang*	文場	yehu*	椰胡
wenchangluo*	文場鑼	yi	乙
wendabo*	文大鈸	yifaan	乙反
wenwusheng*	文武生	yifaansin	乙反線
wuchang*	武場	yinghungbaak	英雄白
wuchangluo*	武場鑼	yiwong	二王
wudabo*	武大鈸	yixiang*	衣箱
wusheng*	武生	Yu Lan*	盂蘭
wuyingu*	五音鼓	yuehu*	粵胡
xi*	戲	yueqin*	月琴
xianshuige*	鹹水歌	zaju*	雜劇
xiao*	簫	zhangban*	掌板
xiaodi*	小笛	zhangtou mu'ouxi*	杖頭木偶戲
xiaoluo*	小鑼	zhangu*	戰鼓
xiaoqu*	小曲	zhazhu*	楂竹
xiaosheng*	小生	zhe*	折
xiezi*	楔子	zhengyin huadan*	正印花旦
xihe dagu*	西河大鼓	zhengzi*	正字
xipi*	西皮	zhezixi*	折子戲
yanbaak	引白	zhonghu*	中胡
yangqin*	洋琴	zhongzhou yin*	中州音
yaoban*	搖板		
yaozi*	咬字		

(* Romanization according to Peking dialect)

Bibliography

1 English

Anderson, Eugene N. *Essays on South China's Boat People*, Asian Folklore and Social Life Monographs, edited by Lou Tsu-k'uang, Taipei: Orient Cultural Service, 1972
Becker, Judith. "A Southeast Asian musical process: Thai *thaw* and Javanese *irama*," *Ethnomusicology*, 24:3 (1980), 453–464
Bolinger, Dwight, ed. *Intonation*, Baltimore: Penguin Books Inc., 1972
Boyce, Conal. "Rhythm and meter of *tsyr* in performance," Ph.D. dissertation, Harvard University, 1975
Brecht, Bertolt. "Alienation effects in Chinese acting" in *Brecht on Theater: The Development of an Aesthetic*, ed. and trans. John Willet, New York: Hill and Wang, pp. 91–99
Brooks, Bruce E. "Chinese aria studies," Ph.D. dissertation, University of Washington, 1964
Burkhardt, V. R. *Chinese Creeds and Customs*, Hong Kong: South China Morning Post, 1953
Chan, Sauyan. "The arrangements of tunes in Nanxi (Southern drama) of the Song dynasty (960–1279 AD)," M.A. thesis, University of Pittsburgh, 1984
 "Improvisation in Cantonese operatic music," Ph.D. dissertation, University of Pittsburgh, 1986
Chang, Hsinpao. *Commissioner Lin and the Opium War*, Cambridge, Mass.: Harvard University Press, 1964
Chao, Yuenren. *The Cantonese Primer*, New York: Greenwood Press, 1947
 "Tones, intonation, singsong, chanting, recitative, tonal composition, and atonal composition in Chinese" in *For Roman Jacobson*, compiled by Morris Halle, The Hague: Mouton, 1956, pp. 52–59
Chomsky, Noam and Morris Halle. *The Sound Pattern of English*, New York: Harper and Row, 1968
Christensen, Dieter. "Inner tempo and melodic tempo," *Ethnomusicology*, 4 (1960), 9–14
Dolby, William. *A History of Chinese Drama*, London: Paul Elek, 1976
Fok, Chan Yuenyuen. *A Perceptual Study of Tones in Cantonese*, Hong Kong: University of Hong Kong, 1974
Han, Kuohuang. "Titles and program notes in Chinese musical repertories," *The World of Music*, 27:1 (1985), 68–75
Hanan, Patrick. "The development of fiction and drama" in *The Legacy of China*, ed. Raymond Dawson, Oxford: Oxford University Press, 1964
Hashimoto, Oikan Yue. *Phonology of Cantonese*, London: Cambridge University Press, 1972
Hightower, James Robert. *Topics in Chinese Literature*, Harvard-Yenching Institute Studies, vol. VI, Cambridge: Harvard University Press, 1950
Hong Kong 1973, A Review of 1972, Hong Kong: Hong Kong Government Press, 1973
Hopkins, Keith, ed. *Hong Kong: The Industrial Colony*, Oxford: Oxford University Press, 1971
Huang, Parker Pofei and Gerard P. Kok. *Speak Cantonese*, New Haven: Institute of Far Eastern Studies, Yale University, 1960
Johnson, Dale. "The prosody of Yuan drama" in *T'oung Pao*, 56:1–3 (1970), 96–146
 Yuarn Music Dramas: Studies in Prosody and Structure and a Complete Catalogue of Northern Arias in the Dramatic Style, Ann Arbor: Center for Chinese Studies of the University of Michigan, 1980
Johnson, David, Andrew J. Nathan and Evelyn S. Rawski, eds. *Popular Culture in Late Imperial China*, Berkeley: University of California Press, 1985
Kagan, Alan. "Cantonese puppet theater: an operatic tradition and its role in the Chinese religious belief system," Ph.D. dissertation, University of Indiana, 1978

Kao, Diana L. *Structure of the Syllable in Cantonese*, The Hague: Mouton, 1971
Kolinski, Mieczyslaw. "The evaluation of tempo," *Ethnomusicology*, 3 (1959), 45–57
Latourette, Kenneth Scott. *The Chinese: Their History and Culture*, 3rd edn, New York: Macmillan, 1964
Levis, John Hazedel. *Foundations of Chinese Musical Art*, 2nd edn, New York: Paragon, 1964
Liang, Mingyue. *Music of the Billion: An Introduction to Chinese Musical Culture*, New York: Heinrichshofen Edition, 1985
Lim, Chewpah. "The two main singing styles in Cantonese opera," M.A. thesis, University of Washington, 1973
Liu, James. *The Art of Chinese Poetry*, Chicago: University of Chicago Press, 1962
Liu, Marjory. "The influence of speech tones in K'unch'ü vocal art," *Selected Reports in Ethnomusicology* (Los Angeles: Institute of Ethnomusicology, University of California), 2:1 (1974), 62–86
Mackerras, Colin P. "The growth of Chinese regional drama in the Ming and Ch'ing," *Journal of Oriental Studies*, 9:1 (1971), 58–91
  The Rise of the Peking Opera 1770–1870, New York and Oxford: Oxford University Press, 1972
  The Chinese Theater in Modern Times, Amherst: University of Massachusetts Press, 1975
Mark, Lindy L., and Fangkuei Li. "Speech tone and melody in Wu-Ming folk songs" in *Essays Offered to G. H. Luce*, ed. Ba Shin, Jean Boisselier and A. B. Briswold, 2 vols., Ascona, Switzerland: Artibus Asiae, 1966
The New Grove's Dictionary of Music and Musicians, ed. Stanley Sadie, London: Macmillan, 1980
Osgood, Cornelius. *The Chinese, A Study of a Hong Kong Community*, 3 vols., Tucson: University of Arizona Press, 1975
Pian, Rulan Chao. "Contribution of the percussion orchestra to dramatic structures in Peking opera," Paper read at the 27th International Congress of Orientalists at University of Michigan, Ann Arbor, Michigan, 1967
  "The function of rhythm in Peking opera" in *The Music of Asia*, ed. Jose Maceda, Manila: The National Music Council of the Philippines in Cooperation with the UNESCO National Commission of the Philippines, 1971
  "Text setting with the shipyi animated aria" in *Words and Music: The Scholar's View*, ed. Laurence Berman, Cambridge: Harvard University Press, 1972, pp. 237–270
  "Aria structural patterns in the Peking opera" in *Chinese and Japanese Music-Drama*, ed. J. I. Crump and William P. Malm, Michigan Papers in Chinese Studies, No. 19, Ann Arbor: University of Michigan Press, 1975, pp. 65–89
  "Rhythmic texture in the opera 'The Fisherman's Revenge'," *Asian Culture Quarterly* 7:4 (Taipei, 1979), 19–26
  "Feng Yeu Guei Jou 'Boat Return in the Rain,' a transcription with commentary," *Don Bang Hak Chi* [Journal of Far Eastern Studies] (Seoul: Institute of Korean Studies, Yonsei University), 23–24 (February 1980), 389–403
  "Musical Elements in the Peking Opera 'Bah Wang Bye Ji'," *Chinoperl Papers*, 12 (1983), 61–83
Riddle, Ronald. *Flying Dragons, Flowing Streams – Music in the Life of San Francisco's Chinese*, Westport, CT: Greenwood Press, 1983
Sachs, Curt. *The History of Musical Instruments*, New York: W. W. Norton, 1940
Schneider, Marius. "La relation entre la melodie et le langage dans la musique chinoise," *Anuario Musical*, 5 (1950), 62–69
Schönfelder, Gerd. *Die Musik der Peking Opera*, Leipzig: Deutscher Verlag für Musik, 1972
Scott, A. C. *The Classical Theatre of China*, London: George Allen and Unwin, 1957
Seeger, Charles. "Versions and variants of the tunes of Barbara Allen," *Selected Reports in Ethnomusicology* (Los Angeles: Institute of Ethnomusicology, University of California), 1:1 (1966), 120–163
  "The music compositional process as a function in a nest of functions and in itself a nest of functions," *Studies in Musicology 1935–1975*, Berkeley: University of California Press, 1977, pp. 139–167. Originally published as "The music process as a function in a context of functions," in *Yearbook, Inter-American Institute for Musical Research* (New Orleans: Tulane University), 2 (1966), 1–36

Tanaka, Issei. "Development of Chinese local plays in the seventeenth and eighteenth centuries," *Acta Asiatica, Bulletin of the Institute of Eastern Culture* 23 (1972) 42–62
"The social and historical context of Ming-Ch'ing local drama" in *Popular Culture in Late Imperial China*, ed. David Johnson, Andrew J. Nathan and Evelyn S. Rawski, Berkeley: University of California Press, 1985, pp. 143–160
Tsim, Taklung. *Chinese Theater in Hong Kong, Proceedings of a Symposium, November 22–23, 1968*, Hong Kong: Center for Asian Studies, University of Hong Kong, 1968
Walton, Susan Pratt. *Mode in Javanese Music*. Athens, Ohio: Ohio University Center for International Studies, 1987
Ward, Barbara E. "Not merely players; drama, art and ritual in traditional China," *Man* 14:1 (March 1979), 18–39
"The red boats of the Canton delta: a chapter in the historical sociology of Chinese opera" in *Proceedings of the International Conference on Sinology*, Taipei: Academica Sinica, 1981
"Regional operas and their audiences: evidence from Hong Kong" in *Popular Culture in Late Imperial China*, ed. David Johnson, Andrew J. Nathan and Evelyn S. Rawski, Berkeley: University of California Press, 1985, pp. 161–187
Wen, Lirong. "Blind songstress of Canton." Translated by Bell Yung as "The blind singers of Guangzhou," *Chinoperl Papers*, 14 (1986), 61–76
Witzleben, J. Lawrence. "Cantonese instrumental ensemble music in Hong Kong: an overview with special reference to the Gou Wu (Gao Hu)," M.A. thesis, University of Hawaii, 1983
"Silk and bamboo: Jiangnan Sizhu instrumental ensemble music in Shanghai." Ph.D. thesis, University of Pittsburgh, 1987
Yeh, Nora. "The Yüeh Chü style of Cantonese opera with an analysis of 'The Legend of Lady White Snake'," M.A. thesis, University of California at Los Angeles, 1972
Yung, Bell. "The music of Cantonese opera," unpublished Ph.D. dissertation, Harvard University, 1976
"Reconstructing a lost performance context: a field work experiment," *Chinoperl Papers*, 6 (1976), 120–143
"A trip to Sok Gu Wan with a Cantonese opera troupe," *Chinoperl Papers*, 7 (1977), 49–59
"Music identity in Cantonese opera" in *IMS: Report of the 12th Congress, Berkeley 1977*, ed. Daniel Heartz and Bonnie Wade, Berkeley: University of California Press, 1981, pp. 669–75
"Popular Narratives in the pleasure houses of the south," *Chinoperl Papers*, 11 (1982), 126–149; 12 (1982), 143–153
"Creative process in Cantonese opera I: the role of linguistic tones," *Ethnomusicology*, 27 (1983), 29–47
"Creative process in Cantonese opera II: the role of tien tz'u (text-setting)," *Ethnomusicology*, 27 (1983), 297–318
"Creative process in Cantonese opera III: the role of padding syllables," *Ethnomusicology*, 27 (1983), 439–456
"Model opera as Model" in *Popular Chinese Literature and Performing Arts in the People's Republic of China, 1949–1979*, ed. Bonnie McDougall, Berkeley: University of California Press, 1984, pp. 144–164
Zhang, Cuifeng. "My life as a drum singer," trans. Rulan Chao Pian, *Chinoperl Papers*, 13 (1984), 7–106

2 Chinese and Japanese

Aoki Masao. *Zhongguo jinshi xiqushi* [History of Chinese drama of the recent centuries], trans. Wang Gulu, Shanghai: Shangwu Yinshuguan, 1936. (Original edition: Shinakinsei Gikyoku Shi, Kyoto, 1930)
Beijing Daxue Zhongguo Yuyan Wenxuexi [Department of Chinese Language and Literature, Beijing University]. *Hanyu fangyin zihui* [A glossary of Chinese characters according to dialects], Beijing: Wenzi Gaige Chubanshe, 1962

Chen Deju. *Guangdong yuequde goucheng* [Structure of Cantonese music], Guangzhou: Guangdong Renmin Chubanshe, 1957
Chen Tianguo. "Guangdong minjian yinyuede qi pingjunlü" [The equal-tempered heptatonic scale of Cantonese folk music], *Zhongguo Yinyue* [Chinese Music], 4 (1981), 7–8
Chen Zhuoying. *Yuequ xiechang changshi* [Guide to writing and singing Cantonese opera], 2 vols., Guangzhou: Nanfang Tongsu Chubanshe, 1952
    Yuequ xiezuo rumen [Introduction to writing Cantonese opera], Guangzhou (publisher unknown), 1956
Cheung Hungnin, Samuel. *Xianggang yueyu yufade yanjiu* [Cantonese as spoken in Hong Kong], Hong Kong: The Chinese University of Hong Kong, 1972
Feng Siyu. *Guangzhouyin zihui* [List of words in Cantonese pronunciation], Hong Kong: Shijie Shuju, 1961
Fu Gongwang. "Longzhou he nanyin" [Longzhou and nanyin] in *Fangyan Wennxue* [Literature written in the dialects], ed. Zhonghua Quanguo Wenyi Xiehui [The All-China Literature and Arts Association], Hong Kong: Xinminzhu Chubanshe, 1949, pp. 42–61
Guangdong xinyu [New reports about Guangdong]. Compiled and written by Qu Dajun, 1700
Guangdongsheng Xiju Yanjiushi [Center for Operatic Research of Guangdong Province], ed. and compiler. *Guangdongsheng xiqu he quyi* [Operas and narrative songs of Guangdong province], Guangzhou: Guangdongsheng Xiju Chubanshe, 1980
    Yueju changqiang yinyue gailun [General discussion of the style of vocal music of Cantonese opera], Beijing: Renmin Yinyue Chubanshe, 1984
Guangzhou fuzhi [Canton Prefecture Gazetteer], compiled by Shi Cheng and Dai Zhaochen, Guangzhou: 1879
Guangzhoushi wenhuaju xiqu gongzuoshi [Center for operatic study of the Ministry of Culture of Canton], compiler. *Yueju luogu jichu zhishi* [Fundamentals of percussion music in Cantonese opera], Guangzhou: Guangdong Renmin Chubanshe, 1979
Hatano Taro. "Etsugeki kanki" [A layman's view of Cantonese opera], *The Bulletin of Yokohama City University*, 22: 2–3 (1971), 76–105
Hu Yun. "Dui Guangdong yinyue 'qi pingjunlü' de yixie yiwen" [Some questions on the 'equal-tempered heptatonic scale' of Cantonese music], *Minzu Minjian Yinyue* [Chinese National Folk Music], 1 (1986), 43–44
Huang Jinpei. "Lun 'yueyue' yifanxian biaoxiande yinyue xingxiang" [On the musical image of *yifanxian* in Cantonese music], *Guangzhou Yinyue Xueyuan Xuebao* [Journal of the Guangzhou Conservatory of Music], 2 (1983), 8–24.
Huang Xiling (Wong, S. L.). *Yueyin yunhui* [A Chinese syllabary pronounced according to Cantonese dialect], Hong Kong: Zhonghua Shuju, 1954
Leung Puikam. *Yueju yanjiu tonglun* [Study of Cantonese opera], Hong Kong: Longmen Shudian, 1982
Li Ji. "Zhengyin huadan yu erbang sanbang" [The principal and the supporting female roles], *Yule Huabao* [Entertainment Monthly] (Hong Kong), 62 (1966), 36–39
Li Yan. *Yuejude chang he zuo* [Singing and acting in Cantonese opera], Macao: Eryashe, 1957
    "'Xian' lun" [Theory on *xian*], *Guangzhou Yinyue Xueyuan Xuebao* [Journal of the Canton Conservatory of Music], 3 (1983), 12–22
Li Yu. *Xianqing ouji* [Incidental memoirs on leisure subjects] (1671), reprinted in *Zhongguo gudian xiqu lunzhu jicheng* [Collection of writings on Chinese classical drama], vol. VII, ed. Zhongguo Xiqu Yanjiuyuan [Institute of Operatic Research of China], 10 vols., Beijing: Zhongguo Xiju Chubanshe, 1959–60
Lu Eting. *Kunju yanchu shigao* [Draft history of the performance practice of *Kun* opera], Shanghai: Wenyi Chubanshe, 1980
Ma Helin and Tong Jingyin. "Yuequde yiluan" [A slice of the Cantonese opera], *Juxue Yuekan* [Theater Study Monthly], 3:9 (1934), 1–13
Mai Xiaoxia. "Guangdong xiqu shilüe" [A brief history of the Cantonese opera], in *Guangdong wenwu* [The cultural things of Guangdong], ed. Guangdong Wenwu Zhanlanhui [Committee on the Exhibition of Cultural Things of Guangdong], 10 vols., Hong Kong: Zhongguo Wenhua Xiejinhui, 1940

Ouyang Yuqian. "Shitan yueju" [A preliminary study of Cantonese opera] in *Zhongguo xiqu yanjiu ziliao chuji* [The first collection of research material for the study of Chinese opera], ed. Ouyang Yuqian, Beijing: Yishu Chubanshe, 1956, pp. 109–157
Pan Xianda. "Interviews," *Xingdao Ribao* [Xingdao Daily News], from May 21 to June 9, 1953
Panyu Xianzhi [Panyu County Gazetteer], compiled by Shi Cheng, 1872
Panyuxian Xuzhi [Supplement to Panyu County Gazetteer], compiled by Wu Daorong, 1911
Qi Rushan. *Guoju yishu huikao* [A study of the art of Peking opera], Taipei: Congguang Wenyi Chubanshe, 1962
Qiao Yannong. *Guangzhouhua kouyucide yanjiu* [A study of the colloquial expressions in the Cantonese dialect], Hong Kong: Huaqiao Yuwen Chubanshe, 1966
Qian Nanyang. *Xiwen gailun* [General study of *xiwen*], Shanghai: Guji Chubanshe, 1981
Qiu Hechou. *Xiange bidu* [Obligatory reading on singing], publication source unknown, 1916
 Qinxian xinbian [A new collection of songs for the struck zither], publication source unknown, 1921
Qu Dajun. *Guangdong xinyu* [New reports about Guangdong] 1700, reprinted Hong Kong: Zhonghua Shuju, 1974
Rong Hongzeng (Bell Yung). "Lun yueju banqiang de tongyixing jiegou chengfen." Chinese version of "Music identity in Cantonese opera" (1981) transl. Chen Yingshi, *Minzu Minjian Yinyue Yanjiu* [Studies in Ethnic and Folk Music], 2 (1983), 58–63
 "Lun shengdiao zai yueju yinyue chuangzuo zhongde gongneng." Chinese version of "Creative process in Cantonese opera I: the role of linguistic tones" (1983) transl. Li Yan and Chen Yingshi, *Guangzhou Yinyue Xueyuan Xuebao* [Journal of the Canton Conservatory of Music], 4 (1983), 69–76.
 "Yueju zhongde chenzi yinyue wenti." Chinese version of "Creative process in Cantonese opera III: the role of padding syllables" transl. Chen Yingshi, *Yinyue Yishu* [Arts of Music, Journal of Shanghai Conservatory of Music], 3 (1984), 23–29
 "Yueju de tianci." Chinese version of "Creative process in Cantonese opera II: the role of t'ien tz'u (text-setting)" transl. Fan Weici, *Yinyue Wenzhai* [The Musical Digest], 1 (1985), 145–153
Shen Ji. *Ma Shizeng de xiqu shengya* [The life of Ma Shizeng as a performer], Guangzhou: Guangdong Renmin Chubanshe, 1957
Shunde Xianzhi [Shunde County Gazetteer], compiled by Feng Fengchu, ed. Guo Yucheng, 1853
Su Yi. "Quanguo juzhong chubu tongji" [A preliminary listing of operatic genres in China] in *Xiju luncong* [Collected Papers on Theater], vol. 1, pp. 215–223, ed. Xiju Luncong Bianji Weiyuanhui, 8 vols., Beijing: Zhongguo Xiju Chubanshe, 1957
Sun Kaidi. *Kuileixi kaoyuan* [The origin of puppet theater], Shanghai: Shangza Chubanshe, 1952
Tanaka Issei. "Mindai no minetzu chihogeki ni tsuite" [An outline of Min Yüeh local drama during the Ming dynasty], *Tohogaku* [Eastern Studies], 42 (August 1971), 82–97
 Chugokku saishi engeki kenkyu [Ritual theaters in China], Tokyo: Institute of Oriental Cultures, University of Tokyo, 1981
Tao Junqi, compiler. *Jingju jumu chutan* [A preliminary compilation of Peking opera titles], expanded edn, Beijing: Zhongguo Xiju Chubanshe, 1963
Tong Fei. *Yuanqu xuanzhu* [Yuan drama with annotation], Taipei: Shangwu Yinshuguan, 1965
Wen Lirong, narrator, Chen Binghan, writer. "Guangzhou shiniang" [Blind songstress of Canton] in *Guangdong quyishi ziliao* [Source material on the history of Cantonese popular narrative song], compiled by Guangdong Yinyue Quyituan, Guangzhou: Guangdong Yinyue Quyituan, 1980, pp. 1–12. Translated by Bell Yung as "The blind singers of Guangzhou" in *Chinoperl Papers*, 14 (1986), 61–76
Wong Shiuhon, compiler. *Yueju juben mulu* [A catalogue of Cantonese opera scripts], Hong Kong: Center of Asian Studies, University of Hong Kong, 1971
Xia Ye. *Xiqu yinyue yanjiu* [Research on operatic music], Shanghai: Wenyi Chubanshe, 1959
Xian Yuqing. "Qingdai liusheng xiban zai Guangdong" [Opera troupes from six provinces in Guangdong during the Qing dynasty], *Zhongshan Daxue Xuebao* [Journal of Zhongshan University], 3 (1963), 105–126
 "Guangdongde xipeng" [The opera sheds of Guangdong], in *Guangdong wenxian congtan* [Documents on Guangdong], ed. Xian Yuqing, Hong Kong: Zhonghua Shuju, 1965, pp. 97–98

Xiong Feiying, Yuan Miaosheng, Yuan Yinghe, Huang Peiying, narrators. "Guangzhou nüling" [Female entertainers of Canton], in *Guangdong quyishi ziliao* [Source material on the history of Cantonese popular narrative song], Guangzhou: Guangdong Yinyue Quyituan, 1980, pp. 13–37

Xu Dishan. "Fanju tili jiqizai hanjushangde diandian didi" [The form of Sanskrit drama and its traces in Chinese drama] in *Zhongguo Wenxue Yanjiu* [Study of Chinese Literature], ed. Zheng Zhenduo, Shanghai: Shangwu Yinshuguan, 1927

Xu Fuqin. *Guangdong minjian wenxuede yanjiu* [The study of folk literature of Guangdong], Hong Kong: Haichao Chubanshe, 1958

Xu Wei. *Nanci xulu* [Memoirs on the southern songs] (1559), reprinted in *Zhongguo gudian xiqu lunzhu jicheng* [Collection of writings on Chinese classical drama], vol. III, ed. Zhongguo Xiqu Yanjiuyuan [Institute of Opera Research of China], 10 vols., Beijing: Zhongguo Xiju Chubanshe, 1959–60

Yang Yinliu. *Zhongguo gudai yinyue shigao* [Draft history of ancient Chinese music], Beijing: Renmin Yinyue Chubanshe, 1982

Yang Zhangsheng. *Menghua suobu* [Miscellaneous recollections on the days of splendour] (1842), compiled by Zhang Cixi in *Qingdai yandu liyuan shiliao* [Historical materials on the theater in Qing dynasty Peking], (1934), vol. II. Reprinted in *Zhongguo shixue congshu* [Compendium of Chinese historical studies], Taipei: Xuesheng Shuju, 1964

Yoshikawa Kojiro. *Genzatsugeki kenkyu* [A study of Yuan drama], Tokyo: Iwanami Shoten, 1948

Yu Huiyong. *Shandong dagu* [Shandong drumsong], Beijing: Yinyue Chubanshe, 1957

Zhang Cuifeng. *Dagu shengyade huiyi* [My life as a drumsinger], Taipei: Zhuanji Wenxue Chubanshe, 1967. Translated by Rulan Chao Pian in *Chinoperl Papers*, 13 (1984), 7–106

Zhongguo dabaike quanshu: xiqu, quyi [Encyclopedia of China: xiqu and quyi], Beijing and Shanghai: Zhongguo Dabaike Quanshu Chubanshe, 1984

Zhongguo Xiqu Yanjiuyuan [China Research Institute of Opera], compiler. *Zhongguo gudian xiqu lunzhu jicheng* [Collection of writings on Chinese classical drama], 10 vols., Beijing: Zhongguo Xiju Chubanshe, 1959

Zhou Yibai. *Zhongguo xijushi* [History of Chinese theater], Shanghai: Zhonghua Shuju, 1953

"Zhongguo xijude xingcheng he fazhan" [The origin and development of Chinese theater] in Zhou Yibai, *Zhongguo xiqu lunji* [Essays on Chinese opera], Beijing: Zhongguo Xiju Chubanshe, 1960, pp. 1–30

Zhongguo xiqu lunji [Essays on Chinese opera], Beijing: Zhongguo Xiju Chubanshe, 1960

"Zhongguo xiqu shengqiangde sanda yuanliu" [The three main vocal styles in Chinese opera], in Zhou Yibai *Zhongguo xiqu lunji* [Essays on Chinese opera], Beijing: Zhongguo Xiju Chubanshe, 1960, pp. 204–229

3 Published notations of Cantonese tunes

Guangdong xiaoqu [Cantonese tunes], compiled by Li Zijun, 4 vols., Hong Kong: Jinhua Chubanshe (no date)

Guangdong yinyue [Cantonese music], Hong Kong: Taiping Shuju, 1963

Guangdong yinyue quji [Collection of Cantonese music], Beijing: Renmin Yinyue Chubanshe, 1981

Guangdong yuequ yibaishou [One hundred pieces of Cantonese music], Jilin: Renmin Yinyue Chubanshe, 1981

Qinxian xinbian [A new collection of songs for the struck zither], compiled by Qiu Hechou, publication source unknown, 1921

Xiange bidu [Obligatory reading on singing], compiled by Qiu Hechou, publication source unknown, 1916

Xinbian qinxian qupu [A new collection of instrumental tunes], compiled by Zhao Yu, 3 vols., Hong Kong: Jinhua Chubanshe (no date)

Yuedong luogu yuepu [Percussion patterns of Eastern Guangdong music], compiled by Tan Rongguang, Dongruan, Guangdong: Jiyouzhai, 1921

Yueyue mingquji [Collection of famous Cantonese tunes], compiled by Li Xiaotian, 3 vols., Hong Kong: Xincheng Shuju, 1971

Yueyue mingqu jinghua [The best of famous Cantonese tunes], Hong Kong: Gangjiu Yinyueshe (no date)
Yueyue quxuan [Selection of Cantonese tunes], compiled by Chen Junying, Shanghai: Wenyi Chubanshe, 1959
Zhongxi xiange fengqin hepu [Songs in Chinese and Western notations], compiled by Shen Yunsheng, Guangzhou: Yinyue Yanjiushe, 1929

Index

absolute pitch, 181 n.2
acrobatics, 11, 20, 42; *see also* battle scene
aesthetics, 91, 150
amateur singer, 34, 38, 39
amplification, 39
aria types, 13, 67–81; comparison with fixed tunes, 136–137; features of, 72–73; invariance, 90; in *The Magic Pearl*, 54; percussion instruments in, 27; titles of, 72–73
Autumn Moon on the Calm Lake, 130

Baan, 72, 118, 132, 157, 184 n.3; see also *ban*
backdrop, 12
ban, 7, 15, 17; in *Naamyam*, 141; see also *Baan*
banghuang, see *bongwong*
banzhu, 32, 42, 43
battle scene, 44; *see also* acrobatics
bayin, 38
Birthday Greeting from the Eight Immortals, 33, 37, 183 n.14
blind songstress, 38
bongji, 67, 180 n.29; compared with *yiwong*, 80–81
Bongji Maanbaan, 50–51, 54, 78, 93–104, 147, 148
bongwong, 13, 67; see also *bongji*; *yiwong*
Brecht, Bertolt, 6

cadential pitches, 127; *see also* line-ending pitches
Cantonese operatic songs, 39
Cantonese rod puppet theater, 40
Chatjiching, 55, 68–71, 73, 82–89; differences among versions, 82–89; identity of, 68–71; in *The Magic Pearl*, 51, 54, 55; in speech-song spectrum, 151, 152; metrical pattern, 70; musical notation of, 69, 153; tempo change in, 153–154, 156–157
Chen Zhuoying, 73, 107
Chinese opera: features, 5; history, 1–5; regional opera, 8; role types, 6
chuanqi, 3, 4
cipher notation, 123, 124, 181 n.4
comic relief, 20
Comic Rhymed Speech, 58–59
comic role, 55, 58
commercial performance, 42, 182 n.6; *see also* secular performance
commercial recording, 40
costume, 12
Cultural Revolution, 10, 33, 180 n.27, 181 n.7
cymbals, 24–25

Dainty Steps: choice of, 130; in *The Magic Pearl*, 48; musical notation of, 16, 17, 55
dance, 6, 11, 42, 44; *see also* movements on stage
dance of promotion, 183 n.14

didactic message, 20
ding, 15, 17, 118, 132
Dinühua, 18, 58, 99
dizi, 3, 29, 30, 31, 143
Dolby, William, 1
drum, 25
duqu, 44

eight tones, 38
erhu, 27, 28, 31, 41, 106, 143; finger position, 109; player, 42, 43, 44, 129
Erhuang, 5

Faaidim, 76, 148–149, 185 n.9; as fast *Chatjiching*, 154; dramatic function of, 54; in *The Magic Pearl*, 47, 55; musical notation of, 76
Faansin Jungbaan, 75, 110; musical notation of, 114–115; popularity of, 149
Faansin Sapji Bongji Jungbaan, see *Faansin Jungbaan*
Faansin Yiwong, 100–101
female entertainer, 38
Feng Yuanzhi, 108
festivals, 35, 36, 38; performances in, 42; *see also* ritual performance
film, 40
fixed tunes, 13, 27, 128–37; identity of, 132–133; in *The Magic Pearl*, 54; in speech-song spectrum, 151, 152; see also *Dainty Steps*

Gaamji Fuyung, 77, 89; musical notation of, 77
Giving the Magic Pearl at Rainbow Bridge, see *The Magic Pearl*
gong, 24–25
gongche notation, 14–18, 123, 156; of *Dainty Steps*, 16
grammatical particles, 59, 63
Gu Jian, 4, 5
guan, 30, 41
guji, 38
Gwanfa, 78–79, 147–149; in *The Magic Pearl*, 46–53; in speech-song spectrum, 151, 152; musical notation of, 79

Haiyan opera, 3
hand shadows, 56
Heavenly Maiden Delivers a Son, 183 n.14
heterophony, 31
Huang Jinpei, 107, 108

improvisation, 42, 63, 72
instrumental accompaniment: function of, 14; in *Chatjiching*, 71; in *Gwanfa*, 78–79; in speech-song spectrum, 151; in *Supported Speech*, 58; in Yuan *zaju*, 3

203

instrumental ensemble, 13; in Peking opera, 14; percussion, 14; size of, 30–31
instrumental interlude, 79
instrumental prelude, 56
instruments, see musical instruments

Jiangnan Sizhu, 16, 157
Jingsin Jungbaan, 72, 110; musical notation of, 112–13
Jingsin Sapji Bongji Jungbaan, see Jingsin Jungbaan
Jingsin Sapji Yiwong Maanbaan, 56, 154–155
Jiugong dachengpu, 2
Johnson, Dale, 98
Jungbaan, see Jingsin Jungbaan

Kai Tak amusement park, 33
Kao, Diana, 85
Kunqu, 4–5, 7–8, 27, 33, 129

Lai Chi Kok amusement park, 33
Li Yan, 107, 108
line-ending notes, 118
line-ending pitches: of *Chatjiching*, 71; of *Muk'yu*, 143; of *Naamyam*, 141–142; see also cadential pitches; linguistic tones
linguistic tones, 13, 62, 82–91, 158–61; and creative process, 89–91; in aria types, 82–91; in fixed tunes, 133–36; in Kunqu, 4; in speech-song spectrum, 151
linguists, 85–86
Long *Gwanfa*, 52, 101, 102, 148
Long *Yiwong*, 52, 80, 102, 103, 147

Ma Shizeng, 101
Magic Pearl, The, 17, 18, 31, 44–53; changes in script of, 44; *Chatjiching* in, 153; fixed tunes in, 128, 130; *Muk'yu* in, 143–144; plot of, 18–20; role types of, 21; script for act 1 of, 45–53, 145–149, 184 n.4; speech types in, 59–65
Mai Bingrong, 42, 66, 148
make-up, 12
manager, 36
Master Zhang, 9
Minister of the Six States, 33, 37
mode, 8, 71, 110, 127; of *nanxi*, 3; of Yuan *zaju*, 2
movements on stage, 21, 26, 44; see also dance
Muk'yu, 143–144, 147–149; in *The Magic Pearl*, 46, 54; musical notation of, 144; in speech-song spectrum, 151, 152
music clubs, 34
musical instruments, 23–31; core instruments, 31; melodic, 27–31; percussion, 23–26, 31
musical notation, 14–18, 34, 42, 91, 180 n.13; literary title as, 55; of *Poetic Speech*, 61; of Yuan *zaju*, 2
muyü (instrument), 24

Naamyam, 31, 139–143; baan in, 141; in *The Magic Pearl*, 48; instrumental interlude of, 143; instrumental prelude of, 142; musical notation of, 140; sin in, 141
Nanyin, 31; see also *Naamyam*
narrative songs, 13, 31, 54, 138–144; see also *Naamyam*; *Muk'yu*
nüling, 38

opera shed, 37, 181 n.3
oral delivery type, 13, 43; in *The Magic Pearl*, 54, 55, 145–149; in speech-song spectrum, 149, 153; in *tigang* [outline], 56
ornamentation, 8
overture, 21

paaiji, 128–129; see also paizi
padding syllables, 92–105, 119; added phrase, 94–95; interlude fillers, 100; multiplets, 98–100; nonsense syllables, 101; phrase-leader syllables, 96–98; tail syllables, 101
paizi, 13, 21, 27, 187 n.1; see also paaiji
Pan Xianda, 37
Patter Speech, 59, 63–64, 66, 148; in *The Magic Pearl*, 45, 54, 55; in speech-song spectrum, 151, 152; musical notation of, 65
Peking drumsong, 95
Peking gongs and cymbals, 24–25, 59, 62
Peking opera: backdrop in, 12; and Cantonese opera, 9, 129, 147, 180 n.29; programming of, 18, 34; role types of, 6, 20; social context of, 5, 8, 33, 34; tune families in, 7
percussion instruments, see musical instruments
percussion music, 6, 21; dramatic functions of, 22, 26–27; percussion patterns of, 27, 43, 44, 53, 54, 59, 62
percussion pattern, see percussion music
Percussion Speech, 59–60, 66; in *The Magic Pearl*, 45, 54, 62, 148; in speech-song spectrum, 151, 152
phrase-ending notes, 118
pipa, 29, 30, 186 n.2
Plain Speech, 57–58, 66; in *The Magic Pearl*, 45–53, 54, 55, 147, 148; in speech-song spectrum, 151, 152
Poetic Speech, 59, 60–62, 66; in *The Magic Pearl*, 45, 148, 149
Powers, Harold, 71
preexistent tunes, 3, 4, 7, 13
principal scale, 122

qinqin, 29, 107
Qiu Hechou, 109, 124, 126, 156, 184 n.3, 187 n.18

Radio Television Hong Kong, 34
rehearsal, 34, 42–44; lack of, 42
Revolutionary opera, 33
Rhymed Speech, 62–63, 66; in *The Magic Pearl*, 47, 59, 148, 149; in speech-song spectrum, 151, 152
ritual performance, 35–37, 42, 182 n.6, 182 n.11, 183 n.14
ritual plays, 25, 33
role types, 2, 11, 20, 21, 73–74
Rowing a Boat, 130
Royal Beauty, The, 18, 58, 99

sanxian, 28, 29, 31
scale, 8, 14–17, 106, 119–122, 181 n.5, 186 n.6
scriptwriter, 39, 42, 43, 72
secular performance, 32–34; see also commercial performance
Shandong drumsong, 93, 95, 98
sin, 70, 89, 106–127; in *Muk'yu*, 143, 144; in *Naamyam*, 141
small gong, 62
Society of Eight Harmonies, 42
song, 43, 150
speech, 6, 150

Index

speech-song spectrum, 149–153
speech types, 13, 21, 22, 57–66; in *The Magic Pearl*, 43, 54
stage 6, 180 n.20
stage manager, 43
stage set, 12, 20
story, 42, 43
Su Weng, 149, 181 n.9, 184 n.3
suite, 2, 7
suona, 21, 25, 27
Supported Speech, 58, 66; in *The Magic Pearl*, 48, 50, 147
Swatow opera, 34, 183 n.14
syllable placement, 70, 118, 119

Taiping Theater, 32, 33
Tanaka Issei, 35
Tang Disheng, 18, 33
tempo, 24
tempo changes, 153–57; in *Chatjiching*, 153–154, 157; and *Faaidim*, 154; in *Jingsin Sapji Yiwong Maanbaan*, 154–155
theaters, 35
theatricality, 6
tigang, 55, 56
tune family, 7
tune title, 3, 44

verse structure, 69–70, 131–132, 151

village performance, 36–37; *see also* ritual performance
voice types, 73–74, 89, 185 n.8, 187 n.16

Wang Chun, 109
wanjia, 38
Wei Liangfu, 4
Western influence, 5, 31, 107, 129, 182 n.6
Western instruments, 31, 37
Western theater, 33
When the Petals Fall, 55
woodblock player, 42, 43
woodblocks, 21, 23–24, 58, 59, 154, 184 n.3

xiao, 30, 143
xipi, 5

yangqin, 29, 30, 31, 107, 124–127
yehu, 28, 143
Yifaansin, Jungbaan, 110, 116–117
Yifaansin Sapji Bongji Jungbaan, see *Yifaansin Jungbaan*
yiwong, 67, 80, 180 n.29, 186 n.9; compared with *bongji*, 80–81
Yiwong Maanbaan, 56
Yu Huiyong, 93, 98
Yuan *zaju*, 1, 2, 7, 33, 93, 98
yueqin, 29, 30, 107

zaju, see Yuan *zaju*